SCOTLAND AND WAR
AD 79–1918

SCOTLAND AND WAR
AD 79–1918

Edited by
NORMAN MACDOUGALL
Senior Lecturer in Scottish History
University of St Andrews

JOHN DONALD PUBLISHERS LTD
EDINBURGH

ISBN 0 85976 248 3

Distribution in the USA by Barnes & Noble Books, 8705 Bollman Place, Savage, Maryland 20763

British Library Cataloguing in Publication Data

Scotland and war: AD 79–1918.
  1. Wars. Scotland, history
  I. Macdougall, Norman
  941.1

Typeset by Pioneer Associates, Perthshire
Printed and bound in Great Britain by
Billing & Sons Ltd., Worcester

DEDICATION

Professor Ian B. Cowan, one of the contributors to this volume, died in December 1990, shortly after the book had gone to press. Professor Cowan's contribution to Scottish historical studies over more than a quarter of a century has been immense, and the editor and co-authors would like to dedicate *Scotland and War* to his memory.

ACKNOWLEDGEMENTS

The editor would like to thank the Director and Committee of St John's House, St Andrews, where the *Scotland and War* seminar was held; Professor T. C. Smout for much practical advice and assistance; Dr Colin Martin for help literally above, and certainly beyond, the call of duty; and Mrs Margaret Richards for sterling support in preparing much of the material for publication.

CONTENTS

CONTRIBUTORS

Gordon Maxwell
Royal Commission on the Ancient and Historical Monuments of Scotland, Edinburgh

Geoffrey P. Stell
Royal Commission on the Ancient and Historical Monuments of Scotland, Edinburgh

Norman Macdougall
Senior Lecturer in Scottish History, University of St Andrews

David H. Caldwell
Royal Museum of Scotland, Edinburgh

Ian B. Cowan
(late) Professor, Department of Scottish History, University of Glasgow

Raymond Gillespie
Office of Public Works, Dublin

Keith M. Brown
Royal Society of Edinburgh Research Fellow, University of St Andrews

Bruce P. Lenman
Reader in Modern History, University of St Andrews

Gerard J. de Groot
Lecturer in Modern History, University of St Andrews

INTRODUCTION

The nine essays published here were given between 1986 and 1988 before the Seminar for Scottish History at St John's House Institute of Advanced Historical Studies of the University of St Andrews. Speakers with specialist interests were invited to contribute papers on the broad theme 'Scotland and War'; and the essays which resulted cover an enormous time-span, from the resistance of the Caledonian tribes to the incursions of Julius Agricola in the first century, through the rearguard actions fought against the English by the medieval and early modern Scottish host, to the carnage of the early twentieth century, when Scots died in enormous numbers in Flanders — in company with their former enemies — for the glory of God and the British Empire. If there is a unifying theme in the book, it is surely the vast discrepancy between the theory and practice of war, between the bullish expectations of rulers, politicians, and generals and the realities faced by those who have to fight their battles. Thus although there are some heroes in the book, this is not a book about heroes, still less about master strategists with infallible battle plans. Instead, many of the chapters which follow demonstrate how often great military struggles are decided by chance, human error, blind faith, invincible stupidity, or combinations of any of the four. A subsidiary theme is the inexorable removal from Scottish control of military decision-making, even at the level of home defence, by a mistrustful and overbearing London executive.

The scene is set by Gordon Maxwell, who defines the geographical parameters of the military contests which occurred within Scotland itself, and stresses the role of Scottish topography in limiting the activities of generals as far removed in time from one another as the third-century Roman Emperor Severus and the thirteenth-century English king Edward I. Edward's chosen Scottish routes and battle sites, and indeed those of later commanders like Somerset, Montrose, Argyll, Mar, and Cumberland, strikingly parallel those of Agricola and Severus. Geoffrey Stell, who also takes the long view of Scottish military history, examines the effects of siege warfare on medieval and early modern strongholds, and warns against the danger of always believing confident written reports of their partial or total destruction. The weather and gradual decay were in the long run equally effective instruments of demolition.

If we except the activities of Scottish mercenaries in foreign — especially French — service, Scottish participation in the various theatres of European war remained small down to the regal union of 1603. The only military threat to the continued existence of the kingdom came from England, and the king's first duty, as the Declaration of Arbroath makes abundantly clear, was to defend his country against the English. On occasions, individual Scottish rulers' interpretations of defence could be thoroughly aggressive: James IV launched the pride of his fleet, the enormous capital ship, the 'Michael', in 1511, a vessel which in 1513 was used as part of a Franco-Scottish war effort to assail the English in Ulster and the Channel. Much more typical of Scottish aggression or defence than the fleet was the host, the medieval predecessor of a national militia, appropriately — if rather optimistically and rarely very efficiently — made up of all able-bodied men between the ages of sixteen and sixty, serving without pay in theory for forty days a year, in practice rarely available for more than a very brief campaign of perhaps half that length. The shattering defeat at Flodden in September 1513 destroyed the military reputation of the Scots, assiduously cultivated by James IV in his skilful use of the host on six swift raids into Northumberland in 1496–7. Even worse, as David Caldwell shows, was the disastrous defensive action fought by the host against the Duke of Somerset more than a generation later, at Pinkie near Musselburgh, on 10 September 1547. This turned out to be the last major battle between the Scots and English; and Dr Caldwell's detailed analysis of it leaves no room for doubt that the unpaid and under-supplied Scottish host was no longer a credible national fighting force.

Twenty years after Pinkie, the natural leaders of the various components of the host, the Scottish magnates, faced the dangerous challenge of choosing sides in the Marian Civil War, a six-year-long struggle analysed by Ian Cowan. Removals of Stewart monarchs by their heirs, or parties using their heirs as figureheads, were of course nothing new; such coups had been carried through in 1384 and 1399, had been attempted (probably) in 1482, and had succeeded spectacularly in 1488. In 1567, however, the struggle was complicated, as Professor Cowan shows, by issues which had not been present before, above all religion and the nobility's response to the rather tenuous advance of Protestantism in Scotland in the early 1560s. But the crucial factor which led to the collapse of Queen Mary's cause in Scotland was the absence of the queen herself after her defeat at Langside in May 1568. In the last analysis, the Marian Civil War without Mary is rather like Hamlet without the Prince.

The seventeenth century, a period of tremendous upheavals and violent change in Scottish society, had as its centrepiece the confused and bloody War of the Three Kingdoms in the 1640s. Raymond Gillespie analyses a specific area of the war, the arrival of the Scottish mercenary army in Ulster in 1642, and the chaotic sequel as its activities were overtaken by rapidly changing political and military events elsewhere. Significantly, the army's commanders, Munro and Leslie, found their arrival most resented by Ulster settlers who had emigrated from Scotland in the early years of the century and who, as Dr Gillespie shows, had by the 1640s evolved as Scots-Irish rather than simply Scots in Ireland.

By contrast, Keith Brown uses an enormous canvas to trace the lengthy survival action undertaken by astute members of the Scottish aristocracy during the century. With the gradual demise of lordship, large numbers of magnates sought to recover their power and status by becoming part of the British military establishment, a fact which played a significant role in increasing Scottish support for the union of 1707. Similar broad treatment is applied by Bruce Lenman to the raising of a Scottish militia in the Restoration period, and its subsequent demise in the eighteenth century. Dr Lenman traces the general overall success of the militia as an effective home defence force until James VII, regarding the majority of his subjects as Protestants and potential rebels, abolished the annual embodiment of the militia in 1685 and duly suffered the consequences three years later. Thereafter, the Scots militia slid into an 'abyss of neglect', to use Dr Lenman's phrase, because King William III had little interest in Scotland other than to provide 'cannon-fodder for Flanders'.

The most notable recipient of human cannon-fodder was General Sir Douglas Haig, the eventual victor in the carnage of the First World War. Dr de Groot's theme is Haig's belief in divine inspiration, which originated in his Scottish Presbyterian upbringing and was sustained in the worst years of the war by another Scot, the Reverend George Duncan, who was deeply impressed by Haig and who in turn exerted an almost Messianic influence on Haig through his sermons. 'The words of

Duncan became the ways of Haig', as Dr de Groot shows, and the commander-in-chief was sustained in his firm belief that he was fighting a just war on behalf of God's Empire, a belief which made him, if not insensitive to appalling losses on the Somme and at Passchendaele, quite prepared to accept them as the price of victory. Dr de Groot concludes that a commander of greater sensitivity and less conviction than Haig might not have been able to endure such losses, and that Haig was the type of commander which such a terrible war required. Thus Scottish presbyterianism, a radical force in the sixteenth century, had become totally geared to the needs of the British establishment in the twentieth, and duly helped to secure the divinely ordained victory of the British Empire in 1918. As Haig himself put it in a letter to his nephew, rejecting his appeals to leave the army and become a farmer: 'Aim at being worthy of the British Empire and possibly in the evening of your life you may be able to own to yourself that you are fit to settle down in Fife.'

Norman Macdougall

1

THE ROMAN EXPERIENCE:
PARALLEL LINES OR PREDESTINATION?

Gordon Maxwell

The first historical and archaeological evidence for the *extensive* practice of warfare in Scotland belongs to the Roman period. It is important, at the outset, to emphasise how slight that evidence is and how brief the period to which it refers. A few chapters of a single work — *de Vita Julii Agricolae* by the historian Tacitus — a paragraph here and there, and a handful of sentences gleaned from more general or epitomised historical accounts represent all that deals specifically with Roman military operations north of the Tyne-Solway isthmus. There is, admittedly, a considerable wealth of Roman monuments and artefacts which have been discovered in Scotland, but the great majority of these, though military in character or association, relate to the phases of occupation; they illustrate the threat of armed force rather than the practice of war. The distinction needs to be made because, in the past, it has been customary to work backwards from the known permanent installations in order to reconstruct the processes which preceded their foundation. Fortunately, some forty-five years of aerial survey[1] have served to demonstrate the richness of the Scottish heritage in terms of temporary works erected by Roman armies on campaign. At the time of writing, there are at least 150 sites in this category, the majority so denuded as to be visible only when they appear as cropmarkings in time of drought. Although relatively few can be assigned to a specific year of campaigning, an appreciable number have been shown to possess characteristics — a common size, proportion, or type of gateway-defence — which allow them to be grouped in series and tentatively associated with historically-attested periods of military activity. The physical distribution of such groupings may then be incorporated with roughly contemporary permanent garrison-posts to provide a schematic picture of Rome's intentions in three separate episodes of colonial aggression.

The first, known as the Flavian, commenced in AD 79 or 80 and continued for at least another four seasons; it saw the governor of Britannia take Roman troops at least as far as the River Spey (fig. 1.1)

1

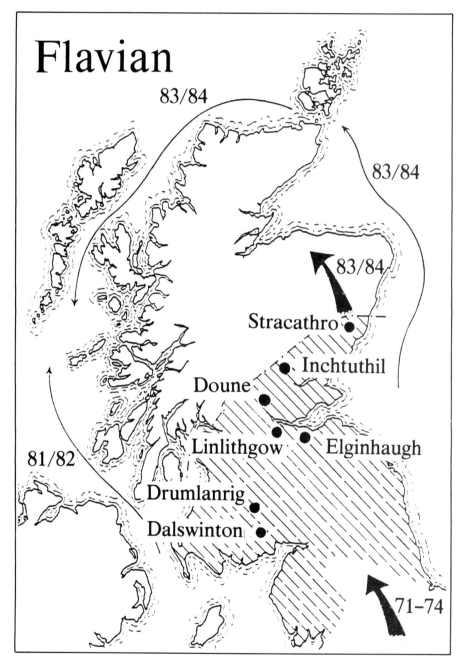

Figure 1. (1.1, 1.2, 1.3). Sketch maps of areas of Scotland affected by successive Roman military operations; hatching indicates occupied territory, arrows the main thrusts of campaigning in the north.

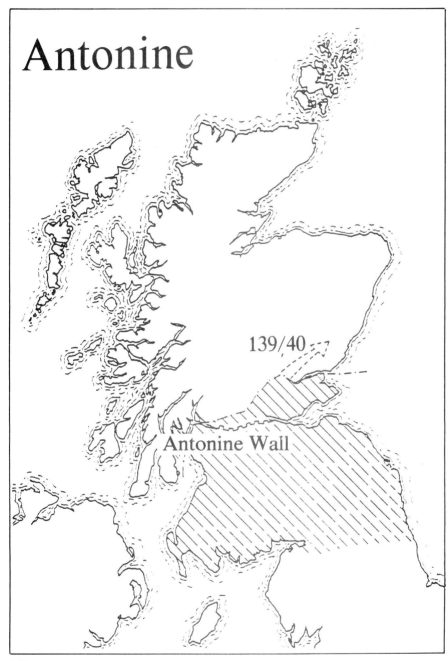

Antonine

139/40

Antonine Wall

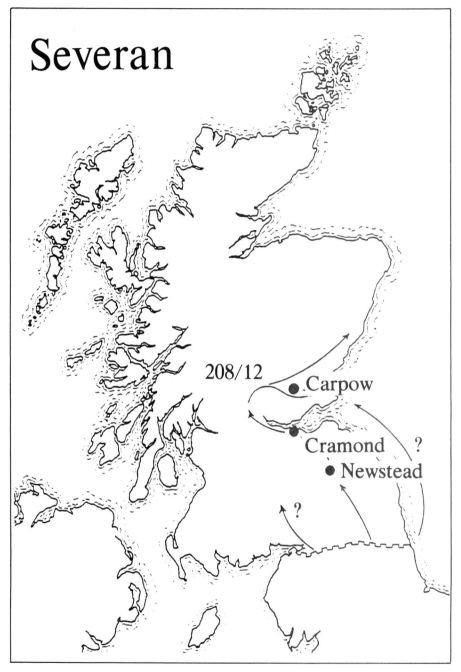

Severan

208/12

Carpow

Cramond

Newstead

?

?

1.3

and inaugurate an occupation embracing all of southern and central Scotland, together with Fife and most of Strathmore, if not beyond.[2] The northernmost conquest probably did not endure beyond 87 and even the southern areas had been abandoned by the early years of the second century. The second period began soon after the death of Hadrian, when his successor, Antoninus Pius, probably *c.* AD 140, commanded the governor Lollius Urbicus to advance northwards again, secure the Forth-Clyde isthmus with a further wall of turf, and occupy eastern Scotland as far north as the Tay;[3] with one brief interval, this occupation lasted until the 160s, when the line of Hadrian's Wall again became the northern limit of the province. The final incursion was perhaps the most intensive, when the emperor Septimius Severus himself took the field at the head of an imperial expedition in AD 209 and, proceeding from York by way of Lauderdale, Pathhead, Falkirk and Stirling, campaigned widely through Fife and Strathmore[4] (fig. 1.3); only brief and restricted occupation appears to have followed these far-ranging operations, however, with legionary and auxiliary garrisons deployed in isolated coastal positions at Carpow on the Tay and Cramond on the Forth respectively.

This fluctuating pattern of invasion and conquest occupied, in total, less than thirty ill-documented years. What interest can it therefore be expected to afford the student of warfare in comparison with many centuries of later Scottish history? The answer lies in the seemingly unending array of parallels it offers to the military operations of those later times. That history repeats itself abundantly in this respect has long been appreciated. For General William Roy, the father of the Ordnance Survey, it was of more than academic significance. Charged with the survey of Northern Britain in the years following the Jacobite Rising of 1745–6, Roy had especially good reason to understand

> that military men, especially those who have been much accustomed to observe and consider countries in the way of their profession, in reasoning on the various revolutions they have already undergone, or in those which, in certain cases, they might possibly suffer hereafter, are naturally led to compare present things with the past; and being thus insensibly carried back to former ages, they place themselves among the ancients, and do, as it were, converse with the peoples of those remote times.[5]

And with even more relevance, he goes on to say:

> The nature of a country will always, in a great degree, determine the general principles upon which every war there must be conducted. In the course of

many years, a marshy country may be drained; one that was originally covered with wood may be laid open; or an open country afterwards enclosed: yet while the ranges of mountains, the long extended valleys, and remarkable rivers, continue the same, the reasons of war cannot essentially change. Hence it will appear evident, that what, with regard to situation, was an advantageous post when the Romans were carrying on their military operations in Britain, must, in all essential respects, continue to be a good one now; proper allowances being made for the difference of arms, and other changes which have taken place between the two periods.

Equally practical, if less momentous, considerations initially moved the author of this chapter:[6] on the one hand, the need to identify the positions of as yet undiscovered Roman forts, and on the other the desire to understand more fully the possible strategic context of known installations. Before the advent of mechanised transport, and, even more, before the widespread adoption of shell-firing artillery, it seemed probable that invading armies would have responded to comparable constraints in similar ways. In particular, the experience and practice of the armies of Edward I and Edward II during the Wars of Independence appeared to be a suitable model for reconstructing the Roman equivalents in the time of Agricola and Severus, as, indeed, of Ecgfrith of Northumbria in 685 and possibly even William in 1072 or the Hanoverian forces under Cumberland in 1746. There is at least a superficial resemblance, for example, between the rate of progress of the 18th-century army between Falkirk and the Moray Firth (10-20 km per day) and that of the Severan legions as indicated by the 15 km average marching-camp interval between Dunipace and the Northeast end of Strathmore.[7]

More specific comparison can be made between the irresistible progress of the Roman imperial army of the early third century (as indicated by the disposition of contemporary marching-camps) and the documented advance of invading forces in the time of Edward I and Edward VI: thus, we know that Severus took three days on the 33 km march from Tweeddale, near Melrose, to the Lothian Tyne (using the 66-hectare camps at Newstead, St Leonards, Channelkirk and Pathhead), while in July 1298 Edward I journeyed *c.* 32 km along the same route from Lauder to Braid in two or three days; in 1547 the army of the Protector Somerset (see below, p. 72) advanced at a rate of between 8 and 14 km each day towards the field of Pinkie. Such progress need not necessarily be considered slow, and attributed to either diffidence or nonchalance. Battle groups numbering upwards of

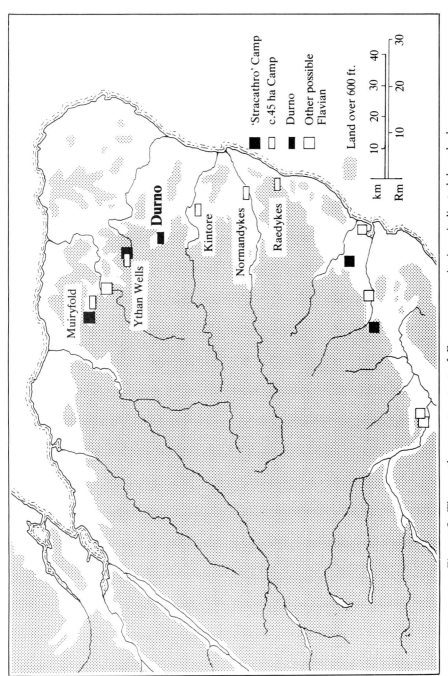

Figure 2. The northernmost extent of Roman campaigning, indicated largely by marching-camps, presumed to be of Flavian date.

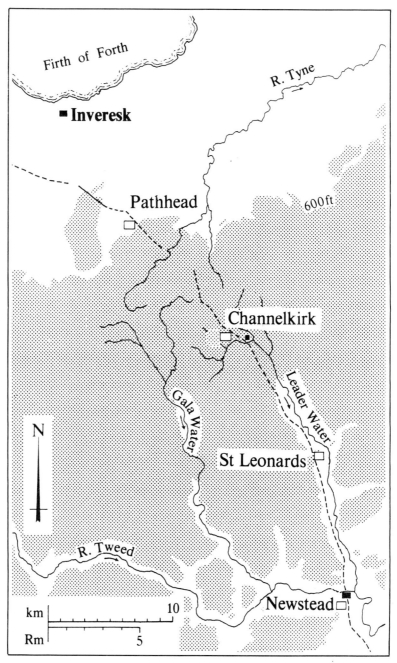

Figure 3. Severan army movements between Tweed and Forth; 67 ha temporary camps of the early 3rd century A.D., marking the daily advance of a battle group, perhaps 50,000 strong.

15,000 men, encumbered with supply columns including wagons and draught-animals, would have found it none too easy to better such rates. When the need arose to march with a siege-train, progress could have been even slower: Edward's operations against Bothwell Castle in 1301, for example, required the transport of heavy equipment from Glasgow, only 12 km distant; the journey by wagon took two days.[8]

The parallels between the Severan invasion and the Edwardian campaigns are particularly interesting, for there seems little doubt that in both cases the invading army used the pre-existing Roman road as an ideal avenue — at least, to the South of the River Tay — for penetration; the main difference lay in the fact that Severus' commanders followed the route by intention, consulting 'file-copies' of Antonine and Flavian itineraries and aligning their rectangular defended bivouac each night with the metalled *agger* of the road. Edward I, on the other hand, was following a track worn by centuries of post-Roman use; had he known of its Roman origin, he would doubtless have been deeply gratified, being himself well-versed in the writings of ancient military authors.[9]

To the north of the Tay, no Roman route has been definitely identified, the northernmost authenticated sector leading across the gravel terrace at Huntingtower towards the fort of Bertha, at the confluence of Tay and Almond, where in Roman times the former river was crossed by bridge or ford. In 1296 Edward appears to have crossed the Tay some 10 km further upstream, on his way to the castle of Clunie.[10] In doing so, he must have passed close to the fortress of Inchtuthil, where a legionary garrison served as the main stronghold of the outer Flavian frontier in AD 83–7; it is quite possible that in this section of his advance he was following a road whose last traces have long since been removed by cultivation, but which once led directly to the fortress. Edward's northward advance took him from Clunie to Forfar and then Montrose, where John Balliol was formally stripped of the blazon of royalty. In the kirkyard of Stracathro, near Edzell, where, shortly before, John had been compelled to perform yet another demeaning act of contrition, a fitting venue had been found for this symbolic statement of external domination; all around at Stracathro, though unrecognised, lay the defaced earthworks of Rome's most northerly permanent outpost,[11] constructed in AD 84 after Agricola had humiliated Calgacus at *Mons Graupius*. From here Edward pushed on by way of the Cowie Mounth to Aberdeen and thence up the River Don to Kintore, eventually penetrating to the coast and proceeding westward across the Spey to Moray. There is a close correspondence in this final sector (where no

Plate 1. Stracathro, Tayside, Angus: in the foreground the churchyard, scene of Balliol's abasement in 1296; to the left the cropmarks of the Agricolan fort-defences and (above) the marching-camp.

Roman road is likely to have been contemplated, far less built) to the line of march indicated by the bold arc of seven great camps, at least 44 ha in area, which housed the troops of either Agricola or Severus at the northern limits of their invasion.[12] In the case of the former, if we are to believe Tacitus (*Agricola*, 29), the immediate goal was the destruction of the Caledonian confederate field army under Calgacus, which thus presented a tactical problem similar to that posed to the 18th-century Hanoverian army by the Jacobite forces at Culloden. For Edward I, in 1296 and in later years, there were other considerations — the reduction of castles held by the enemy and the appropriate treatment of local magnates or power-blocs; in other words, tactical similarities, apparently dictated by terrain, may conceal differing territorial ambitions and strategies. From the point of view of the archaeologist seeking to identify 'new' Roman sites, it may, in any case, hardly matter; within the constraints of geographical determinism the effects of differently-based political contexts could well be irrelevant. Moreover, the interactive illuminating process may work both ways. As an example, one might cite the recent discovery of the Flavian fort at Elginhaugh, where the Roman road Dere Street crosses the North Esk near Dalkeith;[13] the site lies in a parcel of ground called Englishman's Field, situated some way to the northeast of England's Hill. Both place-names are possibly to be associated with folk-memories of the Battle of Roslin in February 1303. On this occasion a strong force of English horse commanded by Sir John Segrave was sent to break up resistance elements massing at Biggar under John Comyn and Simon Fraser.[14] It would seem that the English force, having crossed the Esk at Elginhaugh, was divided into three detachments, which clashed head-on with the Scottish cavalry in three separate engagements. The action, which ended in the routing of Segrave's men, commenced at dawn, the Scottish horse having travelled by night and come upon the foe before they were expected. It is thus highly probable that both sides were using the Roman route that runs along the southern flank of the Pentland Hills from Biggar to the outskirts of Edinburgh; such speedy response at night, and in the depths of winter, scarcely seems feasible otherwise.

Similarly, Edward's decision to halt overnight at the castle of Hallyards, on the right bank of the Almond near Kirkliston, as he made his way to Falkirk in July 1298, may owe less to the hospitality of the Templars than to the probability that the Roman road leading west from Edinburgh crossed the river at an adjacent ford.[15]

It is, of course, impossible to disentangle the later re-use of Roman routes from the need to follow natural corridors of access, but occasionally the parallels are persuasively close. After his victory at Falkirk, for example, Edward eventually retraced his steps to Edinburgh, and, rounding the northeastern end of the Pentland Hills, proceeded by way of Glencorse and West Linton (the route 'pioneered' in the reverse direction by Agricola) to Ayr; his subsequent journey to Lochmaben would have brought him past Dalswinton — then a Balliol castle, but earlier one of the strongest Roman garrison-posts (as well as a much-used campaign base) in southwestern Scotland[16] — and thence by the military way that followed the Water of Ae to link with the main north-south trunk road across the River Annan near Lockerbie. In Edwardian times the passage of the ill-drained ground where Ae and Kinnel Water meander to join the Annan was dominated by the Bruce stronghold of Lochmaben, now strengthened and guarded by an English garrison; the Romans chose to control the same area from the east,

Plate 2. Elginhaugh, Midlothian: Englishman's Field, where Sir John Segrave crossed the Esk in 1303, and where modern parch-marks betray the existence of approach road and internal streets of an Agricolan fort.

building a fort (discovered only in 1989) on the nose of the Ladyward ridge, at the confluence of Annan and Dryfe.[17] The importance of the crossing-point in Roman times may have been heightened by its proximity to a local native, cult-centre, the *locus Maponi* — 'the place of Mabon' (the Celtic Apollo), whose name has come down to us in the little changed form of Lochmaben itself.[18] Even as late as the 16th century this natural cross-roads was still an arena for political and military conflict — the Johnstones of Annandale and the Maxwells of Nithsdale who fought the major Scottish clan-battle in 1593 at Dryfesands[19] doubtless echoed territorial struggles going back to the disputes between local Iron Age tribes, the Novantae and Brigantes — if not beyond.

Plate 3. Dalswinton, Dumfries and Galloway, Nithsdale: cropmarks of double-ditched two-period Flavian fort and (to right) single line of Stracathro-gated camp.

Although it is not the purpose of this chapter to compare the location and character of Roman fortified sites with those of much later periods, even a brief consideration of the relationship between the Roman and medieval works near Lochmaben illustrates the potential value of such an approach. Much deeper examination would be required to determine whether the proximity of sites of different periods reflected similar responses to comparable political and territorial stimuli, or merely the acknowledgement of ineluctable physical constraints.

What relationship, for example, existed between the legionary base at Carpow[20] and the old Pictish capital at Abernethy? Were both brought into being to regulate or control a particularly vigorous local population, now perhaps glimpsed only in the palimpsest of cropmark traces indicating extensive unenclosed settlement at nearby Mugdrum?[21] In contrast, are we overlooking evidence for the local political stimuli which brought into being the 1st-century fortress at Inchtuthil[22] (almost unique in any legionary bases in Britain in its lack of subsequent settlement), and did those stimuli have a medieval or modern counterpart? Tibbers Castle, immediately north-west of Thornhill in Dumfriesshire, played an active role in the Wars of Independence,[23] but formerly it was only the false etymology of antiquaries (Tibbers = Tiberius) that linked it to a Roman past.[24] We now know that it had an early precursor in the Roman fort at Drumlanrig,[25] which guarded the river-crossing of the Roman route linking Ayrshire with the Solway; similar juxtapositions can be seen at the fort of Crawford, adjoining Tower Lindsay motte in Upper Clydesdale,[26] and at Doune on the River Teith, where the discovery of a barely detectable Roman site occupying Castle Hill[27] makes the existence of an early medieval work beneath the 15th-century castle more probable than was once thought.

Such interactive study may even help to locate sites 'missing' from their respective categories. The Edwardian peel at Linlithgow, partly overlain by the much-rebuilt Palace, has been presumed to have overlain the site of a Roman fort or fortlet,[28] partly on the grounds of spacing of Roman garrisons, partly because shreds of late 1st-century *mortaria* were found in nearby St Michael's Kirkyard. Excavations in modern times[29] have failed to reveal positive traces of either Agricolan or Edwardian work, not surprisingly, perhaps, since the ground around the Palace has been landscaped and developed in various ways in the long history of the site.[30] A ray of hope may, however, have been introduced by the summer drought of 1988, when aerial photography[31] recorded patterns of enclosures in the parched lawns to the west of the Palace: one of these may indicate the course of an early (Edwardian) palisade drawn along the crest of the Palace hill, while another, with straight sides and a rounded angle might just possibly represent part of a Roman defensive work. Similar climatic conditions and good luck could conceivably assist in the identification of the Edwardian *castrum de Tarres*;[32] in this case, aerial surveyors might do worse than begin their reconnaissance in the area of the Roman fort of Broomholm on the Tarras Water.

As stated earlier, however, among the most valuable insights afforded by such comparisons are those that lead to a clearer perception of the movement of ancient armies. Thus, Linlithgow demands attention because it may adjoin the road that Agricola took, like Edward I and his son, from Lauderdale to Falkirk. Doune is doubly interesting; it reminds

Plate 4. Drumlanrig, Dumfries and Galloway, Nithsdale: internal street-grid of two-period fort, with extensive ditch system, immediately below the formal gardens of Drumlanrig castle.

us not only that there may have been an alternative route from Stirling to Strathearn, avoiding the crossing of the Forth at Stirling Bridge,[33] but also that, in ancient times, the natural corridor from Dumbarton to north-eastern Scotland *via* the Fords of Frew may have been equally important. Crawford, who presciently pointed out the significance of the Fords in a Roman context, argued that they were also the scene of bitter conflict in early Historic times.[34] As late as the seventeenth century they provided the means by which one of the major battles of the Civil War was fought: Montrose used the Fords to manoeuvre the Royalist army, which had marched from Deeside past scattered opposition, enabling it to occupy the high ground at Kilsyth and win a convincing victory over hastily-reassembled Commonwealth forces.[35]

Plate 5. Crawford, Strathclyde, Clydesdale: the internal street-grid and outer-ditches of three-period fort immediately north (left) of Tower Lindsay medieval motte (in trees).

The events leading up to Kilsyth closely parallel the situation in Agricola's sixth campaign,[36] when the Romans, seeking to occupy the southern fringes of Caledonia, were faced with the threat of an enemy counter-attack, the native forces using their knowledge of the country to outflank the invading army. Agricola's answer was to split his troops into three groups in an attempt to cover all possible avenues of penetration from the north. In a close-run encounter he was eventually successful, mainly as a result of effective reconnaissance; in 1645 Baillie and Argyll moved and thought too slowly — and paid the price.

Seventy years later at Sherriffmuir[37] it was the Jacobite army under the Earl of Mar which played the role of the Caledonian threat in another re-run of the Agricolan campaign. Believing that the Royalist position was insecurely held, Mar gathered together the strong reinforcements from the north and began to march on Stirling; the Duke of Argyll, in the Tacitean phrase *iter hostium ab exploratoribus edoctus,*[38] moved forward to prevent an outflanking movement by way of Doune and the Fords of Frew; in 1715 the result of the battle itself was inconclusive, but for the Royalist cause, which on the same day triumphed at Preston, it had all the effects of a victory — as had Agricola's barely-executed rescue of the Ninth Legion in AD 82.

In these brief sketches of later conflicts we can glimpse something of the reality that lay behind the terse historical accounts of Roman field-operations. But there is more: the possibility of understanding the tactics and strategy of the native forces, to which much of the Roman action was a response. Scottish military history affords a rich harvest of fruitful parallels, but none perhaps more telling than the campaigns of Montrose. His brief military career[39] began in 1644, when armed with King Charles I's commission to raise a royalist army in Scotland, he quickly gathered his forces, won a sudden victory over government troops at Tippermuir at the east end of the Gask Ridge and then marched north through Perth and Strathmore by the time-hallowed route to Aberdeen. Thereupon with equal address he led his troops into the heart of the highland hills, emerging from their mountainous refuge to harry the king's enemies as opportunity offered; that he made the circuit of the Grampian massif twice within six months and still preserved his army's effectiveness amply illustrates his exceptional talents for leadership.

Returning to the fray in March 1645, like Agricola,[40] after the loss of his son (who was buried at Bellie on the banks of the Spey beside the long-supposed site of Agricola's most northerly camp), Montrose marched south-east by Kintore to Stonehaven, probing along the foothills of the Highland Line as far as Dunkeld; he then seized the opportunity of capturing Dundee, but was surprised by superior government forces and with a brilliantly executed retreat extracted all his army from the jaws of destruction to vanish up the North Esk, once more secure in a highland refuge; if the government general Baillie was at all acquainted with the classics the phrase of Tacitus '*quod nisi paludes at silvae fugientes texissent*'[41] must have been in his mind. Once more Montrose used the upland terrain to his advantage, marching and countermarching at will, and in late May, when he and Baillie met face to face, the latter was too weak to take advantage of the situation; as Buchan observed 'Montrose with his highlanders could draw supplies from the countryside; but Baillie could only starve'. The situation neatly

Plate 6. Linlithgow, West Lothian: parching in lawns to west (left) of Palace and church reveals rectilinear ditched enclosure-angle, possibly part of Flavian fortlet.

encapsulates Agricola's advice to his troops before *Mons Graupius*: '*neque enim nobis aut eadem locorum peritia aut eadem commeatuum abundantia*'.[42]

It is another testimony to Montrose's leadership, on the other hand, that by May he could issue from the hills to win a victory at Auldearn, between Nairn and Forres, at the head of an army numbering 1,500 and faced by a strength put at 4-5,000. Between May and June Montrose again sought recruitment and safety in the hills, and, ever alive to opportunity, even descended through Glen Clova into Strathmore in search of prey; it was to check just such penetration of the Flavian frontier that the Romans constructed the intermediate fort recently found by air survey at Inverquharity at the mouth of Glen Clova.[43] However, Montrose, finding it served no useful purpose, retired again into the hills and eventually by skilful manoeuvring forced his opponents into a battle on unfavourable ground at Alford; the victory won here was but the latest in a series of struggles enacted in the cockpit of north-east Scotland. Precursors included such bloody encounters as the Red Harlaw in 1411 and, perhaps, *Mons Graupius* itself.[44]

It should not be forgotten, however, that history also affords several parallels in the field of marine or naval operations. Such diverse commanders as Edward I and the Protector Somerset relied heavily on sea-borne transport for the movement of men, supplies and war-material. The former used a bridge of boats, transported from King's Lynn,[45] to by-pass the contested crossing of the Forth at Stirling — just as Severus in 208–211 may have engineered a *traiectus* of the Tay at Carpow;[46] for the siege of Brechin Castle heavy siege-engines were shipped to Montrose, exploiting, as Agricola appears to have done in his northernmost campaigns, the sheltered waters of the Montrose Basin.[47] Even Agricola's most celebrated naval project, the south-western campaign of AD 81 and the proposed descent upon Ireland,[48] has its 14th-century analogue, the ill-fated invasion of that island under Edward Bruce. We may only ponder on the outcome had Agricola, with his planned force of 'one legion and modest number of auxiliaries', actually attempted what lay beyond the powers of Bruce's experienced veterans of Bannockburn and Loudoun Hill.

In 1547 Somerset employed as many as eighty vessels (see below, p. 68) to support the land campaign which culminated in the battle of Pinkie; the fleet was divided between offensive operations and supply-duties, providing, as they sailed along the Berwick and Lothian coast, reconnaisance facilities and a mobile artillery base from which, during the battle itself, the Scottish army might be harassed with impunity. How many of the defending side, one wonders, recalled the plight of the Caledonians suffering the combined attentions of Agricola's marine and land-forces during the sixth campaign, *'cum simul terra, simul mari bellum impelleretur?'*[49]

Somerset's dispositions after the battle of Pinkie are also of interest. Apart from the garrisons at Lauder and Roxburgh, securing the main land-route from the south, particular attention was paid to deployment along the Firths of Forth and Tay: at Eyemouth, Dunglass, Inchcolm, and Broughty Craig. Recent assessment[50] of the motives lying behind this markedly-skewed pattern of occupation has suggested that

Plate 7. Doune, Central, Stirling: in pasture field between castle and modern buildings, very tenuous cropmarkings indicate part of a Roman fort's triple-ditched perimeter, an ideal bridgehead position on the River Teith.

economic use of manpower, control of the estuaries as seaways, the protection of sympathetic elements in the population, and the provision of convenient springboards for further operations are likely to have been the main considerations. There is thus a striking similarity between the strategic and tactical goals of Somerset and those which we may presume to have been selected by Severus in 208–11. After a successful advance far into Caledonia, the Roman army appears to have been content to withdraw from the conquered territory and establish a legionary base at Carpow near Newburgh on Tay with a major supply fort at Cramond on the south shore of the Forth. To the south only one or two possible stations on Dere Street can even tentatively be identified,[51] to guard the communications with the garrison of Hadrian's Wall and its outposts. The two northern garrisons, which would thus have been mainly supplied by sea, seem likely to have been charged with duties similar to those laid on Somerset's.

As far as is known, it is with these well-equipped and carefully deployed elements that Rome made its last attempt to provide a permanent military solution to the Caledonian question. When they were withdrawn, however, the stage upon which they had played their warlike roles may have darkened, but it did not remain empty. As we have seen, a succession of later actors stood forth to repeat the lines and re-enact the moves of the military drama.

NOTES

1. J.K.S. St Joseph, *Glasgow Archaeol. Journ.*, 4 (1976), 1–28; G. S. Maxwell and D. R. Wilson, *Britannia*, 18 (1987), 1–48.
2. For a recent assessment of archaeological evidence relating to the Flavian occupation of Scotland, see W. S. Hanson, *Agricola and the Conquest of the North* (London, 1987).
3. For a study of the Antonine Wall and its context see W. S. Hanson and G. S. Maxwell, *Rome's North-west Frontier: The Antonine Wall* (Edinburgh, 1983).
4. The third-century evidence is handily summarised in S. S. Frere, *Britannia*, 3rd edition (London, 1988), 167–190.
5. W. Roy, *Military Antiquities of the Romans in North Britain* (London, 1793), Preface, i.
6. Some of the points raised here were included in a paper delivered to the Thirteenth International Congress of Roman Frontier Studies at Aalen in Baden-Württemberg in 1983; see G. S. Maxwell, *Studien zu den Militärgrenzen Roms, III (Forschungen und Berichte zur Vor- und Frühgeschichte in Baden-Württemberg*, 20 (1986), 60–63.
7. Cf. J.K.S. St Joseph, *Journ. Roman Stud.*, 48 (1958), 93; idem, *Britannia*, 9 (1978), 277–87.
8. H. M. Colvin (ed.), *The History of the King's Works, vol. I: The Middle Ages* (London, 1963), 412.
9. It is recorded that Edward was presented by his queen, Eleanor of Castile, with a specially-prepared copy of Vegetius, *de re militari*.
10. For a convenient summary of Edward's campaigning in Scotland cf. G. W. S. Barrow, *Robert Bruce and the Community of the Realm of Scotland* (Edinburgh, 1976), 97–369.
11. See J.K.S. St Joseph, *Journ. Roman Stud.*, 51 (1961), 123.

12. For recent discussions of these sites, see G. S. Maxwell, *A Battle Lost: Romans and Caledonians at Mons Graupius* (Edinburgh, 1990); cf. also J.K.S. St Joseph, *Britannia*, 9 (1978), 271-87.

13. In the course of air survey by the Royal Commission on the Ancient and Historical Monuments of Scotland (afterwards cited as R.C.A.H.M.S.); cf. G. S. Maxwell, *Britannia*, 14 (1983), 172-6.

14. See Barrow, *op. cit.*, 178.

15. For a recent brief account of evidence supporting this view, see G. S. Maxwell, *P.S.A.S.*, 113 (1983), 379-85.

16. See J.K.S. St Joseph, *Glasgow Archaeol. Journ.*, 4 (1976), 7-11.

17. Located by the Royal Commission on the Ancient and Historical Monuments of Scotland.

18. In support of this identification see A. L. F. Rivet and C. Smith, *The Place-names of Roman Britain* (London, 1979), 395-6.

19. T. Henderson, *Trans. Dumfries and Galloway Natur. Hist. and Antiq. Soc.*, 3rd series, 14 (1926-28), 169-73.

20. J.K.S. St Joseph, *Journ. Roman Stud.*, 63 (1973), 220-23; R. E. Birley, *P.S.A.S.*, 96 (1962-3), 184-94.

21. Photographed over several years between 1977 and 1986 in the course of aerial survey by R.C.A.H.M.S.; the complex comprises numerous ring-ditch houses, probably souterrains, and subrectangular, oblong structures — possibly timber 'longhouses'.

22. L. F. Pitts and J.K.S. St Joseph, *Inchtuthil: the Roman Legionary Fortress*, Britannia Monograph Series, No. 6 (London, 1985).

23. The castle of Sir Richard Siward, begun with financial assistance from the royal exchequer in 1298 (Bain, *Cal. Docs. Scot.*, ii, 1005, 1307).

24. E.g. as cited in A. Gordon, *Itinerarium Septentrionale* (London, 1726), 19.

25. Discovered during air survey by R.C.A.H.M.S. in 1984; G. S. Maxwell and D. R. Wilson, *Britannia*, 18 (1987), 19-20, 22.

26. Roman fort excavated 1961-66; G. S. Maxwell, *P.S.A.S.*, 104 (1971-2), 147-200.

27. Discovered during air survey by R.C.A.H.M.S. in 1983 and subsqeuently proved by trial-excavation to be of Flavian date: G. S. Maxwell, *Britannia*, 14 (1983), 167-72.

28. W. S. Hanson, *Scottish Archaeol. Forum*, 12 (1980), 66.

29. L. Laing, *P.S.A.S.*, 101 (1968-69), 134-45.

30. For Edwardian refortification at Linlithgow, see H. M. Colvin (ed.), *op. cit.* (note 8 above), 412-15.

31. During air survey by R.C.A.H.M.S.

32. H. M. Colvin, *op. cit.* (note 8 above), 412, n.3.

33. Cf. G. S. Maxwell, *The Romans in Scotland* (Edinburgh, 1989), 112-14.

34. O. G. S. Crawford, *The Topography of Roman Scotland North of the Antonine Wall* (Cambridge, 1949), 14-15.

35. For a summary of the relevant action, see J. Buchan, *Montrose* (London, 1928), 261-72.

36. Tacitus, *de Vita Julii Agricolae*, xxv-xxvii.

37. A. & H. Tayler, *1715: the Story of the Rising* (Edinburgh, 1936), 94-105.

38. Tacitus, *de Vita Julii Agricolae*, xxvi.
39. See J. Buchan, *op. cit.* (note 35, above), esp. 167–314.
40. Tacitus, *de Vita Julii Agricolae*, xxix, 1.
41. *ibid.*, xxvi.
42. *ibid.*, xxxiii.
43. Inverquharity, about 1 acre (0.4 hectare) in area, is a large fortlet of the type used by the Flavians in North Britain, often in less vulnerable intermediate positions; it was identified during air survey by R.C.A.H.M.S. in 1983; cf. G. S. Maxwell and D. R. Wilson, *op. cit.* (note 1, above), 15–16, 21–22.
44. For a general account of the possible location of the battle of *Mons Graupius*, see G. S. Maxwell, *op. cit.* (note 12, above).
45. The construction and use of this structure is covered in H. M. Colvin (ed.), *op. cit.* (note 8, above), 416–17.
46. The possibility that Severus might have crossed the Tay at Carpow (or some other major river-barrier) by a bridge of boats, as depicted on a medallion bearing the legend *TRAIECTVS*, is discussed *inter alia* by A. S. Robertson, in W. S. Hanson and L. J. F. Keppie (eds.), *Roman Frontier Studies 1979: papers presented to the Twelfth International Congress of Roman Frontier Studies* (Oxford, 1980), 131–40.
47. As appears to be indicated by the small temporary camp (overlooking a former inlet on the north side of the Basin) at Dun; see J.K.S. St Joseph, *Journ. Roman Stud.*, 63 (1973), 225–6.
48. Tacitus, *de Vita Julii Agricolae*, xxiv.
49. *ibid.*, xxv.
50. M. L. Bush, *The Government Policy of Protector Somerset* (London, 1975), 24.
51. As for example at Newstead by Melrose; cf. B. R. Hartley, *Britannia*, 3 (1972), 54.

2

DESTRUCTION AND DAMAGE: A REASSESSMENT OF THE HISTORICAL AND ARCHITECTURAL EVIDENCE

Geoffrey Stell

Warfare in Scotland, as elsewhere, has been a major source of destruction and damage, and accounts of physical destruction have been prominent in the military and political record. From Biblical to modern times, however, such accounts cannot always be taken at face value, and a principal purpose of this essay is to test the reliability and value of these accounts as historical evidence by relating recorded episodes of destruction and damage to the surviving physical remains of medieval and early modern buildings. The selection of case-studies is restricted to those sites that are known to have been subjected to siege warfare, slighting, or other acts of wilful violence, as opposed to natural and generally more potent agencies of destruction.[1] The cases are also principally, though not exclusively, Scottish.

In order to appreciate better the circumstances and effects of such activities, it is first necessary to consider how destruction and damage have been viewed through the ages. The twentieth-century world has been conditioned by the experiences of modern warfare and by knowledge of the awesome effects of bombardment, culminating in the devastation of Hiroshima and Nagasaki in August 1945. There is no lack of modern images and measures of destructive force.[2] It is much more difficult to establish earlier perceptions of destruction, although natural phenomena such as volcanoes and earthquakes clearly set the standards against which man's efforts long appeared puny, and were evidently the main sources of artistic inspiration.

Medieval iconography of destruction is well represented by the Apocalypse Tapestries at Angers woven for Louis, Duke of Anjou, by Nicholas Bataille between about 1375 and 1381.[3] One panel depicts Babylon as a heap of ruined debris, whilst another shows that even Louis IX's mighty fortress-palace at Angers itself, completed in the 1230s, would ultimately succumb to the sounds of the last trumpet as described in the Book of Revelation. The Bible was a never-failing

24

source of destructive imagery, and Genesis Chapter 19 inspired Albrecht Dürer (1471–1528) to the painting, probably in the later 1490s, of Lot and his two daughters fleeing from Sodom and Gomorrah.[4] The two evil cities are shown receiving their promised blast of brimstone and fire from the heavens in the form of dramatic, largely volcanic, explosions.

To the medieval mind, Hell was the main factory of the destruction industry, and no medieval artist depicted it more powerfully than Hieronymus Aken or Bosch (*c.*1450–1516). The right panel of his triptych, *The Garden of Earthly Delights*, probably painted towards the end of his life, shows gloomy castle-like buildings with mysterious attendants, contributing to scenes of blood and destruction that are presented in the usual compelling mixture of realism and gruesome fantasy.[5] A detail from another of his late paintings, *The Temptation of St Anthony of Egypt*, conveys in realistic visual terms how a burning medieval village would have appeared, the collapsing spire emphasising and symbolising the processes of destruction.[6]

Fire was the most potent and feared agency of destruction, but authentic visual records of medieval conflagrations are not plentiful, the most vivid representations generally being heavily romanticised views created long after the events they depict. Prepared for publication in 1838, Thomas Allom's view of the burning of Elgin Cathedral by Alexander Stewart, 'Wolf of Badenoch', in 1390 is typical of this genre.[7] There are some word-pictures of medieval fires but none compares with Samuel Pepys's detailed eye-witness account of one of the biggest and most famous fires of all time, the Great Fire of London of September 1666, or with the detailed views of the fire-damaged buildings produced almost immediately after the event.[8]

Contemporary or near-contemporary pictorial representations of damage, including fire damage, caused by besieging forces are found in a number of scattered sources, ranging from the Bayeux Tapestry (where Duke William's men are shown forcing the surrender of the timber fortress of Dinan in 1064) to those woodcuts in Dürer's treatise of 1527[9] which show an up-to-date fortress keeping at bay a large army which was engaged in the destruction of vulnerable outlying structures. For Scotland, an equally instructive background detail is contained in an English map known as the 'platte of Milkcastle' or 'Map of Castlemilk' which dates from 1547 and depicts major strongholds and frontier towns in the western Anglo-Scottish Borders.[10] Annan is shown with a broken steeple and a terse caption, 'Annand town distroyit', clear reference to the fact that on 11 September 1547, the day after the Battle of Pinkie, Thomas Lord Wharton, warden of the west Marches, battered into submission a Scottish force of 65 men stationed in Annan Steeple.

Pictorial records of the effects of gunpowder artillery in later conflicts become progressively more numerous and more detailed. For the English Civil War, for example, Wenceslaus Hollar's contemporary engraving of Basing House in Hampshire shows 'the tower that is half battered downe' as the Royalist garrison bravely resisted besieging Parliamentary forces from 1643 until October 1645.[11] In Scotland, the damage wrought by the returning Jacobite army in early 1746 was also given clear graphic expression. A Thomas Sandby drawing of Fort Augustus shows the damaged bastion (which housed the gunpowder magazine) and barrack-block which had been slighted by the Jacobites in their successful two-day siege of the fort in March 1746.[12] Even greater damage and embarrassment was inflicted upon the first Fort George at Inverness when, a few weeks before Culloden, the Jacobites had forced the garrison to surrender. A 1750 Board of Ordnance plan of the fort by William Skinner[13] shows buildings described as burnt out, and piles of rubble marking the positions of mines that were sprung after the surrender; the governor's house at the entrance was left 'entirely in ruins'.

Turning from the pictorial to the surviving physical evidence of the buildings themselves, this enquiry must, for the sake of reasonable brevity, be largely restricted in scope to upstanding architectural remains, given that *all* below-ground archaeological excavation is in a broad sense an investigation into the effects — and causes — of damage, destruction or decay.

Among early stone castles in Britain few are as instructive as the 35m-high tower of Rochester Castle in Kent in their possession of clear and measurable evidence of siege damage.[14] This great Norman tower, which was built after 1127 by William de Corbeil, archbishop of Canterbury, has a cylindrical south-eastern turret whilst the other three angle-turrets are square, the reason being that this angle had to be rebuilt in order to make good the damage done by King John's besieging force against a rebel baronial garrison in the autumn of 1215. The collapse of the original turret had been effected by undermining and by firing the timber props shoring up the mine.[15] The work of reconstruction was undertaken at royal expense between 1226 and 1232, and since masons then, as now, would have worked from a stable wall-face the extent of the rebuilding would have been greater than the immediate area of damage. The south-eastern angle was rebuilt on a semi-circular plan in the belief that this would give it greater covering power and strength. Indeed, Rochester did successfully withstand a siege by Simon de Montfort and the rebel barons in 1264.

One of the first recorded sieges on Scottish soil was in 1230 and involved 'a' castle on Bute that is identifiable as Rothesay.[16] After an initial repulse by the Scots garrison, the Norse attackers eventually captured the castle because they 'bound over themselves shields of wood . . . hewed into the wall with axes, because the stone was soft; and the wall fell down after that'; it was added that they had 'hewed the wall out close to the ground'. The siege evidently lasted for three days and appears to have cost about 300 lives. Modern architectural analyses have thus attempted to determine how much of the existing fabric of Rothesay Castle may have formed part of the building besieged and captured in 1230, and whether it still bears the scars of this major episode.

It has been suggested,[17] for example, that the comparatively soft defences referred to in 1230 were of compacted clay on a framework of hurdles, and that the *steinn* was comparable to German *backstein* (brick). But given the nature of medieval stonework on Bute at Rothesay and elsewhere there is little reason to doubt that the earliest of the surviving walling was standing in 1230 when the castle probably consisted of a simple circular enclosure. A further characteristic of the masonry construction is a broad and battered (i.e. sloping) plinth which forms the base of the enclosure-wall except in the eastern sector. This stretch, which is vertical and backed by a later chapel, appears to have been rebuilt and patched; a plausible inference is that this length of walling is where the breach was effected in the 1230 siege. It is equally plausible that the heightening of the enclosure-wall and the addition of the four circular flanking towers later in the thirteenth century were direct responses to some of the shortcomings that the siege had highlighted.

Warfare with England after 1296 rendered a number of major Scottish castles vulnerable to attack, and in the earliest phases of the Wars of Independence there were well-recorded sieges at Stirling, Caerlaverock and Bothwell Castles. After a siege in 1304 the gate of Stirling Castle was found to be 'a great deal' broken,[18] but damage resulting directly from these episodes is otherwise difficult to gauge. There are also problems in assessing the effects of the Scots' policy of demolishing or 'slighting' castles and strongpoints in order to deny their use to the enemy, an activity pursued by Robert Bruce and James Douglas between 1307 and 1314, and by Andrew Murray and William Douglas after 1336. Caerlaverock Castle, for example, was ordered to be demolished in 1312 and levelled in 1357, but much of the castle that stood at the time of the celebrated siege of 1300 is still extant.[19] Clearly, this case demonstrates the need for caution in the ready and literal acceptance of all claims or reports of destruction.

On the other hand, Barbour's *Bruce*, whilst relating slighting activities at Douglas, Roxburgh, Edinburgh and Forfar Castles, as well as the destruction of Perth's town wall, also registers the decision *not* to break down the walls of Berwick town and castle, nor, by inference, those of Dunstaffnage Castle.[20] The condition of the great thirteenth-century cylindrical donjon at Bothwell[21] may also provide a clear physical measure of the Scots' campaign of destruction. Bothwell housed an English garrison from 1296 to 1299, from 1301 to 1314, and again briefly in 1336–7. Upon retaking the castle after Bannockburn, Edward Bruce is reputed to have 'destroyed' the castle (the term is the Lanercost chronicler's), and again in 1337 the Scots under Sir Andrew Murray (lord of Bothwell and rightful owner of the castle) are understood to have undertaken its partial dismantling. After what he described as 'the siege of the tower of Bothwell' the chronicler Fordun added that it was this tower which after its capture was thrown to the ground; in its existing form, the rear half of the donjon appears to have been deliberately dismantled from top to bottom, and it probably lay in this condition until after 1362 when the barony and castle were acquired by Archibald, later 3rd earl of Douglas. He and his descendants chose to redevelop the castle in various ways, including the erection of a cross-wall within the sliced donjon, presumably in order to make it more habitable and secure.

The use of gunpowder ordnance considerably increased the destructive potential of field artillery and siege armies, James II (1437–60) being the first Scottish ruler to make full and enthusiastic use of these armaments. A contemporary account of his siege of Abercorn Castle in 1455 related how 'the king remained at the siege and gart struck many of the towers down with the great gun, the which a Frenchman shot right well and failed no shot within a faldom of where it was charged him to hit'.[22] In his own account of the one-month siege James confirmed that the towers of the curtain wall had collapsed as a result of the continual blows of the 'machines'.[23] Abercorn, which was the most strongly fortified of all the Douglas castles according to George Buchanan, clearly did not survive this onslaught; landscaped in the early eighteenth century, it survives merely as a tree-covered mound in the policies of Hopetoun House, archaeological excavations having failed to give more than a glimpse at the extent and character of the medieval castle.[24] Slightly more survives of the Hamilton stronghold of Inveravon, a few miles further west, which James 'cast down' in the same campaign.[25] Here, associated with some earthworks, is a fragment of a D-shaped tower of probable early fifteenth-century date, mute testimony perhaps to the effectiveness of early gunpowder artillery in the hands of a determined and ruthless monarch.

Most of the recorded moves of the greatest piece of early royal ordnance, Mons Meg, were made in the reign of James IV.[26] It was trundled into action in 1489 when a royal siege-train was assembled against the castles of Crookston, Dumbarton and Duchal. Crookston offered no resistance, and Duchal also must have surrendered quickly, although the slight surviving remains of Duchal Castle may in part have resulted from the attentions of a gun which acquired the name of 'Duchal' in this campaign.[27] Dumbarton eventually succumbed to the threat of force.

Outside Scotland, James IV devoted most of his destructive forces to the English border strongholds, particularly Norham Castle,[28] the centre of the Bishop of Durham's outlying principality of North Durham. James took his first tilt at Norham in 1497 during his military invasion in the summer of that year. The siege lasted rather more than a fortnight and the garrison was eventually relieved by a field army under the Earl of Surrey. Although some repairs and additions to the castle were made afterwards, the Scottish siege artillery may have had little physical effect on this occasion. At James's second attempt in August 1513, however, large artillery pieces laid low the gatehouse and the walls of the outer bailey, and within a week the garrison had surrendered. But within three weeks, in the aftermath of Flodden, the castle was again in English hands. Upon his return, the bishop of Durham found that only the great twelfth-century tower and parts of the east and west curtain-walls were left standing. The greater part of the existing curtain-walls of the two baileys, including a rudimentary form of bastioned defence, date from a major rebuilding campaign concluded in about 1521. The rebuilt defences, which were sufficient to hold off an attempted siege by the Duke of Albany in 1523, are thus a crude measure of the considerable damage done to the castle, from which the Scots could take grim satisfaction in counting the otherwise dreadful cost of the Flodden campaign.

Sixteenth-century warfare left much damage in its wake. Extensive destruction of St Andrews Castle,[29] for example, was caused by the bombardment of July 1547 and the demolition that followed its capture from the besieged Protestant garrison. According to John Knox, one of the inmates, the castle 'was raised, the Blockhouse thairof cast down and the walls round about demolished',[30] both blockhouses at each end of the forework having been newly erected in the Beaton area. The precise extent of the damage is not easy to measure, however, although much of the surviving restoration work undertaken by Archbishop John Hamilton (1549–71) probably occupied an area of destruction on the west side, his hall range and gatehouse replacing the Fore Tower as the main entry and frontispiece of the castle. The Fore Tower itself is considerably less damaged than it might otherwise have been if the mine dug in late 1546 had not been broken into and aborted by the defenders' counter-mine.

What was almost certainly the most destructive phase in the history of Edinburgh Castle occurred in April and May 1573 when the castle was held by Sir William Kirkcaldy of Grange on behalf of Queen Mary against the besieging forces of Regent Morton.[31] Five siege batteries were concentrated on the castle, and the most spectacular effect of the bombardment was to bring down one of the major buildings, David's Tower. This lofty tower fell in two stages, burying the great well of the castle on its second collapse. In the rebuilding operations which followed the siege the much-reduced ruins of the tower were encapsulated within the Half-Moon Battery where they still survive.

In the war zones of southern Scotland the destructive effects of English armies are difficult to distinguish from other dilapidations and vandalism of the Reformation era. Unconfirmed military reports of places burnt or destroyed during the War of Rough Wooing cannot necessarily be taken at their own valuation, nor can the testimony of monastic chroniclers, long known as masters of the hyperbole. A description of Kelso Abbey in 1517, for example, revealed only one small portion of damage attributable to the English, an area of the cloister 'partly covered with lead and partly unroofed through the fury and impiety of enemies'.[32] However, there was no gainsaying or exaggerating what later happened to Kelso at the hands of the Earl of Hertford in the 1540s, it being his professed intention 'to raze and deface this house of Kelso so as the enemy shall have little commodity of the same'.33

That military intelligence could make mistaken judgements in these matters and act upon beliefs rather than facts is demonstrated by the later history of Dunivaig Castle, a stronghold on the south-eastern coast of Islay, Argyll.34 Deprived by the crown of what they considered their rightful inheritance, the later members of the MacDonald family of Dunivaig sought to wrest control of it from successive royal agents. A series of incidents in 1614 culminated in the planning of a punitive royal expedition, and in order to avoid a protracted siege, additional soldiers and heavy ordnance were shipped from Dublin. The artillery was to be sufficient 'for the battery and forcing of the said house of Dunivaig, which we are informed, is a place of good strength, being strongly built of itself, and, besides, it is compassed with three stone walls, each of them containing thirty and six feet in thickness'.35 Such was the belief in the castle's strength that a trial of a petard was made in Edinburgh Castle in November 1614 in order to assess its effectiveness against Dunivaig.

Sadly, the castle failed to live up to its extraordinary reputation. The Commanding Officer of the besieging force, which moved into position on 1 February 1615, later reported to James VI:36 'Three days with the battery we used was powerful [enough] to ruin the whole house, invincible without the cannon and famine'. His account referred to the battering of 'a tower in which the rebels held guard over the port that entered the outer bawn [bailey]', and the debris-strewn entrance gate and shattered facework of the outer curtain is testimony to that. The artillery bombardment also 'yielded such abundance of ruins and rubbish' that the inner bawn and the castle well were completely 'choked up'. The castle survived a later demolition proposal and even withstood a siege in 1647, its shattered ruins still bearing witness to the power of early seventeenth-century siege artillery.

Evidence of localised damage caused by bombardment or deliberate slighting in the Civil War period can also still be seen. At Caerlaverock Castle, for example, the conclusion of the 13-week siege of the Royalist garrison by an army of the Estates in 1640 was marked by the dismantling of the south curtain-wall and the associated hall range which had been newly erected by the earl of Nithsdale. In England, probably the most famous castle-slighting campaigns by Parliamentary forces were at Corfe Castle, Dorset, laboriously and expensively dismantled after March 1646, and at Raglan Castle, Gwent, whose fifteenth-century Great Tower did not yield easily to demolition; a late seventeenth-century account records that 'the great Tower, after tedious battering the top thereof with pickaxes, was undermined, the weight of it propped with the timber whilst the two sides of the six were cut through; the timber being burned it fell down in a lump, and so still remains firmly to this day'.[37]

Tangible evidence of some episodes of seventeenth-century warfare in Scotland are, however, much more enigmatic. Brodie Castle is alleged to have been burnt and destroyed by Montrose's men under Lord Gordon at the time of their victory at nearby Auldearn in 1645, Brodie of Brodie being a prominent member of the Committee of Estates. Much of the late medieval nucleus of this castle still stands, however, and, judging from the surviving architecture, the cautious suggestion that 'some of the ancient parts have been preserved in the restoration which took place thereafter' seems an understatement.[38]

The accuracy of traditions concerning minor damage is usually equally difficult to corroborate. The pitted masonry of the tower of Holy Rude Church, Stirling, for example, which stands only about 300m distant from the outer defences of Stirling Castle, is sometimes taken to be marks of musket fire.[39] In August 1651 General Monk's men, pending the completion of their artillery platform, certainly fired on the castle from the tower of the parish church, and could thus have expected to receive a return of fire directed from the castle. However, the marks occur on all four sides of the tower and are particularly heavy on the west side of the north aisle, where they are hidden from the castle; so the geology of the building stones may provide a less attractive but more plausible explanation. Similar uncertainty surrounds the origins of a high-level scar on the rear wall of Borthwick Castle, Midlothian, which has been attributed to the effects of Cromwell's artillery under the command of General Lambert in November 1650; on the other hand, the author of the article in *The Statistical Account* suggests that either lightning or a defect of building was the cause.[40]

The final shots in this review of military destruction and damage belong to the Jacobite era, and are well illustrated by a violent episode in the history of Eilean Donan Castle, Wester Ross.[41] In May 1719 a Jacobite force with Spanish arms and support sailed into Loch Alsh and set up their headquarters in this late medieval island stronghold. A squadron of government warships was on their trail, however, and later views of the castle show the devastating effects of their bombardment and subsequent slighting. The buildings in which the provisions for the main Jacobite camp had been stored were set on fire and the castle was blown up. The castle eventually emerged phoenix-like from its ruins, however, and between 1912 and 1932 was restored by members of the MacRae clan, constables of the former MacKenzie castle. Hence, what has now come to be regarded as one of the most picturesque and Romantic Scottish castles, was for almost two hundred years little more than a heap of rubble, negative witness to the newly-installed Hanoverian government's fears and firepower.

NOTES

1. Geoffrey Stell, 'Destruction, Damage and Decay: the Collapse of Scottish Medieval Buildings', *Review of Scottish Culture* 2 (1986), 59–69.
2. e.g. J. M. Richards (ed.), *The Bombed Buildings of Britain* (2nd edn, 1947).
3. *La tenture de l'Apocalypse d'Angers* (Cahiers de l'Inventaire, no. 4, 1986).
4. Original painting, Washington, National Gallery of Art.
5. Original painting, Prado, Madrid.
6. Original painting, Museu Nacional de Arte Antiga, Lisbon.
7. William Beattie, *Scotland Illustrated* (1838), ii, opp. p. 153.
8. Etchings by Wenceslaus Hollar, London before and after the Great Fire, 1666, originals in British Museum, London, Q6–57 (Sloane collection) and 1862-6-14-1425.
9. Reproduced in W. Kurth (ed.), *The Complete Woodcuts of Albrecht Dürer* (1927, republished 1963), 344–5.
10. Marcus Merriman, 'The Platte of Castlemilk', *Dumfriesshire Trans.*, Third series, xliv (1967), 175–81 at 179–80.
11. Reproduced in Charles Kightly, *Strongholds of the Realm* (1979), 183 (Fig. 156); original in British Museum, London.
12. Original drawing, Royal Library, Windsor Castle, 147 24; reproduced in David Smurthwaite, *The Ordnance Survey Complete Guide to the Battlefields of Britain* (1984), 208.
13. National Library of Scotland, *MS 1646*, Z2/36; reproduced in Iain MacIvor, *Fort George* (1983), 6.
14. R. Allen Brown, *Rochester Castle* (1969) passim; idem., *English Castles* (1976 edn), 67–9, 71, 180 and refs. cited.
15. Underneath one angle of the largely-demolished tower at Bungay in Suffolk there are two incomplete mining galleries almost ready to bring down the tower, one gallery being about 1.5 long by 0.6m wide. Obviously never finished and fired, they evidently belong to Henry II's siege in 1174 of the newly-built tower of Hugh Bigod, earl of Norfolk (Hugh Braun, 'Some notes on Bungay Castle', *Proc. Suffolk Institute of Archaeology*, xxii (1936)).

16. Anderson, *Early Sources*, ii, 476. For architectural description of Rothesay Castle see especially W. D. Simpson, 'The Architectural History of Rothesay Castle', *Glasgow Archaeol. Trans.*, new series, ix, part iii (1939), 152–83; and ibid., 10 (1941), 78–9. See also idem. in K. Falck (ed.), *Annen Viking Kongress, Bergen 1953* (1955), 73–6.

17. W. M. Mackenzie, 'Clay castle-building in Scotland', *Proc. Soc. Antiq. Scot.*, lxviii (1933–4), 117–27 at 117–19.

18. *Cal. Docs. Scot.*, iv, No. 1825.

19. B. H. St J. O'Neil, *Caerlaverock Castle* (1952), 8–9; cf. W. D. Simpson, 'Caerlaverock Castle', *Scot. Hist. Rev.*, 32 (1953), 123–7 at 126.

20. Barbour, *Bruce*, i, 125–7, 204–7, 220, 225, 242–3; ii, 85.

21. W. D. Simpson, 'The Architectural History of Bothwell Castle', *Proc. Soc. Antiq. Scot.*, lix (1924–5), 165–93 at 168–70 and refs. cited; idem, 'Bothwell Castle Reconsidered', *Glasgow Archaeol. Trans.*, new series, xi (1947), 97–116.

22. *Chron. Auchinleck*, 54.

23. Pinkerton, *History*, i, 486–8.

24. Buchanan, *History*, ii, 159; *Medieval Archaeology*, viii (1964), 261; *Discovery and Excavation in Scotland 1963* (Council for British Archaeology, Scottish Regional Group, 1963), 51.

25. *Chron. Auchinleck*, 12; *Exch. Rolls*, vi, 12; RCAHMS, *Inventory of West Lothian* (1929).

26. Claude Gaier, 'The origin of Mons Meg', *Journal of the Arms and Armour Society*, 5 (1965–7), 425–31, 450–2; J. B. Paul, 'Ancient Artillery: with some notes on Mons Meg', *Proc. Soc. Antiq. Scot.*, 1 (1915–16), 191–201.

27. *Treasurer Accts.*, i, 119.

28. C. H. Hunter Blair and H. L. Honeyman, *Norham Castle* (1966), especially 8–9; Norman Macdougall, *James IV* (1989), 138–9, 271–3 and refs. cited.

29. RCAHMS, *Inventory of Fife* (1933), No. 465; for the mine and counter-mine see especially *Letters and Papers, Foreign and Domestic, of the Reign of Henry VIII*, xxi, II (1910), No. 380.

30. John Knox, *History of the Reformation* (1732 edn), 77.

31. 'Journal of the Siege of the Castle of Edinburgh, April and May, MDLXXIII', *Bannatyne Misc.*, ii (1836), 72–80; see also W. F. Gray in *BOEC*, 16 (1928), 9–14, and RCAHMS, *Inventory of Edinburgh* (1951), No. 1 at pp. 5–7 and refs. cited.

32. A. Theiner (ed.), *Vetera Monumenta Hibernorum et Scotorum Historiam Illustrantia* (1864), 527, cited in RCAHMS, Inventory of Roxburghshire (1956), i, No. 504, at 240–1. For other episodes of destruction in the Reformation era see D. McRoberts, 'Material destruction caused by the Scottish Reformation', *The Innes Review*, 10 (1959), 126–72.

33. *State Papers during the Reign of Henry the Eighth*, v (1838), Correspondence relating to Scotland, part IV, 515.

34. RCAHMS, *Inventory of Argyll*, 5 (1984), No. 403.

35. G. G. Smith (ed.), *The Book of Islay* (1895), 157–283, especially 240–9 and refs. cited.

36. *Ibid.*

37. For Corfe Castle RCHM(E), *Inventory of Dorset*, ii (South-east), I (1970), 57–78 at 64 and note; for Raglan, A. J. Taylor, *Raglan Castle* (1950), 20–22. Other episodes of proposed or actual demolitions of English and Welsh castles between 1642 and 1660 are recounted in M. W. Thompson, *The Decline of the Castle* (1987), 138–57, 179–93.
38. D. MacGibbon and T. Ross, *The Castellated and Domestic Architecture of Scotland*, vol. iv (1892), 63–4.
39. RCAHMS, *Inventory of Stirlingshire* (1963), i, No. 131 at p. 133, and No. 192 at pp. 187–8.
40. RCAHMS, *Inventory of Midlothian and West Lothian* (1929), No. 3 at p. 5 and note; *The Statistical Account of Scotland*, xiii (1794), 633.
41. W. K. Dickson (ed.), *The Jacobite Attempt of 1719* (SHS, vol. 19, 1895), xlv–xlix and refs. cited. For a description of the castle in ruins see D. MacGibbon and T. Ross, *The Castellated and Domestic Architecture of Scotland*, iii (1889), 82–5.

3

'THE GREATTEST SCHEIP THAT EWER SAILLIT IN INGLAND OR FRANCE': JAMES IV's 'GREAT MICHAEL'

Norman Macdougall

On the evening of St Andrew's Day, 30 November 1512, the ship carrying Charles de Tocque, Seigneur de la Mothe, ambassador of Louis XII of France to his ally James IV of Scotland, attempted to anchor off Leith in a great storm. The ambassador's arrival was keenly awaited by the Scottish king, for De la Mothe was bearing not only gifts to King James and Queen Margaret, but also the final version of the Franco-Scottish alliance, signed by King Louis, and — more important still — secret instructions from the French king, indicating how much Louis would contribute in return for Scottish armed assistance against Henry VIII of England. De la Mothe fired off two guns, followed by eight, to announce his arrival at Leith, but succeeded only in causing great alarm in Edinburgh, whose citizens believed themselves under attack from the English. The foul weather made it impossible to disembark at Leith, and De la Mothe's ship was driven westwards up the Forth, beyond the Queensferry narrows, until she found a calmer anchorage at Blackness, where the royal warship 'Margaret' was lying. Towering over the 'Margaret' was a second ship, a huge capital ship which de la Mothe had not seen on his previous visit to Scotland, the vessel launched at Newhaven in October 1511 as the 'Michael', referred to in royal accounts and by the English as the great ship, and by later chroniclers as the 'Great Michael'.[1]

The ambassador was received on board the 'Michael' by James IV himself, duly presented his credentials, and no doubt staggered gratefully ashore to begin a visit to the Scottish court which was to last some 2½ months. In this effective piece of theatre, the wily Scottish king had shown himself as a valuable ally in time of war, an ally whose services might have a higher price placed on them by King Louis. De la Mothe was suitably impressed; when he returned to France, late in February 1513, he described the 'Michael' to Louis in such terms as to lead the French king to request the services of the ship 'si puissante qui

36

ne s'en treuve une telle en chrestienté', and to increase substantially his initial offer to the Scots in return for active support by land and sea.[2]

The superlatives lavished on the 'Michael' by the French in 1513 have been used ever since to describe the ship, to the extent that many Scots who know or care little about the reign of James IV are familiar with her name, and have gazed wonderingly at models of the 'Michael' in the Royal Museum and Edinburgh castle. In its own way, this is a remarkable tribute to King James's propaganda; for from beginning to end, the career of the 'Michael' in Scottish service was short, a mere 2½ years from her launch to her purchase by the French in the spring of 1514. Furthermore, much of the first year following her launch was spent fitting out the ship; from late August 1513 to April 1514 she was on hire to Louis XII of France; and she fired her guns in anger on only one known occasion. Her posthumous reputation therefore requires some explanation.

In spite of a wealth of contemporary official material about her, the 'Michael' is undoubtedly best known through descriptions of her in late sixteenth-century narratives. Bishop John Lesley, whose vernacular history was completed around 1570, mentions the 'Michael' briefly as one of the three principal ships in the Scottish fleet during the war of 1513; and he states that in that year James IV sailed in her as far as the Isle of May in the Forth.[3] George Buchanan, whose *History* was published in 1582, begins in the same vein, mentioning 'three vessels of very large bulk, besides others of smaller dimensions', as the nucleus of James IV's fleet; but he then goes on to remark that one of these 'far exceeded, in size, cost, and equipment, any ship that had ever been seen on the ocean.'[4] Although Buchanan does not name the ship, he is clearly referring to the 'Michael'; and his superlatives about her provide a curious echo of Hector Boece's description of that other famous late medieval Scottish ship, Bishop Kennedy's 'Salvator', which Boece called 'the biggest [ship] that had been seen to sail upon the ocean.'[5] Thanks to the work of Dr A. W. K. Stevenson, we now know that the 'Salvator' was a vessel of 500 tons,[6] and Boece was therefore wildly exaggerating her size in relation to contemporary European shipping. Is Buchanan doing the same thing in his description of the 'Michael'?

The *locus classicus* for the 'Michael' is not, however, Buchanan, but the Fife chronicler Robert Lindsay of Pitscottie, whose *Historie* — at least for the century following 1437 — is as quotable as it is generally unreliable; and one is at first tempted to dismiss as fiction Pitscottie's lengthy description of what he sees as one of the glories of the reign, 'ane great scheip callit the greit Michell quhilk was the greattest scheip and maist of strength that ewer saillit in Ingland or France.' But it is worth reading on. 'This scheip', according to Pitscottie, 'was of so greit statur and tuik so mekill timber that scho waistit all the wodis in Fyfe except Falkland wode, by (besides) all the tymmer that was gottin out of Noraway. Scho was so strang and wyde of length and breid that all the wryghtis of Scottland, yea, and money uther strangeris was at hir devyse be the kingis commandement . . .'[7] The chronicler then becomes even more precise. The 'Michael', he says, was 12 score feet long and 35 feet broad between her walls, which were each 10 feet thick. The total cost to the king of building and equipping her — not counting her artillery — was £30,000 Scots. The artillery, according to Pitscottie, consisted of 12 cannons on each side, together with three great basilisks, one forrard and two aft, 300 smaller pieces — medium-sized cannons (mayans), 'batterit falcons and quarter falcons' — and an array of slings, serpentines, and 'doubill doggis' (perhaps 'daggis', horse-carbines or hand-guns), hagbuts and culverins, crossbows and longbows. Her crew numbered 300 sailors, there were 120 gunners to work the artillery, and she could carry a thousand troops.[8]

To lend credibility to this detailed information, Pitscottie claims as his sources Sir Andrew Wood and Robert Barton, respectively quartermaster and master skipper of the 'Michael' according to the chronicler. Superficially the naming of those famous sailors of James IV's day appears to add considerable authority to Pitscottie's narrative; but neither Barton nor Wood, nor even Wood's son, was a contemporary of the chronicler, who was not born until about 1532. While it is clear, therefore, that Pitscottie acquired his knowledge of the 'Michael' through information passed on by the Barton and Wood families, with the passage of time it probably became rather less than exact, and the natural tendency for later writers, looking back on a kind of golden age and a ship of great size, must have been to exaggerate. Thus we must doubt the great length of the 'Michael' as described by Pitscottie — an enormous 240 feet, 5 or 6 times as long as she was broad, double the overall length of the 'Triumph', the largest ship in Elizabeth's navy. But the later 16th century had seen a reaction against huge capital ships; and if we go back to the early 15th century, it would appear that Henry V's 'Grace Dieu', built at Southampton to carry troops to Normandy, had a keel of almost 200 feet in length.

Lacking any firm contemporary evidence as to the ship's length, we have to turn back to Pitscottie himself. As though anticipating objections, the chronicler immediately produces a curious piece of evidence to prove the 'Michael's' great size. 'If ony man beleiffis that this descriptioun of the scheip be not of weritie as we haue writtin', he says, 'lat him pase to the yeit of Tillebairne (Tullibardine) and thair affoir the samin he will sie the length and breid of hir planttit witht hathorne againe be the wryghtis that helpit to mak hir.'[9] This remarkable statement is borne out by Thomas Hunter, writing about the forests of Perthshire in the 1880s.[10] Hunter, admittedly relying on the Second Statistical Account of 1837, which in turn drew some of its information from Pitscottie, had actually seen the 'Michael' excavation. He locates it close by the remains of the old castle of Tullibardine, a few miles north of Auchterarder in Perthshire, and describes it as an excavation of the exact length and breadth of the 'Michael', planted in hawthorn. Since the 1837 Statistical Account, at which time only three of the hawthorns still survived, the excavation had been almost completely filled in, but in the late 1850s the shape of the ship survived as an ornamental pond in which acquatic plants and birds luxuriated; and it was still distinctly visible to Hunter in 1883.

A century later, nothing is clearly visible to the casual observer. Indeed, Tullibardine castle, in front of which the 'Michael' excavation is supposedly to be found, had disappeared completely by the early 19th century, its ruins being used in the building or rebuilding of nearby cottages and farmhouses. But the site of the castle is marked clearly on the first edition of the Ordnance Survey, prepared for this area in the early 1860s, so that it is possible to work out the exact site of the excavation.[11] In July 1990, Dr Colin Martin photographed the site from the air (Fig. 1); both the remains of the castle and the 'Michael' excavation are visible, though only further work on the ground — and perhaps further aerial photography under better weather conditions — could produce an accurate estimate of the length and breadth of the ship.

The historian's question — as distinct from that of the archaeologist — about the 'Michael' excavation is why the knight of Tullibardine should have chosen to plant the exact shape of James IV's great ship in hawthorn outside his castle gate. Tullibardine is after all about as far from the sea, east or west, as one can reach in Scotland. There is no clear answer; but it may have something to do with the connection between the families of Murray of Tullibardine and Colquhoun of Luss. The heraldic arms of both families are to be found impaled in Tullibardine chapel, founded by Sir David Murray of Tullibardine, who

Plate 1. Tullibardine, Perthshire: The site of the 'Michael' excavation, photographed by Dr Colin Martin in July 1990. The remains of Tullibardine castle are just visible at the junction of the farm tracks in the bottom centre of the photograph. The 'Michael' excavation lies across the track (just above the castle remains in the photograph) leading to Tullibardine chapel (centre right). (University of St Andrews Department of Scottish History aerial Photographic Collection).

died around 1452. His eldest son seems to have married Margaret, daughter of James III's Chamberlain, Sir John Colquhoun of Luss.[12] Colquhoun was a shipowner — indeed, restitution for the seizure of one of his vessels by the English was one of the by-products of the Anglo-Scottish treaty of 1474[13] — and his successor Humphrey Colquhoun sold a ship for £130 Scots to James IV in 1489.[14] So the Colquhoun connection *may* explain the Murray interest in the navy in general, and in particular, in the 'Michael' and her remarkable size.

Returning to Pitscottie's description of the 'Michael', we find that much which he has to say is wholly credible. On the subject of the ship's big guns, Pitscottie's twelve cannon on each side and the three basilisks — a total of 27 — may be compared with the 21 bronze cannon on Henry VIII's 'Henri Grace à Dieu', launched a year after the 'Michael' and possibly built in imitation of her;[15] and some of Pitscottie's claims for the 'Michael's' big guns can be substantiated from contemporary sources. Thus the chronicler's three great basilisks are surely to be identified with the 'iij gret gunnys' transported from Edinburgh castle down to Leith in August 1512, to be put aboard the 'greit schip'.[16] These guns, cast in the castle foundry, presumably under the supervision of the king's 'master meltar' Robert Borthwick,[17] were only a small proportion of the output of the royal foundry in 1512–1513; but latterly, with the approach of the Flodden campaign, it becomes impossible to distinguish between guns forged to accompany the army and those intended for the navy. There is, however, sufficient evidence to show that the 'Michael', in spite of her vast range of small weaponry down to culverins and crossbows, was essentially a big gun ship whose main armament was a small number of major artillery pieces newly forged, which were intended to inflict massive damage at a distance, either on other vessels or on fortresses which could be attacked from the sea. In this respect the 'Michael' strikingly anticipates the 'Henri Grace à Dieu' but differs sharply from an ageing English capital ship of comparable size, the 'Regent', which fought her last fight in August 1512 grappling with her French opponent, the 'Cordelière', with troops on both sides shooting at each other at close range with handguns, crossbows and longbows, until both ships were consumed by fire.[18]

Two of Pitscottie's other claims for the 'Michael' are easily dealt with. First, he states that, at full strength, the ship had a crew of three hundred; this is exactly correct, as the royal naval accounts of 1512–13 demonstrate. Remarkably, we know the names of every crew member on board the 'Michael' in the summer of 1513 with the exception of the cooks, who remain anonymous.[19] Secondly, the chronicler's claim that the 'Michael' could carry a thousand troops is certainly no wild exaggeration, and may in fact be very close to the truth. A useful comparison is Robert Barton's French-built 300-ton 'Lion', the first ship in James IV's navy to reach France in the late summer of 1513, carrying 260 men, soldiers and sailors.[20] The crew probably numbered about sixty, the remainder being soldiers in the Scottish expeditionary force to France. If the 'Lion' could carry two hundred troops — possibly more[21] — it is not unlikely that the thousand-ton 'Michael' could accommodate up to a thousand in addition to her crew of three hundred.

Indeed, in August 1512, one of Louis XII's largest capital ships, the 'Cordelière' of 790 tons, is to be found carrying a total complement of 1254.[22]

As to the cost of the 'Michael', Pitscottie's round figure of £30,000 Scots — excluding the ship's artillery — is probably fairly accurate. Although we lack the Treasurer's accounts for 1509 and 1510, when the 'Michael' was under construction, and cannot therefore arrive at any exact figure, we know that the ship was finally sold to the French, in April 1514, for 40,000 francs — about £18,000 Scots.[23] It is unlikely that the Scottish government after Flodden, with no great interest in the fleet, the king dead, and facing acute financial problems, received anything like cost price from Louis XII for the 'Michael'. Thus an initial cost of £30,000 Scots, or something very close to it, seems not unreasonable.

Remarkably, Pitscottie could on occasions be guilty of understatement. His comment that timber for the 'Michael' 'waistit all the wodis of Fyfe except Falkland wode' is to some extent borne out by the Treasurer's accounts; and the chronicler does not even mention further supplies of oak for royal shipbuilding brought from forests in Ross-shire, Darnaway in Moray, Cambuskenneth, Cawdor, Kincardine, and Tulliallan.[24] Further timber was imported, not only from Norway but also from France and Denmark; and much of the ship's outfitting was foreign, with brass pulleys from Denmark, some of the larger guns from Flanders, rigging from France and the Low countries, compasses from Middelburg.[25] Some of the outfitting, however, was of Scots origin, for example the leather lining the gun port-holes to prevent the woodwork being singed when the cannon were fired.[26] The ship's huge standards, bearing at least one enormous St Andrews Cross, a Lion, and a Unicorn, cost £72 Scots, and some if not all were painted by Andrew Chalmers.[27]

The first reference to the 'Michael' in the Treasurer's accounts comes as early as 12 August 1506 — more than five years before her launch — when James Wilson, an expatriate Scot in Dieppe, was paid £42 for the freight of a vessel carrying 'planks and trees' for what is described as 'the great ship'.[28] About the same time shipwrights, including Jacques Terrell from Normandy, were brought from France to Scotland to plan and build the 'Michael'.[29] For some time the king had been dissatisfied with shipbuilding facilities at the royal dockyard of Leith — as early as 1504, he had looked for a new haven with deeper water — and the existence of sandbanks at the mouth of the Water of Leith, which had created problems at the launching of the 'Margaret' in 1505, may finally have convinced him that 'the great ship' must be built elsewhere.[30] The New Haven of Leith, about a mile to the west, was the king's choice. Construction of a new dockyard started in 1504, craftsmen were imported from France, Flanders, Denmark, and Spain, and in 1507 a chapel dedicated to the Virgin and St James was completed in the centre of the small village of Newhaven which served the dockyard.[31] In March 1511, the city of Edinburgh, perhaps fearing Newhaven as a rival to its own port of Leith, received a grant of it from the king.[32]

Seven months later, on 12 October 1511, the 'Michael' was launched at Newhaven, with music playing and fanfares provided by three trumpeters.[33] Months of outfitting, and the erection of her masts, followed, and it was not until 18 February 1512 that the great ship was towed out into the Forth. Three days later James IV dined on board; and in March the 'Michael' sailed the few miles up to Queensferry.[34] Subsequently the ship appears to have travelled, or been towed, even further west, probably as far as the new dockyard at 'Polertht' — Pool of Airth opposite Kincardine-on-Forth — for further outfitting, and at the beginning of June 1512 the king sailed up the Firth from Bo'ness to visit her.[35] Further royal visits followed in July, and on 3 August, surrounded by tapestries brought from Falkland for the occasion, James IV and Margaret Tudor dined on board.[36] Almost ten months after her 'out-putting' or launch, the 'Michael' was at last out of the hands of the wrights and outfitters.

If the cost of building and outfitting the 'Michael' was enormous, the continuing expense of paying wages to her crew, victualling her, and maintaining her in a seaworthy state was no less daunting. The wages of the crew averaged 35/— per man per month,[37] a figure which compares favourably with contemporary English wages of 5/— sterling — about 20/— Scots per month — and possibly reflects the difficulty of attracting skilled seamen to the Scottish fleet. With these wages, the 'Michael' with her full complement of three hundred would cost James IV more than £500 Scots per month. As royal annual income in 1512–13 was only in the region of £30,000–£40,000, King James's anxiety to have the 'Michael' and the remainder of the Scottish fleet reach France as swiftly as possible, and so become a charge on his ally Louis XII, is easily understood.

As for victualling, an idea of the cost is provided by an account (Table 1) covering a full seven days from Sunday 17 July 1513, when

TABLE 1
The Victualling of the 'Great Michael'

Sunday, 17 July — Saturday 23 July 1513

Crew of 200 on board.

Sunday	2 marts:	£ 2. 0. 0.
	600 loaves;	£ 6. 0. 0.
	1 last ale	
	(144 gallons):	£12. 0. 0.
Monday	1½ marts:	£ 1. 14. 0.
Tuesday	2 marts:	£ 2. 2. 0.
Wednesday	400 fish:	£ 0. 13. 4.
Thursday	2 marts:	£ 2. 6. 0.
Friday	400 fish:	£ 0. 13. 4.
Saturday	400 fish:	£ 0. 12. 0.

Total: £28. 0. 8. (Scots)

[*Source: T.A.,* iv, 485–6]

English comparison

The 'Regent', 1000 tons.
10 days victualling, spring 1512
Total: £33 *sterling* for 300 mariners (Biscuit, beer, beef, fish)
= approx. £132 *Scots* (10 days)
= £88 *Scots* for 200 mariners
= £62 *Scots* for 7 days.

the 'Michael' was lying off Leith with 200 men on board. A week's victuals total about £28 Scots; fully commissioned with 300 men on board, the cost would therefore be around £42, that is £168 per month.

We must of course be cautious in attempting to estimate James IV's expenditure on the 'Michael' and his other ships. The accounts make clear that for much of the time they were manned by skeleton crews; and the fleet was only fully commissioned and rigged for war from July of 1513. Likewise relatively few of the Scottish warships of 1513 were James's personal responsibility, most being hired from, or owned by, his captains, Wood, the Bartons, Brownhill, Merrymouth, and Chalmers. Even so, the 'Michael' alone, costing little short of £700 Scots a month for victuals and wages, was James IV's biggest single

TABLE 2
Expenditure on the navy: 1488-1513

The figures below are drawn from the Treasurer's accounts, which are incomplete (e.g. there are no accounts at all for 1508 — 10). Apart from the final figure, the totals given include building, buying, repairing and victualling of ships, together with wages for shipwrights and labourers in the royal dockyards.

1488 — 1498:	*Total* expenditure	£1486. 12. 10.
i.e.	*Average* per annum (total includes £500 for a rowbarge built at Dumbarton)	£ 140. 0. 0. (approx.)
1501 — 1504:	*Average* per annum	£ 600 (approx.)
1505 — 1507:	*Average* per annum	£5000 (approx.)
1507 — 1508:	*Total* for the year	£7279
1511 — 1513:	*Average* per annum	£8710. 10. 0.

[The last figure is an underestimate, as it excludes much victualling, building and wages]

expense by far, possibly the largest warship in northern Europe until the launching of Henry VIII's 'Henri Grace à Dieu', of similar size, in 1512.

Why was the 'Michael' built at all? It would be easy — too easy — to dismiss her simply as a dramatic demonstration of royal Stewart megalomania, the effort of the king of a remote and impoverished kingdom to compete in terms of prestige with his vastly richer and more powerful European neighbours. However, such an explanation ignores the fact that the 'Michael' was built not as an isolated showpiece, but towards the end of a long reign of 25 years which was characterised throughout by unprecedented and constantly growing expenditure on the royal navy. Table 2 illustrates that the most dramatic increase in King James's outlays on ships occurred shortly after the turn of the century, and that it coincided with the arrival in Scotland of the French shipwrights Lorans and Diew, the real creators of the royal fleet. By the end of a reign during which crown income increased by perhaps 2½ times, annual royal expenditure on the navy multiplied more than sixty times. The 'Michael' and her role can therefore only be understood in the context of James IV's plans for the navy as a whole.[38]

These plans are most explicitly heralded in a remarkable letter from King James to Louis XII of France, dated 13 August 1506. Looking both to the past and to the future, the Scottish king described his building of a fleet to defend Scotland as a project of long standing, and claimed that he was constructing more ships at home under the auspices of Louis. He assured the French king that he had only to command, and James, his subjects, and the Scottish fleet would serve Louis wherever he might have need of them. The letter concludes by impressing on Louis the continuing importance and value of the ancient alliance between the French and Scots.[39]

Even allowing for diplomatic rhetoric, this letter makes clear beyond any real doubt the purpose of the Scottish fleet. It was clearly designed for something more than a static defence of the Scottish east coast, the pursuit of pirates, or the 'daunting' of the Western Isles. These objectives could be achieved much more effectively by delegation of authority to trusted captains like Wood or the Bartons, whose ships might be hired or bought by the Crown for service in specific crises. The minority governments of James IV had in any case long ago built fortalices and gun emplacements at the Queensferry, and on the island of Inchgarvie at the narrows, to prevent any repetition of the naval depredations of John Lord Howard, who had sailed unchecked up the Forth in 1481, attacking and burning Blackness; and the reconstruction of Dunbar castle from 1497 onwards, on the orders of the adult James IV, was a further indication of a government committed to the effective defence of Scotland's vulnerable south-east coast.[40] But the 'Michael', and the other newly-built or acquired ships in James's navy, suggest a more belligerent purpose. On land, as the campaigns of 1496–7 had shown, the Scottish king had adopted a very aggressive view of the defence of his country, with some success. At sea, as his letter of 1506 to Louis XII indicates, his construction of a navy, 'a project of long standing', may be seen to have got under way in 1502, shortly after the conclusion of the Anglo-Scottish treaty of 'Perpetual Peace'. That treaty gave James IV a modest dowry paid over three years, an English wife, and a solemn commitment to peace on land with his former enemy; but the building of a fleet 'under the auspices of Louis' — that is, with French shipwrights and French timber — gave the Scottish king a chance to avail himself of a loophole in an English treaty which was never popular in Scotland, and to pursue an independent policy on the sea.

That policy was of course closely bound up with the needs of the King of France. As the 1506 letter indicates, James was prepared to support Louis with his subjects and the Scottish fleet — but at a price. The French king finally met that price in May 1513, a year after the formal renewal of the Franco-Scottish alliance and in the face of an English invasion of north-eastern France by the young Henry VIII in person. Louis would equip and victual the Scottish fleet, and deliver 50,000 francs — about £22,500 Scots — to James IV, and would offer to the Scots king the services of the war galleys of his most able admiral, Gaston Prégent de Bidoux. In return King James would invade England as soon as Henry VIII had crossed to France, and would at the same time send the Scots fleet to France, if possible reinforcing his ships with others drawn from the navy of the King of Denmark.[41] This was therefore a hard-headed bargain entered into by a Scottish king who could not afford to equip and victual his fleet throughout the course of a lengthy war, and who could certainly make use of a large pension from King Louis to help him clear his annual deficit on current expenditure. It was in this context that the 'Michael' and her companions set sail for France towards the end of July 1513.

Whether they would have sailed at all if Henry VIII had paid for the Scottish king's neutrality in the forthcoming war is arguable; but the situation simply did not arise. It is probably significant that James IV's final deal with Louis XII was struck only a few weeks after Henry VIII's ambassador to Scotland, Nicholas West, Dean of Windsor, had returned home without any commitment from King James to honour the Anglo-Scottish treaty and remain neutral when Henry invaded France. West had had nothing to offer but threats; in his various conversations with James, he warned the Scottish king that he should fear the loss of Henry VIII's favour, that Margaret Tudor's legacy would not be paid to her unless James gave a written guarantee to remain neutral, that the English king might turn his army against the Scots rather than the French, and that in any case King Henry had the power both to invade France and to resist the Scots.[42] Coming on top of renewed English claims of overlordship over Scotland in 1512, and the English-inspired excommunication of James IV for breaking the Anglo-Scottish treaty, in 1513,[43] West's maladroit diplomacy was unlikely to produce the Scottish neutrality which his royal master was seeking. West's behaviour was probably largely the result of frustration at his unrewarding ambassadorial task, made worse by his dislike of the Scots, an antipathy which was heartily reciprocated.

In his efforts to avoid returning south empty-handed, West took some time off from pursuing the elusive King James to go down from Holyrood to Newhaven to spy on the Scottish fleet. However, he failed to find the 'Michael', and wrote disparagingly — and inaccurately — about the remainder of the fleet. Worse still, his visit was revealed to James IV, who spent his subsequent interview with the wretched ambassador taunting West with the size of the 'Michael' — she carried more ordnance on board, according to the king, than Louis XII had ever brought to a siege — and with the prior claim which the French king had to the ship, in spite of Henry VIII's demand for her in a written requirement which West read to James word for word. Even West's efforts to sound out the Scottish king's counsellors, hoping for a more favourable response, were a failure; indeed, the royal Secretary, Patrick Paniter, normally a smooth and diplomatic courtier, summed up Anglo-Scottish relations in a sentence when he told West roundly that if the English needed the Scots they made 'importunate suit' to them, but when they did not need them, they despised them and did them all the harm they could.[44]

In one of West's final altercations with James IV, probably on 6 April 1513, the Scottish king told him that he was aware of the impending papal interdict directed against his kingdom, and remarked that he intended to appeal from the letters of execution. West replied that no appeal was possible, as no-one stood above the Pope. James declared that he would appeal to the apostolic authority of the King of the French and to 'Préjean' — Gaston Prégent de Bidoux, Louis XII's formidable admiral.[45] His words were prophetic; less than three weeks later, on 25 April, Henry VIII's manic admiral, Sir Edward Howard, who had boasted to his king that Prégent and his men would have 'broken heads that all the world shall speak of it', boarded the French admiral's galley off Brest and was hurled overboard to his death.[46] For Thomas Wolsey, Henry VIII's almoner, charged with the mammoth task of organising the safe transport of English troops into northern France only a few weeks later, the omens were not good. Two English ventures on the Continent, in 1511 and 1512, had failed disastrously; and as the servant of a young and belligerent monarch determined to restart the Hundred Years' War in the summer of 1513, and to take part in it himself, Wolsey must have realised that his career was at stake, for only military success in France, and safe passage across the Channel in each direction for his huge expeditionary force, could satisfy Henry VIII. Morale in the English fleet was bad, especially after Sir Edward Howard's death; and as late as June, the month in which King Henry crossed to Calais, the new English admiral, Howard's brother Thomas, reckoned that the Scottish and Danish fleets might join the French in the Channel.[47]

In the event, no such triple alliance materialised. James IV's Danish uncle, King Hans, who had embarked on a sizeable naval building programme towards the end of his reign, died in February 1513;[48] and in spite of efforts by the Scottish king to spur Hans' successor Christiern into action the following month,[49] no Danish ships were forthcoming, and the naval alliance was confined to Scotland and France. King James's fleet would not be ready to sail from the Forth until late July, by which time Henry VIII was safely in France.

However, the English king had also to recross the Channel safely, and Franco-Scottish correspondence during the summer makes it clear that Louis XII hoped to use the fleets of both nations in order to 'faire quelque bonne exécucion sur mes ennemys' — though the objective of the combined navies is nowhere explicitly revealed. As the summer advanced, however, the French king became increasingly impatient, 'aultrement la saison s'en va passée.'[50] No doubt various schemes were mooted. As the allies intended to use not only the Norman and Breton fleets, Prégent's war galleys, and Scottish vessels headed by the 'Michael', but also sizeable French and Scottish expeditionary forces carried by all these ships, perhaps the intention was to launch a direct assault on Henry VIII's transports at Calais, to prevent the English king returning safely from Picardy in the autumn.

In three consecutive days towards the end of July 1513, James IV committed himself to all-out war against the English. He summoned the lieges on 24 July to muster at Ellem in Berwickshire for an invasion of Northumberland, and on the 26th he despatched Lyon King of Arms to France with an ultimatum to Henry VIII. On 25 July, the 'Michael' and the remainder of the fleet, numbering at least eleven ships, sailed from the Forth en route for France.[52] Preparations for this occasion had been under way for months, and are revealed in detail in a series of fascinating shipbuilding accounts.[53] What the records also reveal, however, in addition to the victualling, arming, and crewing of the ships, is that the fleet was expected to carry a large number of soldiers to France. Thus between 16 and 20 June, James IV sent messengers to the north and west, to Galloway, Stirlingshire, Clydesdale, East Lothian, the Merse, and Teviotdale, 'for the furnesing of men to the schippis.'[54] A letter from the king to William, Lord Livingston, on 13 July, reveals both that there had been a general call-up throughout the realm to supply young men for James's seaborne army, and that the prospect of service abroad

Plate 2. Carrickfergus, County Antrim: the principal English stronghold in Ulster, attacked by a Scottish seaborne army en route for France, headed by the 'Michael', in the summer of 1513; much later, in the 1640s, Carrickfergus served as one of the principal Irish bases for Robert Munro's Scottish mercenary army (Ch. 6).

was unattractive to some.[55] Nevertheless, if three or four ships of modest size were able to carry about two thousand troops to Denmark in 1502,[56] it seems likely that a fleet of eleven or more, including a monster like the 'Michael' and large vessels such as the 'Barque

Mytoune' and the 'Margaret', would find accommodation for at least three times as many. Thus in spite of her big guns, and the presence on board of the king's redoubtable master gunners, Jacob and Henrik 'Cutlug',[57] the 'Michael's' principal function in her only campaign in Scottish service was as an enormous troop transport.

It appears, however, that James IV intended his 'armée de mer' to perform an additional task in Scottish service before proceeding to France. The fleet, having sailed north from the Forth on 25 July under the command of King James's cousin James Hamilton, earl of Arran, turned west and south — presumably by way of the Pentland Firth and the Hebrides — and launched an attack on Carrickfergus, the principal English stronghold in Ulster. Unfortunately no strictly contemporary account of this episode survives; however, Pitscottie, claiming the authority of Sir Andrew Wood — albeit two generations removed in time — as his source, sees the Carrickfergus raid as a foolish piece of private enterprise by Arran, who 'keipit no derectioun of the king his maister bot passit to the wast sie wpoun the cost of Ireland, and thair landit and brunt Caragforgus witht wther willagis, and than come foranent the toune of Air and thair landit and repossit and playit them the space of xl dayis.' Thereafter, according to Pitscottie, the furious king sent the veteran Sir Andrew Wood with heralds to Ayr to dismiss Arran, James IV swearing that the earl should be forfeited for disobeying his commands. The prudent Arran, anticipating arrest, set sail for France, only to be further delayed when his fleet was scattered by a storm.[58] A variant of this story, conveying essentially the same information, is to be found in Buchanan's history.[59]

Surprisingly, a more convincing account of the Carrickfergus raid is to be found in Sir David Lindsay's 'Historie of Squyer Meldrum', an epic poem written probably about 1550, towards the end of Lindsay's life.[60] Though not concerned to describe in detail the events of 1513 except in so far as they relate to the martial deeds of his hero, William Meldrum of Cleish and Binns, Lindsay is immediately more believable than the later sixteenth-century chroniclers; for in 1512, as a young man, he had been appointed as usher or chief page to the infant James V, and was presumably at court a year later when the Carrickfergus raid took place. Indeed, he may have had an account of it from Meldrum himself.[61]

Thus the 'Historie of Squyer Meldrum' does not fall into the post-Reformation trap of attempting to slight the Hamiltons; on the contrary, James Hamilton, earl of Arran, is described as 'baith wyse and vailyeand', and there is no suggestion that the Carrickfergus raid was anything other than planned by king and council from the outset.[62] There is, in fact, a great deal of evidence to suggest that this was the case; for on 25 June Hugh O'Donnell of Tyrconnell in Ulster, in the course of a three-month visit to the Scottish court, made a treaty with James IV. This is couched in the most general terms: King James took O'Donnell under his protection and promised him ships and men if the Irish leader asked for them.[63] Yet it is inconceivable that the treaty did not have a specific and immediate objective in view. O'Donnell had been trying to involve James IV in Ulster politics since the spring of 1507,[64] and the Scottish king had had dealings with O'Donnell's father as long before as 1495, at the outset of James's personal rule.[65] As in 1495, so also in 1513, King James's intention seems to have been to incite and make use of Irish rebellion in order to bring pressure to bear on a hostile English government.

Nor was a siege of Carrickfergus anything new to the Scots. During the Bruces' campaigns in Ireland in the years 1315–18, the castle had been surrendered to Edward Bruce, King Robert I's brother, in 1316, following a dour siege lasting almost a year.[66] In the early fifteenth century the boot was on the other foot: in a suggestive but obscure episode in March 1428, the exiled James Stewart, the only survivor of James I's wholesale extermination of the Albany Stewarts in 1425, allied himself with Niall O'Donnell of Tyrconnell, the objective of both men apparently being to use a Scottish Highland army to attack Carrickfergus as a first step to launching an invasion of southern Scotland, removing James I and putting James Stewart in his place. In the event, the attack never took place, probably because Stewart died in 1429; but the scheme itself must have brought home to James I very forcefully the potential danger of the close links between Ulster chieftains and those in the Highlands and Islands of Scotland.[67]

In 1513 James IV was clearly ready to turn internal dissensions in Ulster to his advantage. An earlier attempt by O'Donnell, in the spring of 1507, to elicit armed assistance from James − in the shape of four thousand men led by MacIan of Ardnamurchan − had been side-stepped by the Scottish king, probably because he had only recently accomplished the 'daunting of the Isles' and had no wish to become embroiled in an Irish war with his then ally, Henry VII of England.[68] Six years later, with war all but declared and Henry VIII on the point of sailing to invade France, the political situation was radically different. If a Scottish seaborne army assailed Carrickfergus and then joined up with the forces of Louis XII of France while James IV himself ravaged Northumberland, the pressure on the English king to break off the French war would be substantially increased. King James must also have been aware that the Anglo-Irish lord deputy, Gerald Fitzgerald, eighth earl of Kildare, who had dominated Irish politics for more than a generation, was a broken man, his reputation for invincibility shattered by a heavy defeat in County Limerick in 1510 at the hands of Toirdhealbhach Donn O'Brien of Antrim. In the event Kildare, who had been wounded in action the following year, died on 3 September 1513 after a period of slow physical decline; so there appeared to be an opportunity for the Scots to enlist the forces of Irish Gaeldom against their English enemies with some chance of success.[69]

For his part, Hugh O'Donnell of Tyrconnell must have been relieved to be assured of James IV's assistance, for at the Limerick defeat in 1510 he had been — unusually — on Kildare's side, and by 1513 may have felt in considerable danger from the O'Briens, the traditional enemies of his house. But the Scottish king's aid could not be purchased lightly; for when O'Donnell left the court for the west coast on 15 July, he took with him not only a gift of £160 Scots from James IV, but also artillery, ammunition, a French wright, smiths, carters, and quarriers 'for undirmynding of wallis', at a cost to James of a further £200.[70] Clearly the Irish leader was expected to take part in a siege at an early date, and cooperation with the Scots in an assault on Carrickfergus by land and sea seems the most likely objective.

This is further suggested by the remarkable witness list appended to the O'Donnell treaty of 25 June. It is by far the longest sederunt of its kind for the entire reign, containing no less than nineteen names rather than the usual seven or eight, and eleven of these names do not appear on any other royal grant of 1513. The eleven consist of four western earls with an obvious geographical proximity to Ireland — Arran, Angus, Eglinton, and Glencairn — three lords of parliament from the Lothians — Seton, Lindsay of Byres, and Sinclair — and four clerics, John Hepburn, prior of St Andrews, George Crichton, abbot of Holyrood, James Stewart, abbot of Culross, and Robert Forman, dean of Glasgow.[71]

The common factor bringing many if not all of these eleven individuals together is their connection with the navy, for some of them with the 'Michael' itself. James Hamilton, earl of Arran, the king's cousin, was of course the Admiral of the Scottish fleet who, with his flag on the 'Michael', would lead the Carrickfergus raid. Archibald, fifth earl of

Angus, was a disgraced Chancellor struggling back into favour with James IV; on 27 November 1511, shortly after the launch of the 'Michael', he was to be found playing cards with the king at Newhaven, and tactfully losing 26 ducats.[72] George, Lord Seton, was a royal familiar whose family had naval interests going back at least two generations; it was his kinsman John's seamen who brought King James by boat from the 'Michael' to Leith in March 1512; and it was Lord George's brother who was sent, in July of the same year, 'to fee marinaris beyond the water' — presumably from France.[73] As for Henry, Lord Sinclair, as Master of the royal artillery he had been responsible for the transport of artillery from Edinburgh castle down to Newhaven on 13 September 1511. The guns' destination may have been the 'Michael', which was launched the following month; certainly Sinclair had an interest in the ship, as he helped to supply her in July 1513.[74] So also did another of the eleven, John Hepburn, prior of St Andrews, great-uncle of the Earl of Bothwell, a former Privy Seal and firm supporter of the French connection in the early 1490s, who supplied the great ship with 500 gallons of ale;[75] while yet another witness, Robert Forman, dean of Glasgow, had made a contribution of £20 towards the raising of the 'Michael's' mast in February 1513.[76]

Thus the witnesses to the O'Donnell treaty of 25 June 1513 were individuals who had Irish interests and/or were familiars of James IV; most, perhaps all, of them had naval connections, some with the 'Michael' itself. All this evidence points to the Carrickfergus raid having been planned in a large war council about the time of the O'Donnell treaty; and it is surely significant that William Elphinstone, bishop of Aberdeen, Keeper of the Privy Seal for over twenty years, and according to his biographer Hector Boece a committed opponent of the war,[77] is not to be found as a witness to the treaty, although his name is to be found on every other royal sederunt of 1513. The nineteen signatories fall broadly into categories: those like the Archbishop-Chancellor, Alexander Stewart, the Earls of Argyll and Lennox, and Secretary Paniter, who would accompany the king to Northumberland in August; and the eleven others, who were in some way — either by supplying, leading, or actively supporting — connected with King James's 'armée de mer' en route for Carrickfergus and France. O'Donnell was about to receive his four thousand men (at least), six years later than he had asked for them and probably with a different objective in view than that which he had originally intended.

As the Scottish fleet had sailed from the Forth on 25 July, exactly a month after the O'Donnell treaty had been made, it had presumably arrived in Belfast Lough by early August at the latest. From the scanty evidence available, however, it appears that what followed was not the bombardment of Carrickfergus castle but rather the burning and ravaging of the town and neighbourhood by the Scots host. As Sir David Lindsay puts it:

> '. . . as they passit be Ireland coist,
> The Admirall gart land his oist,
> And set Craigfergus into fyre,
> And saifit nouther barne nor byre.'[78]

If James had intended a coordinated attack on Carrickfergus castle by the 'Michael' and other Scots ships, together with an Irish force under O'Donnell using Scots guns and quarriers, he must have been disappointed. The scheme may have been ruined by the Irishman at an early stage; for in mid-August O'Donnell abandoned his Scottish artillery at Glasgow, and James IV had to spend £47 dragging the guns back to Edinburgh,[79] where they arrived on 24 August, too late to be used by the Scottish host, which had reached its target, Norham castle, on the English East March. O'Donnell's reasons for leaving his guns behind are not clear. He may have been concerned about their transport in bad weather — according to the contemporary Irish annalist he encountered great (but unspecified) peril at sea on his voyage home.[80] Alternatively he may have felt that he could not raise support amongst his own people for a siege of Carrickfergus castle, which was a very tough nut to crack. So he left the Scots to their own devices; and probably obeying the spirit rather than the letter of King James's instructions, Arran sacked the town but did not seek to take the castle,[81] a decision which must have been popular with the Scots host, if not with the king.

After the raid, according to the later chroniclers (but not Sir David Lindsay), the fleet returned to Ayr. Considering the western provenance of many of those who had witnessed the O'Donnell treaty — and who may indeed have sailed with the fleet — a return to Ayr seems not unlikely. Arran may have required to take on fresh victuals or ammunition, or perhaps wanted to deposit booty taken from Carrickfergus; and he may also have been concerned about attacks by English ships on the Firth of Clyde and Ayrshire coast, the threat of which had brought James IV himself to Ayr and Ailsa Craig the previous year.[82] In any event, it is perhaps possible to reconcile the stories of Pitscottie and

Buchanan — that Arran was disobeying orders from the beginning by attacking Carrickfergus, and that the king sought to have him arrested when the earl returned to Ayr and wasted time there[83] — with the known facts. Clearly the Carrickfergus raid had been much less spectacular than the intensive royal planning in the month preceding it suggested that it would be; the sack of an Ulster town was not going to bring Henry VIII, or units of his army, hurrying back from France. Furthermore, so long as the 'Michael' and her companion vessels were in Scottish waters, they were a charge on James IV's treasury rather than on that of Louis XII of France. Thus there were good reasons for the Scottish king's anger, and for Arran's hasty departure from Ayr en route for France, probably around the end of August or beginning of September.

If Pitscottie is to be believed, ill-fortune dogged the fleet to the end, with a storm scattering the ships and delaying their arrival in France.[84] This is possible; but contemporary records suggest that the storm in question occurred *after* the joining up of the French and Scottish ships, about mid-September.[85] As Henry VIII did not re-cross the Channel from France until October, an assault on his ships at Calais would still have been possible. But in spite of the skill of her French pilot, Philippe Roussel, the 'Michael' ran aground shortly after completing her journey from Brest up the Channel to Honfleur at the mouth of the Seine.[86] She was refloated by November 1513; but by that time James IV was two months dead, and Arran left his former master's ship and her crew to be paid and victualled by the French while he himself hurried home to secure his position in the government of the infant James V.[87] That government showed no interest in maintaining a ruinously expensive navy, and one of the first of its cuts, on 2 April 1514, was the sale of the 'Michael' to Louis XII for 40,000 livres (£18,000 Scots).[88] From her launch to her sale, the 'Michael' had been only 2½ years in Scots service.

Thus April 1514 is probably an early date in the history of the ship; for her career in the French navy — as a new ship bought at a bargain rate, but still a very large sum — in her role as 'La Grande Nef d'Ecosse' is likely to have lasted at least as long as that of Henry VIII's 'Henri Grace à Dieu', launched only a year after the 'Michael' and still in action in the 1540s. The great ship's French service still requires investigation.[89]

But those Scots who, in August 1513, watched the 'Michael' sail out of Ayr harbour and disappear into the south-west, were in effect witnessing the end of an era. The ship was sold off because her value to an impoverished government engaged in a real war simply did not justify her enormous cost. On the other hand, her propaganda value in pre-war diplomacy was considerable. Those who had seen the 'Michael', like the French ambassador De la Mothe, left Louis XII in no doubt as to her size and power; while those who had not, Henry VIII's ambassadors Dacre and West, and the English king himself, were given the impression of something heavily-armed, vast and menacing. Undoubtedly the best judges of all were the hapless inhabitants of Carrickfergus.[90]

NOTES

1. *The Letters of James the Fourth, 1505–1513*, ed. R. L. Mackie (S.H.S., Edinburgh, 1953), No. 498; *Letters and Papers, Foreign and Domestic, of the Reign of Henry VIII*, vol. i (1509–1514), ed. J. S. Brewer (London, 1862), No. 3577.

2. *Flodden Papers 1507–1517*, ed. M. Wood (S.H.S., Edinburgh, 1933), pp. 66–72. (Louis XII's instructions to De la Mothe, dated at Blois, 5 March 1513).

3. John Lesley, *The History of Scotland from the Death of King James I in the Year 1436 to the Year 1561* (Bannatyne Club, 1830), 86–7.

4. George Buchanan, *The History of Scotland*, trans. J. Aikman (Glasgow and Edinburgh, 1827–9), ii, 241.

5. Annie I. Dunlop, *The Life and Times of James Kennedy, Bishop of St Andrews* (Edinburgh, 1950), 328.

6. A. W. K. Stevenson, 'Trade between Scotland and the Low Countries in the Later Middle Ages' (Aberdeen University unpublished Ph.D. thesis, 1982), 171.

7. Robert Lindsay of Pitscottie, *The Historie and Cronicles of Scotland* (S.T.S., Edinburgh, 1899), i, 251.

8. *Ibid.*, 251–2.

9. *Ibid.*, 252.

10. Thomas Hunter, *Woods, Forests, and Estates of Perthshire* (Perth, 1883), 324–5.

11. In 1976, A. C. McKerrachar wrote an entertaining if rather inaccurate article on Tullibardine and the 'Great Michael' in which he reached the conclusion that the excavation 'has now vanished into oblivion': A. C. McKerrachar, 'In Search of the "Great Michael"', *The Scots Magazine*, No. 106 (1976–7), 376–381.

12. Sir William Fraser, *The Chiefs of Colquhoun* (Edinburgh, 1869), i, 54.

13. *Calendar of Documents relating to Scotland*, vol. iv (1357–1509), ed. J. Bain (Edinburgh, 1888), No. 1429.

14. *Accounts of the Lord High Treasurer of Scotland*, [*T.A.*], edd. T. Dickson and J. B. Paul (Edinburgh, 1877–1902), i, 125–6.
15. The size, armament, and ship's complement of the 'Henri Grace à Dieu' are strikingly similar to those of the 'Michael' as recorded both by Pitscottie and in contemporary Scottish shipbuilding accounts (*T.A.*, iv, 451–507 *passim*). The two ships have in common a tonnage of 1,000, a crew of 300, and a similar number of large artillery pieces. Much of this information about the 'Henri Grace à Dieu' comes from the much later Anthony Roll of 1546, by which time the ship was 34 years old and had undergone some modifications. In the war of 1512–13, she was expected to carry 400 troops and 20 gunners, who were drawn from the crew: Alfred Spont, *Letters and Papers relating to the War with France, 1512–1513* (Navy Records Society, 1897), 79. By 1546, however, the number of gunners had shot up to 50 in addition to the crew, and the number of troops which the ship could carry had dropped to 329.
16. *T.A.*, iv, 451.
17. David H. Caldwell, 'Royal Patronage of Arms and Armour Making in Fifteenth and Sixteenth-Century Scotland', in David H. Caldwell (ed.), *Scottish Weapons and Fortifications 1100–1800* (Edinburgh, 1981). For artillery in general, see *T.A.*, iv, 508–522.
18. Spont, *op. cit.*, xxv–xxvi, 49–50, 52–3.
19. *T.A.*, iv, 502–5.
20. *James IV Letters*, No. 565.
21. In May 1513, the 'Lion' sailed from Harfleur to Scotland with a total complement of 300 men: Spont, *op. cit.*, 169 n.2.
22. Spont, *op. cit.*, 49–50.
23. *Flodden Papers*, 113 n.1; *Acts of the Lords of Council in Public Affairs, 1501–1554*, ed. R. K. Hannay (Edinburgh, 1932), 39.
24. *T.A.*, ii, lxxxvii–lxxxviii; iii, 132, 134, 190; iv, li–lii.
25. *T.A.*, iv, 289–307 *passim*.
26. *Ibid.*, iv, 529.
27. *Ibid.*, iv, 295, 477.
28. *Ibid.*, iii, 295.
29. *Ibid.*, iii, 208, 295–6; iv, 313.
30. *Ibid.*, ii, 432; iii, lxiii, 204.
31. *Ibid.*, iii, iv, *passim*.
32. *R.M.S.*, ii, No. 3551.
33. *T.A.*, iv, 313.
34. *Ibid.*, iv, 331, 332, 336.
35. *Ibid.*, iv, 347.
36. *Ibid.*, iv, 351, 355, 356.
37. *Ibid.*, iv, 502.
38. For details of the size and uses of James IV's navy, see Norman Macdougall, *James IV* (Edinburgh, 1989), 223–246.
39. *James IV Letters*, No. 42.
40. For details, see Macdougall, *James IV*, 225–8.
41. *Flodden Papers*, 79–83.

42. *James IV Letters*, No. 539, Appendix II.
43. *Statutes of the Realm*, 3 Henry VIII, c.23; *James IV Letters*, Nos. 552, 568.
44. *Ibid.*, Appendix II.
45. *Ibid.*, No. 544.
46. Spont, *op. cit.*, 145–154.
47. *Ibid.*, 169–170.
48. *James IV Letters*, No. 536.
49. *Ibid.*
50. Louis XII to the Grand Master of Brittany, 12 August 1513: B.N. MS. français 5501 f.274 v.
51. *T.A.*, iv, 416–17; *James IV Letters*, No. 560.
52. *T.A.*, iv, 417. The number of ships in the Scottish fleet is uncertain. It is unlikely to have been less than eleven — the 'Michael', 'Margaret', 'James', John Barton's barque, the Spanish barque, Brownhill's ship, Chalmers's barque, the 'Barque Mytoune', the 'Barque of Abbéville', the 'Mary' and the 'Crown'. There were certainly others which do not figure in the Treasurer's Accounts — for example Robert Barton's new 'Lion', which had reached Honfleur by 24 August 1513 with 260 men — soldiers and sailors — on board: *James IV Letters*, No. 565. For the fleet in general, see *T.A.*, iv, 495–504.
53. *T.A.*, iv, 451–507.
54. *Ibid.*, iv, 413–14.
55. *James IV Letters*, No. 559.
56. For details of the Danish expedition, see Macdougall, *James IV*, 229–232.
57. *T.A.*, iv, 507.
58. Pitscottie, *Historie*, i, 257–8.
59. Buchanan, *History*, ii, 245.
60. The poem's full title is 'The Historie of ane nobill and vailyeand squyer, William Meldrum, umquhyle Laird of Cleishe and Bynnis'. It is printed in full in David Laing (ed.), *The Poetical Works of Sir David Lyndsay* (Edinburgh, 1879), vol. i, 159–220.
61. For Lindsay's early court career, see Laing, *op. cit.*, xii–xvi.
62. *Ibid.*, 162–166.
63. *R.M.S.*, ii, No. 3586.
64. *James IV Letters*, No. 104.
65. *T.A.*, i, 242.
66. Ranald Nicholson, *Scotland: The Later Middle Ages* (Edinburgh, 1974), 93–4.
67. Art Cosgrove, 'Ireland beyond the Pale, 1399–1460', in Art Cosgrove (ed.), *Medieval Ireland, 1169–1534* (Oxford, 1987), 575–6.
68. *James IV Letters*, No. 104.
69. For details of the Irish political situation at this time, see D. B. Quinn, 'The Kildare Hegemony, 1494–1520', in Art Cosgrove (ed.), *op. cit.*, 654–6.
70. *T.A.*, iv, 527.
71. *R.M.S.*, ii, No. 3586.
72. *T.A.*, iv, 317.
73. *Ibid.*, iv, 334, 353.

74. *Ibid.*, iv, 310, 489.
75. *Ibid.*, iv, 484.
76. *Ibid.*, iv, 472.
77. *Hectoris Boetii Murthlacensium et Aberdonensium Episcoporum Vitae*, ed. J. Moir (Aberdeen, 1894), 105.
78. Lindsay, 'Squyer Meldrum', in Laing, *op. cit.*, 162.
79. *T.A.*, iv, 527.
80. MacCarthy, B. (ed.), *Annals of Ulster*, iii (1379–1541) (Dublin, 1895), 506-7.
81. Lindsay, 'Squyer Meldrum', 162–166.
82. *T.A.*, iv, 343–5.
83. Pitscottie, *Historie*, i, 257–8; Buchanan, *History*, ii, 245.
84. Pitscottie, *Historie*, i, 258.
85. Spont, *op. cit.*, 183–4, 188–9.
86. *Ibid.*, 176 n.4.
87. *Ibid.*, 188.
88. *Flodden Papers*, 113 n.1.
89. Legions of writers, following Buchanan's lead (Buchanan, *History*, ii, 245), have confidently asserted that the 'Michael', on being sold to the French in 1514, was left to rot at Brest. But Buchanan's *History* was not published until 1582, none of it appears to have been written before the 1550s at the earliest, and his disparaging remarks about Arran (whom he significantly styles 'Hamilton') in the context of the Carrickfergus episode, suggest that the section on the 'Michael' was written after the Reformation, probably in the 1570s when Buchanan could allow his anti-Hamilton bias free rein. So there is no reason to believe that the 'Michael' was *immediately* left to rot; she might indeed have taken part, under her new French name, in the French raid on the Solent in July 1545, the occasion of the sinking of the 'Mary Rose'.
90. I am in general indebted to Roger MacWee, who has been studying the 'Michael' for some years, for his generous sharing with me of the evidence which he has collected on the ship; and I owe thanks to my friend and colleague Dr Colin Martin of the Scottish Institute of Maritime Studies for his many helpful suggestions, and in particular for his kindness in photographing the 'Michael' excavation at Tullibardine from the air.

4

THE BATTLE OF PINKIE

David H. Caldwell

Word reached London on the seventeenth of a great victory in Scotland the previous Saturday, 10 September 1547. A large Scottish army had been convincingly defeated in pitched battle a few miles to the east of Edinburgh, and even then many of the Scottish dead lay stripped and unburied, the colour of their skins changed greenish.[1]

Pinkie[2] now has a firm place in the canon of great battles, its place doubly assured by the impressive array of contemporary pictorial and documentary evidence, and its significance as the last major set-to piece between Scotland and England as independent countries. So why yet another account of it? For two good reasons. Despite the richness of the source material much of it has not been used to the full, and secondly there has been an over-concentration on the actual battle at the expense of an understanding of why it happened and what the consequences were.

The major source for the campaign and battle is a contemporary printed account, complete with battle plans (Fig. 1), by William Patten, who along with the young William Cecil was a 'Judge of the Marshalsey' in the army. He was obviously free to look around and follow events closely. He hero worships the English leaders, particularly the Duke of Somerset, but was not close enough to them or important enough to know their strategy and plans. Everything happens because Somerset has decided that is how it should be. He is very condescending about the Scots whom he characterises variously as cowardly, cruel, braggards and sleverers. He does, however, give a very complete account of the whole campaign, describing events on a day by day basis.[3]

Another important eye-witness account is that of Sir John Berteville,[4] a French protestant in the service of the Earl of Warwick who not surprisingly is portrayed in a good light as a prime contributor to the success of the battle. The work is dedicated to King Edward VI and Berteville himself figures prominently in Patten's book. A further unpublished manuscript in the Harley Collection in the British Library

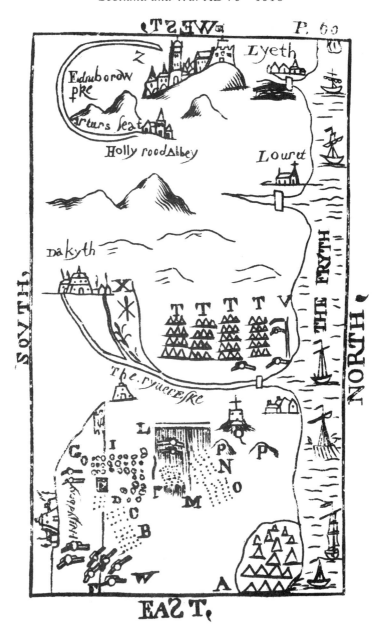

Figure 1. The second of the illustrations of the Battle of Pinkie from Patten's *Expedicion*.
A the English camp; B, C, D the English foot; G Somerset; I the English horse attacking
Angus; L the lane; M the Scottish forward and horsemen; N the Scottish battle; O the
Scottish rearward; PP two hillocks; Q Inveresk Church; R Musselburgh; TTTT the
Scottish tents; V turf wall; W the English baggage; X marsh.

would appear to be the work of an unidentified Englishman on the expedition, from internal evidence originally written soon after the event,[5] while the writer of a Latin manuscript in the Bibliothèque Nationale in Paris, evidently post-dating 1549, relies heavily on 'his friend', Patten.[6] This work is described, not altogether accurately, as an old copy, the work of '(?) Starcerius aulae Peckualrensis scholasticus Oxonii, tempore regis Henry VIII'.[7] Patten has also been much used by other early historians like Holinshed and Hayward.

The Imperial Ambassador in London, François Van Der Delft, reported on the battle,[8] but he was heavily dependent for his information on Sir William Paget, the English Controller, to whom, incidentally, Patten's book was dedicated. Of more interest are the reports of the French Ambassador in London, Odet de Selve, giving the views of the Earl of Huntly, one of the Scottish commanders.[9]

The battle is fully dealt with by four Scottish sixteenth-century historians, John Leslie, George Buchanan, John Knox and Robert Lindsay of Pitscottie.[10] Of these only Leslie is fully sympathetic to the Scottish case as the others adopt a protestant, Anglophile viewpoint at odds with the pro-French policy then being pursued by the Scottish Government. Indeed Knox sees the battle as God's judgement against the 'perjured' Governor and those that assisted him in 'an unjust quarrel'.[11] Pitscottie interestingly portrays Somerset as feeble and irresolute and Warwick as the saviour of the day for the English.[12]

Over and above these written sources are a series of drawings of the battle rediscovered in the Bodleian Library, Oxford, by Sir Charles Oman[13] (Fig. 2). There are five in all, representing different phases of the fighting on the ninth and tenth of September, joined together in a roll one foot deep and over eight feet long. A seventeenth century inscription apparently identifies this as the work of one 'John Ramsay gentyll mane with out mony.' Oman assumed he must have been a renegade Scot wielding his pen if not his sword for the English. His perspective from an artistic point of view would imply a vantage point in the sky above the waters of the Firth of Forth and his sympathies are evident from an image of God Almighty smiting the fleeing Scots.

The drawings are surprisingly detailed and inspire confidence that the artist was actually present at the battle. He has taken trouble, even at such a small scale, to show different types of weapons. Not just the English artillery is depicted but sponges, ladles, shot and powder, and there are little touches like a Scottish steel bonnet abandoned in flight on Musselburgh bridge. Where they are significantly lacking in detail is

Figure 2. Section IV of the roll of drawings in the Bodleian Library. It depicts both the disordered withdrawal of the English horse from the attack on the Scottish vanguard and the start of the collapse of the Scottish foot. Note how the Scottish army is shown as one solid mass. *Photo courtesy of the Bodleian Library, Oxford.*

with the Scottish army. Indeed, it may be argued that at the height of the battle the artist has failed to observe how the Scottish battle and rearguard were positioned and has mistakenly represented the vanguard as the whole Scottish army — appropriately scaled up in size for this purpose.

These drawings are the source of a print assumed to be of the sixteenth century (Fig. 3). It is in the National Army Museum, London (accession no 7102–33–296) and is the print known to Oman as being in the possession of Colonel C. de W. Crookshank. It is possibly the same print as that reproduced by the Bannatyne Club in 1825 along with Berteville's *Expedition*. In style it is not incompatible with the sixteenth-century date suggested for it, but the paper on which it is printed is of much later date, and one has to wonder if the representation of twin barrelled cannons with the Scottish army is the sort of mistake a recent copyist would make rather than a quirk indulged in by a

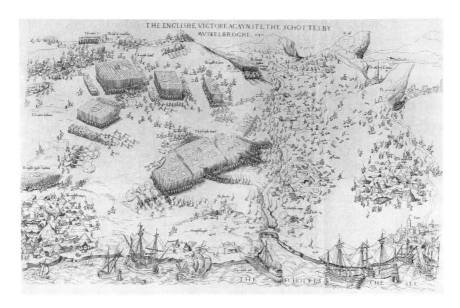

Figure 3. Detail from an engraving of the battle based on the Bodleian drawings.

contemporary artist. The form of words on it suggest an English rather than a Scottish origin.[14] It compresses all five of the Bodleian drawings into one composite representation of the battle and otherwise lacks the precision and detail of its model.

Of recent interpretations of the battle the most influential and most widely known are the two versions published in 1934 and 1937 by Sir Charles Oman.[15] He relied almost totally on Patten and the Bodleian drawings. There are also noteworthy accounts by Sir James Fergusson and W. K. Jordan.[16]

Relations between Scotland and England had not been good for several years. On the death of James V in 1542 there had been diplomatic attempts, resulting in the Treaty of Greenwich of 1 July 1543, to bind the two countries together by the marriage of the baby Mary Queen of Scots to Henry VIII's son and heir Edward.[17] When the Scots repudiated the treaty the following December Henry declared war on them. Although they suffered heavy English raids in 1544 and 1545 the successes were not all on the one side, and the Scots were strengthened by French money and an expeditionary force under Lorges de Montgomery. Then the French saw to it that Scotland was included in the cessation of hostilities resulting in the Treaty of Camp made between them and the English in June 1546.[18]

Neither the Scots nor the English could have imagined this treaty would hold and the Duke of Somerset, ruling England in the name of the young Edward VI, was if anything more obsessed than Henry VIII with bringing Scotland into line by realising the Marriage Treaty. There was conflict at sea in the winter following the Treaty of Camp, with the Scottish ship the 'Lion' being taken by Sir Andrew Dudley. In May 1547 the Bishop of Ross was sent to London but apparently nothing came of this diplomatic initiative.[19] Somerset was preparing for war, as the Scots fully realised, and all they could do was make their own preparations for an English invasion by sea.[20]

What the Scots were not fully aware of was Somerset's intention to initiate a totally different military strategy. He appreciated the futility of sending expensive expeditions into Scotland year after year, which did some damage and then retired again. It seemed that the Scots had a remarkable ability to recover from even the worst raids. Even defeats in battle, although they wounded Scottish pride, did not bring more solid gains in their wake. Now he intended to establish a 'pale' in Scotland, an area pinned down with great artillery fortifications. The Scots within this area would be brought over to the English viewpoint and the Scottish Government would be forced to the negotiating table.

In the years from 1543 to 1546 the Scottish Governor, the Earl of Arran, had conducted sieges of several Scottish strongholds held against his government — the castles of Dalkeith and Glasgow, Coldingham Priory, the castles of Caerlaverock, Lochmaben, Dumbarton and St Andrews. Most of them did fall to him, even if, as he admitted to the Pope in the case of Dumbarton, it was by a miracle.[21] His resources in money and equipment, however, were always meagre and the ineffectiveness of his efforts, especially in his unsuccessful attempts against the newly fortified St Andrews Castle, must have been apparent to Somerset.

In any case, the artillery fortifications envisaged by Somerset were very different from the stone and mortar towers and walls that had provided a ready target for Arran's guns. They were earthwork fortifications with large pointed bastions. Ramparts and bastions of no great height, largely masked from view by broad deep ditches and earthen counterscarps, presented little for enemy guns to bite into while concealing gun platforms from which all parts of their defensive circuit and hundreds of yards beyond could be raked by fire. They are called *trace italienne* fortifications after the country of their origin and they were to revolutionise military strategy and be a basis of European power throughout the world. Both the English and French were erecting forts of this type round Boulogne two or three years before Pinkie,[22] and before 1547 was out, the English were building the first *trace italienne* fort in this island, on Scottish soil at Eyemouth.[23]

Perhaps it was the complexity and expense of Somerset's proposed military initiative that caused delay, but the invasion Arran feared in May did not materialise, and instead, by mounting an expedition against the castle of Langholm in July he provided the English with a useful *cassus belli*. Langholm was a towerhouse of the Maxwells which had had an English garrison in it since before the Treaty of Camp. It was not significantly greater in size or strength than hundreds of others the length and breadth of the country, and was held by a garrison of fifty or less. It yet required the Governor to call out the Scottish host, an army of over 20,000 men, for a period of at least two weeks.[24]

It was probably no coincidence that as Arran forced the surrender of Langholm, the only English garrison on Scottish soil, a French fleet arrived off St Andrews to batter its castle into submission. The castle there had recently been refortified and supplied by Cardinal Beaton, making it one of the strongest in the country, but it was now held by his murderers — protestants and anglophiles funded by Somerset — and was a considerable thorn in Arran's side. Whereas Arran had failed to induce its surrender after months, either by negotiation, bombardment or tunnelling his way in, now the French forces, under the able leadership of Leon Strozzi, Prior of Capua, had his cannon reduce it to ruins in less than six hours.[25]

This was the second time within two years that French troops had intervened in Scotland on behalf of the Scottish government, and the probability that they would do so again if he invaded that country does not seem to have weighed heavily in Somerset's immediate decision to mobilise his forces. With the loss of the last two centres of English power in Scotland, the falling away of potential support amongst the Scots nobility, and the Scots victory at Lilliard's Edge (Ancrum) in February 1544/5 still rankling, Somerset was in no doubt that a major English initiative in Scotland was overdue.

The attack on Scotland was to be two-pronged. The main army, supported by a fleet, was to enter by the East March. A smaller force led by the English Warden Lord Wharton and the exiled Earl of Lennox was to invade the South-west. The army which mustered at Berwick-upon-Tweed at the end of August largely consisted of men levied for the enterprise from the northern counties. In April the commissioners of musters in all the shires had been instructed to survey the available weapons and military stores and to warn all those obliged to keep horses for military service to have them in readiness.[26] In August commissions were granted for raising men, and the Earl of Warwick was made lieutenant and captain general for the counties from Shropshire, Stafford, Derby, Nottingham and York northwards. Lord Seymour of Sudeley was similarly appointed for the southern counties to be in readiness to see off any trouble while his brother Somerset was in Scotland.[27]

Contemporary accounts of the size of the English army are remarkably consistent, varying from 15,300 to 19,000.[28] Patten gives a total of 16,800 fighting men plus 1,400 pioneers. As was the norm the foot soldiers were divided into three divisions or battles, the main battle being commanded by Somerset himself as general of the army. It had 4,000 men. The Earl of Warwick as lord lieutenant led the forward and Lord Dacre the rearward. Both of these battles were 3,000 strong. Lord Gray of Wilton was appointed high marshall of the army and was also captain general of all the horsemen. These consisted of 2,000 light Border horse under Sir Francis Bryan and 3,000 men at arms and demilances under Sir Ralf Vane. There was also a mercenary force of 200 mounted hagbutters under a Spanish captain, Pedro de Gamboa, and the royal pensioners and men at arms under Sir Thomas Darcy. There was a further force of 600 mercenaries on foot armed with hagbuts commanded by an Italian Piero Malatesta, and the train of artillery, including fifteen large guns, under Sir Francis Fleming. Besides this there were 900 carts and also several wagons to carry supplies.[29]

This train of carts and wagons was not enough to carry all the food and supplies for the army for the whole duration of its stay in Scotland, probably never intended to be longer than about thirty days. More space than normal had to be provided for the picks and shovels necessary to start work on the forts. There was obviously a difficulty in finding enough carts and wagons though perhaps it would not have been practical to move many more at the one time.[30] Somerset's strategy, therefore, was to carry a lot of his supplies by sea. A list made up in August indicates that there were to be eighty ships in all, mostly quite small ones. Patten lists sixty-five, of which only the galley and twenty-four others were 'war ships'. They were under the command of Lord Clinton and contained some 9,000 men.[31]

Some of the foot soldiers were armed with bills — heavy bladed long-shafted weapons derived from the agricultural implements of that name — while others were provided with pikes (long spears). The latter had long been preferred on the Continent and in Scotland and it may be were already in the ascendancy in the English army despite the conservative tendencies of many English captains when it came to adopting new weapons. There were also archers with long bows who were grouped separately from the pikemen and billmen. Ideally the pikemen and billmen wore armour to the knees and each had a sword and dagger, but the archers were normally lightly clad. It is likely there were few hand guns apart from those in the hands of the mercenaries.

Most of the horsemen were armed with lance and sword. Only the royal bodyguard and men at arms were armoured from head to foot and had armoured horses. There was a shortage of horses big and strong enough for such service, and in any case lighter more mobile troops were often of more use. These, the demilances, had unarmoured horses and lighter armour. Many of the Border horse wore mailshirts or jacks and brigantines (jackets reinforced with metal plates) rather than breast and back plates.

Charles Oman noted that this army had a high proportion of horse (about a third) and correctly saw this as a new departure. He deduced that this was the result of experience gained in continental warfare.[32] This may well be true but presumably many of the horsemen were intended to man the forts.[33]

Most of the shire levies must have been of rather unpredictable quality, in many cases men pressed unwillingly into service. The hagbutters, on foot and horse, however, were professional forces and many of the demilances had seen service at Boulogne. The senior commanders were also experienced men. Dacre was well inured to warfare in the north while Somerset and Warwick had already led expeditions in strength into Scotland, particularly the devastating raid of 1544 in which their army landed at Granton, sacked Edinburgh and returned overland to England. They, like Lord Gray of Wilton and several of the junior officers, had also been involved in the fighting around Boulogne.

The other English army mustered at Carlisle under Wharton and Lennox was merely a diversionary force, consisting of 2,000 foot and 500 horse, of which 200 were Scots in English service.[34] As events turned out there was little substance in Glencairn's confident assumption that all Ayrshire, much of Renfrew and the Lennox would flock to support Lennox, and it is clear from the Pinkie casualty list that many from those parts fought for the governor.[35]

As his forces gathered Somerset put a stop to the less than serious efforts of the Scottish government to find a diplomatic solution by pretending affront at their lack of trust in the safe-conduct offered to their negotiators.[36] He had a proclamation drawn up, addressed to the Scottish people, appealing to them to honour the marriage compact of 1543 for the good of both countries. He asked them to join with his army which he hoped would pass through their country amicably and with little damage apart from what was necessary for forage.[37] Six of these proclamations were sent to the Earl of Glencairn and others to be set on the gate of Stirling Castle, the door of St Giles in Edinburgh, the door of Glasgow Cathedral, and in Dumfries.[38] More purposefully, on Thursday 1 September while his army lay at Berwick, Somerset rode six miles into Scotland with a small retinue to view the port of Eyemouth and have work started on the first of the new forts[39] (Fig. 5).

Despite Somerset's assurances that he sought a peaceful solution to the differences between the two countries very few Scots joined his army. Patten mentions the Laird of Mangerton in Berwickshire with forty other gentlemen of the East Marches.[40] The intelligence reports, however, that Somerset received from Scotland during August seemed to indicate that many of the Scots were reluctant to muster yet again that year. The anglophile Earl of Glencairn wrote to Lennox and Wharton in early September to say that few of the Scots had as yet obeyed the governor's summons to muster at Fala Moor the preceding 31 August and that Arran feared his own people more than the English. What is more, having already called out the host for the siege of Langholm Castle he could only ask for twenty days more service and was scared his army might dissolve before the English threat materialised.[41]

Arran had been making preparations for an English invasion for some time. The royal castles of Edinburgh, Stirling and Dunbar had been strengthened and supplied with guns, provisions and men, and garrisons were put in the steeple of Annan Church and Hume Castle.[42] He had also issued new instructions for the maintenance of the system of bale fires and posts to give warning of an invasion.[43] On 3 August letters were sent out advising the fencibles to be ready to muster at eight hours' notice. The actual letters ordering the musters went out from 17 August with reminders and threats in the days following. As a

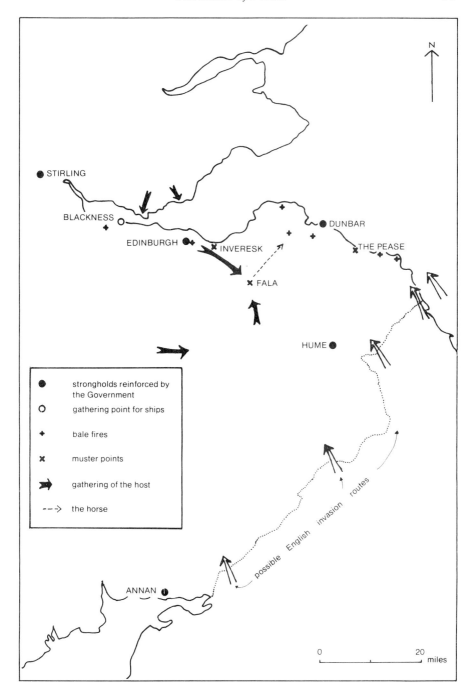

Figure 4. Scottish preparations for invasion by the English.

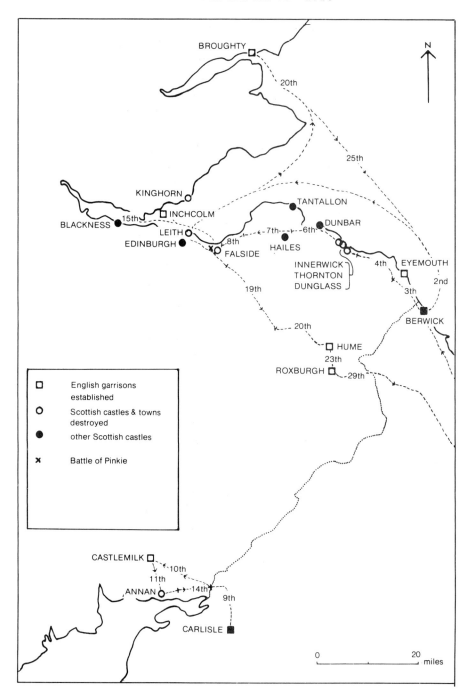

Figure 5. The English invasions in September 1547.

sign of the seriousness of the situation orders were given that fiery crosses were to be sent round.[44] It is clear that Arran intended as full an army as possible. He arranged for contingents from the different quarters to muster at Fala severally from the twenty-eighth to the thirty-first of the month. Those from north of the Forth were apparently organised in Edinburgh after clearing the bottleneck caused by the ferries.[45]

Arran's choice of Fala might seem surprising. He was obviously aware that he faced a double invasion but he must have been expecting the main force to come an inland route rather than by the east coast. His prickers (light border horse) first made contact with Somerset's army near Dunbar on Tuesday 6 September,[46] by which time it was abundantly clear that Fala was the wrong place to be. In fact Arran had apparently realised his mistake a few days earlier. He is reported to have left Edinburgh on Thursday 1 September to go and haste his army to the Pease, by Dunglass in Berwickshire, but on Monday the fifth he was still sending out messengers with letters desperately charging the lieges to join him at Fala.[47] Obviously he was delayed at Fala by the late arrival of many of his troops and he was thus denied all opportunity of protecting Edinburgh other than by making a stand at Inveresk, about nine miles away.

Somerset's strategy of keeping Wharton and Lennox at Carlisle, poised to mount an attack into the South-west, paid dividends in discouraging some from going off to join the army. The lairds reluctantly went in person but left their men behind to defend their property. This explains why Alexander Dunbar of Cumnock in Ayrshire was present at the battle and yet twenty-six tenants, inhabitants and indwellers from about Cumnock were prosecuted for staying away.[48]

Nevertheless the Scottish army at Pinkie is likely to have been one of the largest ever mustered. Estimates of its strength vary considerably as one has come to expect. Patten gives it as above 26,000 fighting footmen, 1,500 horsemen and 4,000 Highland archers.[49] Other sources make the Scots number 40,000, but perhaps the most reliable is the figure of one of the commanders, the Earl of Huntly, who claims that they were only 22,000 or 23,000.[50] Interestingly Edward VI's *Chronicle* also gives the figure of 23,000, later changed to 36,000.[51] With them they had a train of between twenty-five and thirty pieces of field artillery.[52]

This army, with the exception of a small band of gunners, carters, pioneers and other craftsmen for servicing the artillery, was an amateur organisation. Theoretically all able bodied men between the ages of sixteen and sixty including burgesses, town dwellers and churchmen, had to serve, if required, for a maximum of forty days in any one year. Unlike their English counterparts they were obliged to do this armed and fed at their own expense. In practice the lowest tiers in society, those with no considerable investment in land or wealth, were hardly considered and were never a significant element in the army. Thus when the full host was mustered in the sixteenth century it was never much more than twenty thousand strong.[53]

The Scottish foot, like the English, was arranged in three divisions. The main battle was led by Arran, the forward by the Earl of Angus and the rearward by the Earl of Huntly. It was the practice for the contingents to be mustered on a territorial basis. The churchmen and burgesses, however, seem largely to have been in the main battle while the men from the south-west were with Angus who otherwise had Angus, Fife and the Mearns.[54] This reflects the political reality of the time. Angus had until recently been a leader of the Anglophile party and many in the west had protestant and/or English leanings. The churchmen, on the other hand, readily perceiving the threat to their beliefs, property and positions from protestant England, were more eager than on many occasions to come and fight. Patten describes one of the Scottish flags as having the Scottish Church personified as a woman kneeling before a crucifix with a church in the background and the inscription AFFLICTAE SPONSAE NE OBLIVISCARIS (Forget not your afflicted wife).[55] Nor was Arran unsuccessful in raising men from the Highlands and Islands — Macleans, Macleods and MacKenzies, according to Pitscottie. On the other hand several of the MacDonalds, including Clanranald, Glengarry and Knoydart, the Gunns of Braemore in Caithness, a MacGregor and Argyll's brother John Campbell of Lochnell, were later respited for non-attendance.[56]

As at Flodden thirty-four years earlier, the Scottish foot was armed with pikes. It was therefore absolutely essential that the battles be well drilled and keep formation as twenty foot long pikes were useless in individual combat. Although there were few or no guns,[57] many also carried daggers, swords and bucklers. These last were small shields gripped with the left hand and used with a sword to parry blows. They must have been strapped to the back while the pikes were in use.

The Scots were sensibly not overburdened with heavy armour. The Earl of Huntly attracted attention by being clad in plate armour from head to foot, described by Holinshed as 'gilt armour inameled'. Most, however, had jacks. They wore simple steel bonnets or skulls and might have plate defences (splints) on their arms and legs, or else chains of latten wound round their limbs as a defence against cutting.[58] Even Arran wore a jack with splints on the arms and an apron of plate, all covered with purple velvet with an embroidered gold cross. The nails on the splints and apron were gilt.[59]

The Scottish horse, essentially from the Borders, was all light and armed with lances. The main problem with the horse was that there was not enough, nor was there a force of hagbutters. There were instead the contingents of Highlanders and Islanders led by Argyll, armed primarily with bows rather than pikes. Some would also have had mail shirts and two-handed swords (claymores). On the day of the battle Arran used these Highlanders to flank the left of his army rather than split his force of horse for this purpose.

The artillery train included battards, moyens and falcons — that is guns of no great size. One English source gives it as fourteen iron bases, twelve pieces of brass with the arms of Scotland or the conjoined arms of Scotland and France, while another lists thirty pieces in all, including a culverin, three sakers, nine smaller pieces of brass and of iron and seventeen other pieces mounted on carriages.[60] This was obviously quite a respectable train intended for use in the field.

The Scottish commanders were by no means inexperienced, nor incapable of winning battles. The most experienced and able was Angus, aged about fifty-eight, who with Arran had gained a substantial victory over an English force at Ancrum (Lilliard's Edge) in 1545. Huntly, in his mid thirties, had also shown his mettle as a warden, not least in defeating another invading force at Haddenrig in 1542. Arran was younger still, only about thirty, and especially with the benefit of hindsight, can be seen as weak and vacillating, but he had shown considerable resolve in dealing with sieges and his dynastic rival Lennox, and could share the glory of Ancrum with Angus.

On Thursday, 8 September, at the Scottish camp at Monktonhall, a property belonging to the Abbot of Dunfermline, Arran, with the advice of the Lords of Council, issued an act guaranteeing that the heirs of anyone slain in the forthcoming struggle would not have to pay the feudal casualties of ward, nonentry, relief or marriage on taking up their lands and property, and the nearest kin of churchmen who died in the conflict could dispose of their benefices. This act was no doubt intended to reassure the Scots and strengthen their resolve, but it must have reminded many of the previous time such enactments had been made, immediately prior to Flodden.[61]

On Friday, 2 September, the English fleet put to sea from Berwick, and two days later the army set out in good order, marching that first day to Reston, a distance of nine miles (Fig. 5). The next day, Monday the fifth, the army camped at the Pease defile, an unbridged ravine a further eight miles onwards. This was an ideal place for the Scots to have opposed the invasion but the pass was undefended, though there was ample evidence of a recent attempt to cut defensive trenches, apparently at the instigation of Sir George Douglas, Angus' able brother. The adjacent castle of Dunglass was taken and on the Tuesday two further minor strongholds at Thornton and Innerwick.[62] Somerset seems to have been concerned only to clear the line of his communications back to England and the surrounding country was not scoured by raiding parties as in previous English incursions. In 1548 a fort had to be erected at Dunglass as a staging post for the garrisons further north.[63]

Also on Tuesday the sixth, the army marched on within gunshot of the burgh of Dunbar, nine miles from Dunglass. Now the Scottish horse came into sight and there was some skirmishing involving the mounted hagbutters. Dunbar was the best port between Berwick and Leith and should have been Somerset's main objective as a base in Scotland, but with its strong castle, a sophisticated artillery blockhouse and outer earthwork defences,[64] it was evidently too strong for him to tackle and he marched on. Instead he was to settle for the strategically less important Haddington, and with the French installed in Dunbar faced desperate problems relieving its garrison.

Patten's claim that the army camped on the night of the sixth near Tantallon Castle, a further nine miles along the coast from Dunbar, is probably an exaggeration. Near the bridge over the River Tyne at East Linton is more likely.[65] The mention of Tantallon, however, is interesting as this exceptionally strong castle belonging to Angus was the one other base to the east of Edinburgh which should have been high on Somerset's list of priorities for placing a garrison. Again it was presumably deemed too strong to be attempted. That night the Scottish horse kept the English on their guard by raising an alarm.

On the morning of 7 September the Scottish horse again threatened and skirmished with the English army as it crossed Linton Bridge.

Somerset determinedly avoided giving chase and that night camped at Longniddry, some ten miles from the bridge.

The Scottish horse, now keeping pace with the invaders on the hills further inland, was effectively limiting Somerset's actions. On Thursday the eighth he made for the coast at Preston to consult with his admiral, Lord Clinton. He had already sailed his fleet up to Leith, no doubt discovering that defensive measures had been taken to keep him out.[66] All the Scottish shipping in these waters seems to have retired to the safety of Blackness further up the firth, not before an encounter in which two Scottish ships are said to have been taken and one English sunk. The Scottish ships at Blackness were later bombarded from the sea, not without considerable loss to the English, in revenge for which they burned Leith.[67] Now on the eighth, however, Clinton could report that a large Scottish army was encamped nearby at Inveresk, ready to contest the crossing of the River Esk, a fact confirmed by the English light horse.

Somerset must now have realised that his situation was critical. With the exception of Eyemouth, he had so far failed to identify and take the bases he required to carry out his new strategy. He was reliant on his fleet for supplies for his army but with a large enemy force in the field nearby he was being denied access to the best ports, though according to Patten his army was supplied from the ships on Friday the ninth, perhaps at Morison's (or Acheson's) Haven which used to be less than a mile south-west of Prestonpans.[68]

The Scottish army was in a strong position, in a well ordered camp with four rows of tents, presumably arranged as the main divisions in the army. In front of their camp was a steep slope down to the River Esk. Inland there was marshy ground and on the seaside the Scots had erected a turf rampart as a defence against the guns of the English ships. The bridge across the river, nearer the sea than the camp, was defended by some pieces of artillery. The range of hills overlooking the English encampment was commanded by the Scottish horse.

On Friday the ninth, Somerset took action. While his foot remained in camp at Preston he sent out some of his horse to deal with the Scottish forces which commanded Falside Hill. According to Berteville the English consisted of 1,000 light horse and 700 men at arms.[69] The Scots were eventually seen off and in the chase several were killed and as many as 800 taken. Their leader, Lord Hume, was hurt in a fall from his horse and had to be carried off to Edinburgh Castle, while his son, the Master of Hume, was amongst those taken prisoner. On the other hand three of the English captains, Sir Ralf Bulmer, Thomas Gower, the Marshall of Berwick, and Robert Crouch, were captured by the Scots, and as many as a hundred English lost overall, dead or captured.

This fight was a severe blow to the Scots, not least because it now allowed Somerset unimpeded access to the land between his camp and the river. From Carberry Hill with his chief commanders and a small guard he could now get a good view of the Scottish dispositions. He descended from there into a lane, presumably now the line of Inveresk main street, viewing, but not going as far as Inveresk Parish Church, situated on a small hill opposite the Scottish camp. He then turned back to go to his camp.

At this point, according to Patten, the Scots sent out a herald and a trumpeter, the former to enquire about prisoners and to offer conditions of peace if Somerset would return to England without causing any more damage, the latter to offer a challenge on behalf of Huntly to settle the nations' quarrel by fighting Somerset man to man. Both offers were dismissed.[70] The story as told by the Scottish historians, and followed by Holinshed, is rather different. Somerset is said to have sent a letter to Arran offering negotiations instead of battle. Provided the Scots agreed to marriage between Mary and Edward, he may have gone so far as to suggest that the Scots queen should remain in Scotland until she was of marriageable age, and that he should not only withdraw his army in a peaceable manner but that compensation should be paid for any damage caused.[71]

That Somerset should have this one last try at negotiation is not unlikely. It was his avowed intent to engineer a peaceful union between the two countries and he could hardly have been confident of the outcome of a pitched battle with a well-positioned army. If, as is most likely, his strategy in this campaign had been influenced by the supposition that Arran would have great difficulty fielding any army, the evidence was now before his eyes that his actions had caused the Scottish nobility to close ranks behind their governor.

Arran's brother John was now archbishop of St Andrews in place of the murdered Beaton and like his predecessor exercised great influence on the Governor. The Scottish historians agree that Arran's council was dominated by churchmen and through their influence the letter was suppressed. Apart from the fact that they had no wish to negotiate their queen away to a heretic nation they had every reason to think the letter was a sign of weakness on Somerset's part.

Somerset's reconnaissance had shown the Scots were in a very strong position. He could not turn their right flank owing to the marshy ground and if he tried making a wide detour round them they could cross the river and cut his lines of communications. He had a considerable force of fighting men on board his ships which might have been landed behind the Scots so that they could be attacked simultaneously from front and rear — if only they could be disembarked safely. This does not seem to have been practical. The course of action chosen by Somerset was to mount a frontal attack on the Scottish camp. On the side of the Esk opposite the camp there was a considerable eminence of ground, the site of the church of St Michael's of Inveresk. Here, and behind the turf embankments of the lane stretching southwards from it, Somerset intended to plant his artillery for a bombardment of the camp. The fleet had already tried firing on it from the sea and could apply more pressure from that quarter.

Saturday the tenth was an overcast September day which turned to rain about eight in the evening.[72] At eight in the morning the Scottish notaries were still doing business recording last wills and testaments as the English army was on the move.[73] Long before they got to Inveresk the English to their considerable surprise realised that the Scots were crossing the river towards them. Angus was first to cross, to the south of the church along with the main battle. The Bodleian drawings show some contingents crossing by the bridge and going through Musselburgh.

The decision to advance was apparently Arran's alone, taken against the advice of Angus and Huntly, and he has been much criticised for it. It has been suggested that he acted through overconfidence and a supposition that the English were in retreat. It is more creditable that Arran saw the danger his army faced from a frontal artillery assault at close range. Now that his horse had been worsted and driven from Falside Hill it would have been no bad plan to draw up his army on that hill with his guns, and perhaps another force at Inveresk Church to contest the crossing of the river. The Bodleian drawings show Scottish guns heading for the church and some are stationed here on the derivative engraving (Fig. 3). In such a plan the English would be taken in flank by the main army if they attempted to go for Edinburgh, or if they attempted to climb the hill against the main army they could be taken in flank by the force at the church.

Now that each commander was aware that the other was on the move, each had to make rapid decisions. The English army was advancing with its three foot divisions one behind the other. The Scots on the other hand had theirs side by side. Arran drew up his army to the east of the church as the English army continued its advance. The English galley and other ships were close in and firing on the Scots. The Bodleian drawings show the galley making a direct hit on one division of the Scots, presumably Argyll's, as it was on the march to the north of the church. Arran's assessment must have been that there was still time for him to gain the height of Falside Hill before the English and he set his army off to do so, at such a pace that it seemed to his opponents that they went like horsemen. His smaller pieces of artillery were pulled along in front of the foot battles by men.

As the Scottish army moved south-eastwards they had marshy ground to their left. The slopes of Carberry Hill which they were traversing were fallow ground, the ridges and furrows running east-west, thus making progress difficult. Elsewhere in the surrounding countryside the crop of bere had not yet been taken in.[74] The three battles were intended to march alongside each other, Arran in the middle with Angus to his right and Huntly to his left. The horse should have flanked the foot on the right but, now sadly depleted in numbers and its confidence gone as a result of the mauling it received the day before, hung well back. If he had had enough horse Arran would no doubt have split it and positioned half on his left wing. Instead he put the Islesmen and Highlanders here under the command of Argyll.

Somerset had his army drawn out in line of march. Some pieces of artillery led the way and behind came the vanguard, battle and rearward in that order. Each had a contingent of archers in its left wing[75] and hagbutters on its right. The horse, in three divisions, was to the south of the foot and to the rear of them came the rest of the guns and the baggage train. The crest of Falside Hill was actually nearer the English than it was to the Scots but Somerset faced the not inconsiderable problem of wheeling his divisions round to the left and getting his baggage to safety in the rear.

Somerset ordered Gray of Wilton forward with half his force of horse — 1,800 men at arms and 1,600 demilances — to stay the Scottish advance while he manoeuvred the rest of his army so that his three foot battles would line up opposite the Scots (Figs. 6, 7). It is evident from Patten's account[76] and the Bodleian drawings that he was well short of achieving this when the climax of the battle actually came. His foot then stood in order of march on the slope of Falside Hill and on a northeast/south-west alignment. The contingents of hagbutters thus stood nearest the Scots, now with pieces of artillery in the gaps between them. The

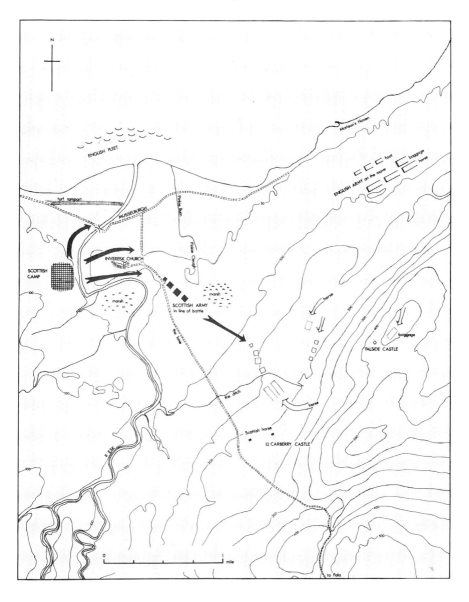

Figure 6. Pinkie, c.10.00 hours, 10 September 1547.

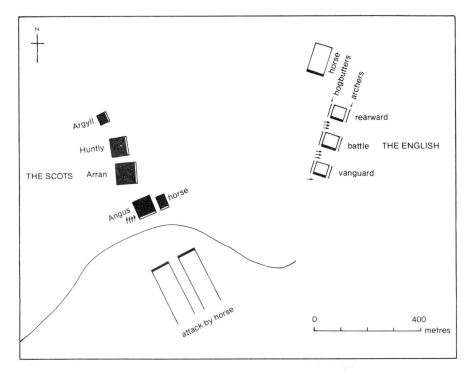

Figure 7. Pinkie, c.11.00 hours, 10 September 1547.

rest of his horse appear to be shown in the Bodleian drawings well to the north of the rearguard, moving thence to the brow of Falside Hill, too late to give pursuit to the Scottish horse. Somerset had by then got his baggage and also some of his artillery on to the top of Falside Hill. Here he himself took up position where he could view the whole course of events. Twenty years later when Queen Mary's army stood on Carberry Hill in opposition to the rebel lords she is said to have occupied the 'trench' that the English had had at the Battle of Pinkie,[77] meaning presumably the Prehistoric ramparts still visible today. It seems much more likely, however, that Somerset and the artillery were placed on Falside Hill, nearer Falside Castle.

Gray came down on the right flank of the Scottish forward from the top of Falside Hill. As the Scots were aware of this impending attack they stopped their advance. Angus was further on than the other two battles at this point but owing to the speed at which they had been pressing forward all three formations had become more dense and closer together than was wise. About a 'stone's throw' from the

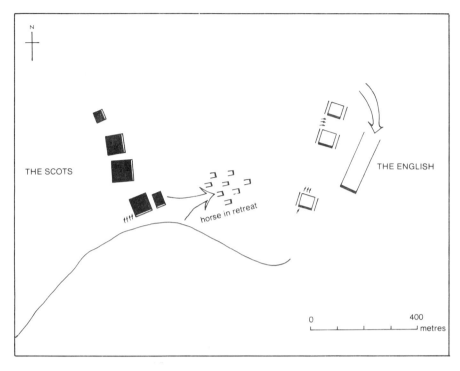

THE SCOTS

THE ENGLISH

horse in retreat

0   400
metres

Figure 8. Pinkie, c.11.30 hours, 10 September 1547.

vanguard, to the south, was a ditch or slough, most probably the small burn that still flows from near Colton Dean into the River Esk between Smeaton House Farm and Whitecraig. Angus lined up along this with four or five pieces of artillery to the east. Patten is the only source that there was some 400 Scottish horse to his east.[78] This meant that the main battle was now bunched behind the vanguard with the rearward alongside it and further to the east.

Gray's advance was slow across the furrows and the slough proved a considerable obstacle. Angus' men received the English resolutely with their long pikes and saw them off, killing and wounding several of them. The horse retired in some disorder, in small groups, making for the main English lines which were rather unsettled as a result. It was with some difficulty that they were brought back into some sort of order and funnelled into a gap created for them between the English vanguard and battle. Some men from Arran's battle, described by Patten as Highlanders, broke ranks to plunder the dead English. Meanwhile an artillery duel was developing between the armies, now only 'two bow

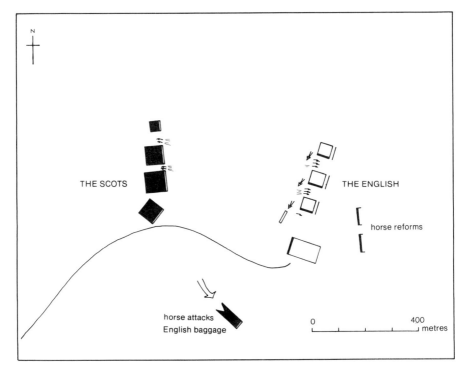

THE SCOTS

THE ENGLISH

horse reforms

horse attacks
English baggage

0   400
                      metres

Figure 9. Pinkie, c.12.30 hours, 10 September 1547.

shots' asunder, and according to Pitscottie an English gun was dismounted.[79] Some 500 Scottish horse also came eastwards along the hill to attack the English artillery being positioned there. They dispersed after a few shots as the English carters were hastily arming themselves with pikes, bills and bows.

The Scots now had to form a better line of battle (Fig. 8). Arran and Huntly moved forwards. Angus could not make more progress southwards because of the ditch and therefore wheeled to the left. The Scottish foot was now only a 'bowshot' from the English and it had every reason to be in good heart after its repulse of the English horse. The Scots had been using pikes now for over half a century and on a man to man basis they were likely to be every bit as resolute as the English. Indeed the English foot was very much an untried force.

In the event the English foot was never put to the test. The Scots were now being fired upon by the English artillery in front and in flank,[80] and contingents of hagbutters had been brought forward by Malatesta and Gamboa to fire into the Scottish vanguard from across

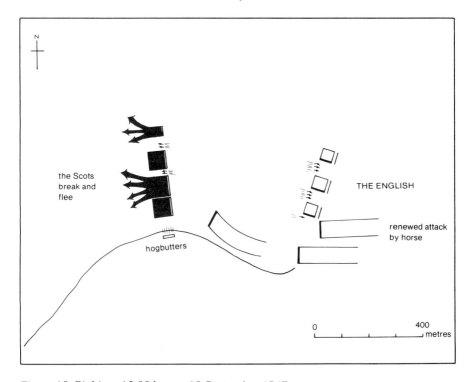

the Scots
break and
flee

THE ENGLISH

renewed attack
by horse

hogbutters

0   400
metres

Figure 10. Pinkie, c.13.00 hours, 10 September 1547.

the ditch. Angus' turning movement was apparently interpreted by the men in the main battle as a retreat and the artillery was particularly unsettling the Highlanders, said to be the first to panic and flee.

The panic spread remarkably quickly, particularly through the battle where Arran, if we are to believe his detractors, was soon calling for his horse and was off. Somerset was quick to capitalise on this turn of events and according to Berteville himself led a renewed attack by the horse[81] (? the contingents not so far involved in the fighting). The Spanish ambassador was fed information by Sir William Paget to the effect that Warwick had led the horse in a surprise attack on Huntly's rear[82] (? the contingents hitherto led by the now wounded Gray of Wilton). Whatever happened, for a short time at least, it seems that Angus and Huntly managed to keep their forces together, the former attempting to manoeuvre his into line with Huntly's after the battle had totally disintegrated. By then confusion was so complete that Huntly's men thought Angus' men were a force of advancing English.[83] Holinshed has it that Huntly stood firm with his rearguard until the chase was

past him and then withdrew.[84] Although the collapse of the Scottish
army was spectacular there is some information to suggest it was not
complete. Some of the horse regrouped to the west of Cousland and
agreed to hold a treist at Ancrumwoodhead two days later.[85] Buchanan
claims that the Highlanders, meaning perhaps in this case Huntly's
men rather than those serving under Argyll, formed a circle in good
order, and retreated without loss, unassailed by the English horse who
were attacking the dispersed fugitives.[86]

The chase lasted from about one o'clock to almost six. Many of the
Scots threw away their pikes and shed their armour in order to run the
faster, some in the direction of Edinburgh, others along the sands to
Leith, but most towards Dalkeith, the English horse being unable to
follow them there owing to the marshes. Many drowned in the River
Esk or ran themselves to death. Where they had stood was covered with
pikes 'like a wood of staves strewed on the ground as rushes in a
chamber, unpassable (they lay so thik) for eyther horse or man'[87] (Fig.
2). English estimates put the slaughter as high as 15,000 Scots killed
and 2,000 taken, but Huntly's figure of 6,000 dead is probably nearer
the truth. Of these he claimed 4,000 were 'gentlemen'.[88] Patten
condescendingly claims that so many men of quality would not have
been killed if they had been better dressed and could have been readily
distinguished from the mere peasants.[89]

The most notable Scottish casualties included the Master of Buchan,
Lord Cathcart, William Cunynghame of Glengarnock and his son, the
Laird of Lochleven, Lord Elphinstone, the Master of Erskine, Lord
Fleming, James Gordon of Lochinvar, the Master of Graham, the Master
of Livingston, the Master of Methven, Duncan MacFarlane of that ilk,
the Master of Ogilvy, the Master of Ruthven, the Master of Ross and
George Stirling of Glovat. Whole families and kin groups were cut
down together — at least seven Gordon lairds, eight Kennedy lairds,
nine Ramsays, a whole generation of Ogilvies and seven sons of Thomas
Urquhart of Cromarty. Official status did not save a trumpeter of
Italian origin, Julian Drummond, and no sympathy was shown to men
of the cloth. The English borderers, however, were suspected of being
lenient to their sparring partners from across the border, and there were
some prisoners taken, English estimates of these varying from 500 to
2,000. The most notable of these was the Earl of Huntly but they also
included Lord Hay of Yester (Sheriff of Peebles), Thomas Crawford of
Jordanhill, the Laird of Luss, the Master of Sempill, Robert Hamilton of
the Briggs (Captain of Dunbar Castle), Sir John Wemyss of Wemyss

and John MacKenzie (ancestor of the Earls of Seaforth). All but Huntly were freed soon afterwards.[90]

The English on the other hand lost only a few hundred, perhaps no more than the 800 reported from London on 18 September. Officially it was given out that losses were only 200 though the rumour about the English court, fed by private letters from those in the army, indicated that 500 to 600 was more likely.[91] The French ambassador, Odet de Selve, was no doubt not alone at the time in concluding that the defeat of the Scots was by an unbelievable misfortune which he thought no one living could have had any good reason to have predicted.[92]

Arran's decision to cross the Esk has often been criticised, but in the final analysis it was not so much an order by Arran that lost the battle but the fact that the Scots in the main battle, en masse, decided to turn and fly. A question mark must hang over Arran's role in precipitating this flight by his own eagerness to be away, just as three years earlier he had abandoned the siege of Coldingham Priory in not very seemly haste on the approach of an English relieving force.[93] The finger of suspicion has also been pointed at Angus and Huntly who stand accused of treacherously allowing the English to win. Initial confused reports sent to London about the battle were mindful of the former's recent adherence to the English interest while later Scottish historians, to whom Huntly's later doings were abhorrent, found it too tempting not to blame him for Pinkie as well.[94] These suspicions and rumours about these two commanders are best seen, however, as ill informed and unnecessary slander. Pinkie was not in any way a repeat of the debacle at Solway Moss in 1542, where there is every reason to think that many of the Scots nobility deliberately gave themselves up without a fight.

The English superiority in horse obviously played an important role in the Scottish defeat. It is likely that almost all the Scottish casualties were caused by the horsemen in the chase at the end of the battle. What of the role of guns? The early report by the French ambassador that the English and Scots were so mixed together that their artillery could not be of any use seems to be a misunderstanding of the role it played.[95] Arran had sensibly brought guns light enough to keep up with his army and they were used to some effect. He also anticipated the threat from the guns on the English ships by fortifying his camp against them.

The English guns certainly had an effect in unsettling the Scots and causing casualties, not just the artillery with the main foot divisions but the other pieces mounted on top of Falside Hill. The lack of an adequate force of horse to deal with this latter problem and later to chase off the

English hagbutters and archers was a serious handicap to Arran. It must have been of particular regret to him that he could muster so few hand gunners himself and had to rely so heavily for his missile arm on the Highland archers, who, when it came to the battle, were found to be lacking. It was only in the years following Pinkie that the Scots fully realised the potential of hand firearms and it is not unlikely that the memory of the part played by the English hagbutters at this time acted as an inspiration to many a Scot to take more interest in these weapons.

Bad leadership, lack of horse and a mauling from the English artillery and hagbutters were all significant factors in the Scottish defeat. Perhaps the single most important cause of the Scots' discomfiture was their lack of training. Fighting with pikes was best done by professional armies since it demanded a complex structure of command and long training. The English were the first to recognise that the Scots were stout warriors but the prowess of individuals could find itself ill at ease when incorporated into large battles, forced to act in unison with thousands of others in complicated sequences of moves, on orders of bewildering complexity. Drill work which the modern army recruit finds difficult enough on the parade ground, the Scot of the sixteenth century had to learn on the field of battle with disastrous results. It may be that the English foot at Pinkie were no better than the Scots, but Somerset never had to put them to the test.

The day after the battle Somerset marched on to camp at Leith. He stayed there until 18 September when he left for England, leaving garrisons at Broughty Craig on the Tay, on Inchcolm in the Forth, at Eyemouth, and at Roxburgh on the border of the East Marches. He also started to fortify Leith but abandoned the project on his departure.[96] Meanwhile Lennox and Wharton made little progress and attracted little support in the south-west.

It might seem remarkable that Somerset failed to take greater advantage of his victory but the truth of the matter is that he probably lacked the time — before his supplies of food ran out — and the men to do so. No attempt was made on Edinburgh itself and it is hard to believe that this was altogether 'for consideracions moovying hym to pitee'.[97] Edinburgh was defended by walls and may have harboured much of the defeated Scottish army. It was also overshadowed by the castle which Somerset did not think was worth attempting. Even the holding of Leith seemed to be beyond his abilities and he settled for the remoter and securer Inchcolm instead. It has been suggested that the reason Leith was not fortified was because it had been rendered useless by being burned,[98] but it was not the houses in Leith which were of importance but its position and harbour. That it could be readily defended was proved soon afterwards by the French.

Nor had a crushing defeat totally subdued the Scots. Arran was soon getting an army together again to try to drive out the English garrisons, and there were, in any case, two other inevitable consequences of Somerset's victory: first, the removal of Queen Mary to France and ultimately her marriage to the Dauphin, and secondly the arrival of a French expeditionary force in June 1548. This, and Somerset's unwillingness to invest enough money and men in his Scottish enterprise, doomed his policy to failure. Both sides erected sophisticated earthwork fortifications and campaigned all year round, the French with considerable support from the Scots. From November 1548 the English were almost totally on the defensive, blindly hoping that something would turn up that would give them the upper hand. From August of the following year, with uprisings at home to contend with and a renewed French attack on Boulogne, they held on only to have something to bargain with when the negotiations for peace would inevitably be forced upon them — at Boulogne in April 1550.[99]

Pinkie, as has often been remarked, was the last major battle between the Scots and English as separate countries. Political, religious and dynastic considerations later in the century brought the two countries together, eventually into a union in 1603. The Scottish host was, therefore, never put again to such a test as Pinkie. This battle and first hand experience of working with the professional well-supplied French forces must have brought it home to many Scots that their host was not a credible fighting force except for purely local struggles. The only way to make it credible was to make it in some measure more professional and train more horsemen and hand gunners. That would have cost more money than any Scottish government of the time could ever command.

NOTES

1. *Acts of the Privy Council* (England), ii, 517; Patten, *Expedicion*, 82.
2. The battle is now called Pinkie or Pinkiecleugh, and was so called at the time. It was also referred to as the battle of Inveresk, Musselburgh or Falside.

3. W. Patten, *The Expedicion Into Scotlande of the most woorthely fortunate Prince Edward, Duke of Soomerset* (London, 1548). It has been reproduced in W. Dalyell, *Fragments of Scottish History* (Edinburgh, 1798), the pagination of which is given in these notes.

4. *Recit De L'Expedetion En Ecosse L'An MDXLVI Et De La Battayle De Muscleburgh Par le Sieur Berteville* (Bannatyne Club, 1825).

5. British Library Harl. MS 540 ff. 70, 71. 'The moste fortunate & victorious procedinge of the . . . . Duke of Somerset . . . into Scotland'.

6. 'De expeditione in Scotiam commentarius', printed in *Papiers d'etat, pieces et documents inedits ou peu connus relatifs a l'histoire de l'Ecosse au XVIeme siecle*, ed. A. Teulet (Bannatyne Club, 1852), i, 124–58. The manuscript, now in the Bibliotheque Nationale, Paris (C. V. Colbert 35) is in a 16th or early 17th century hand. It appears to be a much corrected copy of the original and the errors (corrected) in it, e.g. Werronico for Berovico (Berwick) suggest the copyist was not English.

7. Could this be a copy of a manuscript by the English archivist and collector, Ralph Starkey (died 1613)? See *DNB*, sv Starkey for an account of him. 'Aulae Peckualrensis' has proved difficult to identify, but I am grateful to Mrs M. Clapinson of the Bodleian Library, Oxford, for pointing out that there was a Peckwater Inn in Oxford, the building of which was incorporated into Christ Church. I know of no evidence of Ralph Starkey's connection with it.

8. *Cal. State Papers. Spanish*, ix, 150–2.

9. *Correspondence politique de Odet de Selve, ambassadeur de France en Angleterre, 1548–49*, ed. G. Lefevre-Pontalis (Paris, 1888), 203 ff.

10. Buchanan, *History*, ii, 364–68; Pitscottie, *Historie*, ii, 91–101; Knox, *History*, i, 98–101. Leslie is most accessible in translation in Dalrymple, *Historie*, ii, 296–301.

11. Knox, *History*, i, 101.

12. Pitscottie, *Historie*, ii, 98.

13. They were published by C. W. C. Oman, 'The Battle of Pinkie, Sept. 10, 1547', *Archaeol. Journ*, xc (1933), 1–25. They are no. 30492 in F. Madan, *A Summary Catalogue of Western Manuscripts in the Bodleian Library at Oxford* (1905).

14. I am grateful to Michael Ball of the National Army Museum for information on the paper, and Harry Watson, Editor of *The Dictionary of the Older Scottish Tongue*, for advice on the inscriptions. The print has also been published by C. de W. Crookshank in 'Military Battle Prints', *Journ Soc Army Hist Research*, xii (1933), 102–3.

15. C. W. C. Oman, 'The Battle of Pinkie, Sept 10, 1547', *Archaeol. Journ*, xc (1933), 1–25; *A History of the Art of War In The XVI Century* (London, 1937), 358–67.

16. J. Fergusson, *The White Hind* (London, 1963), 11–13; W. K. Jordan, *Edward VI: The Young King* (London, 1968), 246–63.

17. *Foedera*, xiv, 792–6.

18. *Henry VIII. Letters & Papers*, xxi, i, no. 1014; *Foedera*, xv, 93–98.

19. *The Chronicle and Political Papers of King Edward VI*, ed. W. K. Jordan (New York, 1966), 6.

20. *RPC*, i, 73.

21. *Henry VIII. Letters & Papers*, xxi, ii, no. 6.

22. See L. R. Shelley, *John Rogers. Tudor Military Engineer* (Oxford, 1967).

23. See M. Merriman, 'The Fortresses in Scotland' in *The History of the King's Works*, ed. H. M. Colvin (London, 1963-), vol. 3 (1485-1660).

24. *CSP*, i, 9; *TA*, ix, 85-94; *Cal State Papers. Spanish*, ix, 126; *Cal State Papers. Domestic* (1601-1603) Add. 1547-1565, 327; *Henry VIII. Letters & Papers*, xxi, ii, no. 695; *State Papers*, V, no. 582.

25. Knox, *History*, i, 96.

26. *Cal. State Papers. Domestic*, i, 36.

27. *Acts of the Privy Council*, ii, 118-19.

28. The lowest figure is from Berteville, *Expedetion*, 8, the highest is given by Van Der Delft, *Cal. State Papers. Spanish*, ix, 129, but this includes about 3,000 fighting men on the ships.

29. Patten, *Expedicion*, pp. xxv-xxvi.

30. C. S. L. Davies, 'Provisions for Armies, 1509-50; a Study in the Effectiveness of Early Tudor Government', *The Economic History Review*, 2nd ser., xxvii (1964), 234-48, makes much of the lack of carts in the north as a factor hindering Tudor attempts to impose a Union in Scotland.

31. *CSP*, i, no. 29; Patten, *Expedicion*, p. xxvi. Instructions drawn up in August speak of 8,000 men for the ships, of which 2,000 would be mariners, the other 6,000 to be set on land. See *CSP*, i, no. 31.

32. Oman, *The Art of War*, 359.

33. See *CSP*, i, no. 31, instructions drafted in August, specifically saying that the 1,800 light horse it envisaged included the garrison men.

34. *CSP*, i, no. 42.

35. *Ibid.*, no. 41. For Ayrshire casualties see J. Fergusson, *The White Hind* (London, 1963), 34-40, where 45 are listed. From Renfrewshire and the Lennox the following can be added:

William McGrory, Knock	SRO CS7/3/2 fol 277
John Maxwell of Cowglen	W. Fraser, *Memorials of the Maxwells of Pollock* (Edinburgh, 1863), i, 292
Duncan MacFarlane of that ilk	J. MacFarlane, *The History of*
Walter MacFarlane of Ardleish, and other MacFarlanes	*Clan MacFarlane* (Glasgow, 1922), 59
George Stirling of Glovat	SRO CS6/24 fol 93

The Master of Buchanan is also given in Dalrymple, *Historie*, ii, 300; but this is a mistake for the Master of Buchan, as given by Lesley. See I. Leslaeus, *De Origine, Moribus, et Rebus Gestis Scotorum* (Rome, 1578), 487. The following were taken prisoner:

Robert Colquhoun of Luss	*CSP*, i, no. 55
Thomas Crawfurd of Jordanhill	W. Fraser, *The Chiefs of Colquhoun* (Edinburgh, 1869), i, 91.

36. *CSP*, i, no. 35.
37. See Jordan, *Edward VI: The Young King*, 252-3.
38. *CSP*, i, no. 34.
39. Patten, *Expedicion*, 29.
40. *Ibid.*, 27.
41. *CSP*, i, nos. 34, 40, 41.
42. *TA*, viii, 463; ix, 56, 99-106, 111, 144, 163; *CSP*, i, no. 10.
43. *RPC*, i, 73-74.
44. *TA*, ix, 106-111.
45. *RSS*, iii, nos. 2460, 2518, 2576; iv, no. 1872; *CSP*, i, no. 34; *TA*, ix, 107.
46. Patten, *Expedicion*.
47. *CSP*, i, no. 40; *TA*, ix, 120.
48. *CSP*, i, no. 41; *ADCP*, 574; *RSS*, iii, no. 2769.
49. Patten, *Expedicion*, 47, 60.
50. Pitscottie, *Historie*, ii, 92; *Cal. State Papers. Spanish*, ix, 150; Selve, *Correspondance Politique*, 204, 219.
51. *The Chronicle of Edward VI*, 7.
52. Patten, *Expedicion*, 78; BL Harl. MS 540, fol. 71; *TA*, ix, 115-16.
53. See D. H. Caldwell, 'The Use and Effect of Weapons: the Scottish Experience' in *ROSC*, iv (1988), 53-62.
54. Knox, *History*, i, 199; D. Hume, *The History of the Houses of Douglas and Angus* (Edinburgh, 1648), 272.
55. Patten, *Expedicion*, 96.
56. Pitscottie, *Historie*, ii, 96; *RSS*, iii, no. 2924; iv, nos. 808, 2046, 3067.
57. Alexander Fraser of Aberdeen, who died in the battle, actually possessed a handgun (a culverin) but evidently left it at home when he went off with the army: *Aberdeen Council Register*, i, 458.
58. R. Holinshed, *Chronicles of England, Scotland, Ireland* (London, 1808), v, 551; Patten, *Expedicion*, 69.
59. *TA*, ix, 97-98, 112.
60. BL Harl. MS 540, fol. 71; Patten, *Expedicion*, 78; *TA*, ix, 115-16.
61. *APS*, ii, 599-600.
62. Patten, *Expedicion*, 29ff.
63. J. de Beaugue, *Histoire de la guerre d'Ecosse: pendant les campagnes 1548 et 1549* (Maitland Club, 1830), 70.
64. For Dunbar Castle and blockhouse see I. MacIvor, 'Artillery and Major Places of Strength in the Lothians and the East Border, 1513-1542' in *Scottish Weapons and Fortifications 1100-1800*, ed. D. H. Caldwell (Edinburgh, 1981), 94-152.
65. BL Harl. MS 540, fol. 71.
66. Leith already had defences in 1544. See 'The Late Expedicion in Scotlande .... 1544', reprinted in Dalyell, *Fragments*, 5.
67. Selve, *Correspondance Politique*, 203, 212; *Cal. State Papers. Spanish*, ix, 168-9.
68. Patten, *Expedicion*, 46: For Morison's Haven see A. Graham, 'Morison's Haven', *Proc. Soc. Antiq. Scot.*, xlv (1961-2), 300-303. Graham notes the tradition recorded by the Ordnance Survey's offices in 1853 that there was

a fort by the Haven 'built about 1547 by a certain John Acheson' who had served in the Scots Guard in Paris. Was this in fact the site of the English Camp in September 1547?

69. Berteville, *Expedetion*, 12–13.
70. Patten, *Expedicion*, 49–50.
71. Pitscottie, *Historie*, ii, 92; Buchanan, *History*, ii, 365; Knox, *History*, i, 98; Holinshed, *Chronicles*, v, 549.
72. Patten, *Expedicion*, 55, 75.
73. The last will and testament of Master Thomas Sluthman of Edinburgh was witnessed on the lands of Monktonhall about 8 a.m. on 10 September: SRO NP1/2A fol. 123. David Barclay of Cullerny had his will drawn up at Musselburgh on 8 September: SRO NP1/169 fol. 23. John French of Cloverhill, dwelling in the parish of Bothwell, had his done in the camp at Musselburgh: SRO CC9/7/1 fol. 5.
74. SRO CS7/3/1 fol. 198; CS7/3/2 fols. 344, 346, etc.
75. This is the arrangement shown in the Bodleian drawings but Patten says the archers were on the right.
76. Patten, *Expedicion*, 62.
77. Knox, *History*, ii, 211.
78. Patten, *Expedicion*, 60.
79. Pitscottie, *Historie*, ii, 99.
80. At this point the English ships were too far away to have fired effectively at the Scottish army — under any circumstances over one mile and probably over two.
81. Berteville, *Expedetion*, 16.
82. *Cal. State Papers. Spanish*, ix, 151–2.
83. Pitscottie, *Historie*, ii, 100.
84. Holinshed, *Chronicles*, v, 551.
85. W. Fraser, *The Scotts of Buccleuch* (Edinburgh, 1878), ii, 185–7.
86. Buchanan, *History*, ii, 368.
87. Patten, *Expedicion*, 66.
88. Selve, *Correspondance Politique*, 206, 218. Cf. *Ibid.*, 222.
89. Patten, *Expedicion*, 69.
90. This paragraph is based on an analysis of the main sources on the battle (notes 3–6, 8–10, 54, 57), a survey of the printed *ER, RSS, RMS, Retours, ADCP*; the manuscript Acts & Decreets (SRO CS7), Acts of the Lords of Council and Session (SRO CS6), Glasgow Testaments (SRO CC9/7/1) and the collection of Protocol Books in the Scottish Record Office; and also various published genealogical sources. In particular for the Ogilvies and Urquharts see H. Tayler, *A History of the Family of Urquhart* (Aberdeen, 1946), 93, 138. From all the above a list of some 230 Pinkie casualties can be made, mostly, of course, men of some substance. Owing to the partial survival of contemporary records and their uneven geographical spread, I have not seen fit to subject this list to any more detailed analysis. It is also abundantly clear that the information that someone died at Pinkie was not invariably recorded in documents even where there was some legal point in demonstrating that feudal casualties

need not be, or had not been, paid because of this. If the records were searched for men who had died about the time of the battle, the list would be very much longer.

91. *Cal. State Papers. Spanish*, ix, 150, 152. Cf. Selve, *Correspndance Politique*, 222.

92. Selve, *Correspondance Politique*, 222.

93. *Henry VIII. Letters & Papers*, xix, ii, no. 707; *Diurnal of Occurrents*, 36; Pitscottie, *Historie*, ii, 30.

94. *Cal. State Papers. Spanish*, ix, 152; J. Balfour, *Annales of Scotland* (Edinburgh, 1824), i, 288.

95. Selve, *Correspondance Politique*, 206.

96. Patten, *Expedicion*, 80.

97. *Ibid.*, 82.

98. M. L. Bush, *The Government Policy of Protector Somerset* (London, 1975), 24.

99. M. H. Merriman, *The Struggle for the Marriage of Mary Queen of Scots: English and French Intervention in Scotland, 1543–1550* (London University PhD Thesis, 1975), 212.

5

THE MARIAN CIVIL WAR, 1567-1573

Ian B. Cowan

The Marian civil war led to few battles of any consequence. The first encounter at Carberry in 1567 commenced with a series of fruitless chivalric parleys and ended without bloodshed after the flight of the earl of Bothwell and the capitulation of the queen.[1] The final stage of the conflict, the taking with English assistance of Edinburgh castle in 1573, proved to be an equal anti-climax to a struggle, the outcome of which had become increasingly predictable.[2] The execution of Kirkcaldy of Grange, commander of the castle, and some of his principal associates may be seen as a salutary reminder of the newly established authority of James VI, but the bulk of the garrison, who were not considered a threat to future national security, were allowed without condition to leave their stronghold, 'with their armour, bag and baggage'.[3] The prospect of any continuation of the conflict between the supporters of Mary queen of Scots and those of her son was at an end.

How inevitable was this outcome? Paradoxically it would appear that the result of the Marian civil war was predetermined at its onset. Carberry, which led to Mary's imprisonment and enforced abdication, was an engagement which should never have been contemplated. Dunbar would have provided a safer refuge from which the errant queen could have mustered support for her cause.[4] The nucleus of a Marian party certainly existed. Supporters unshaken by the Bothwell marriage included among their number the earl of Huntly, Lords Fleming and Seton and, representing the powerful house of Hamilton, John Hamilton, archbishop of St Andrews.[5] Few of those were, however, at Carberry, although Lord Seton, who had absented himself from the queen's marriage to Bothwell, nevertheless marched with her to Musselburgh.[6] Delay would have brought more recruits to her side, but the premature and impetuous appeal to arms followed by her subsequent surrender left the queen's allies confused and without an immediate cause.[7]

The encounter at Carberry had, however, produced several positive advantages: it not only freed the queen from the clutches of Bothwell, but in many cases led to personal hostility towards Mary being replaced, following her enforced abdication and coronation of her son on 29 July 1567, by anxiety for her safety.[8] Such considerations further weakened the fragile anti-Marian confederacy, the unity of which had always been in doubt, and led to early desertions by reluctant supporters such as Archibald, fifth earl of Argyll, Alexander Gordon, bishop of Galloway, and Lords Boyd, Fleming and Herries amongst others.[9] Many who joined the queen's party at this juncture were swayed by the argument that the queen had abdicated under duress. Among those who favoured this point of view was Kirkcaldy of Grange, to whom Mary surrendered at Carberry and who subsequently pursued Bothwell to Shetland to rid the queen of the latter's influence, only to find that his efforts, far from freeing the queen, had led to her incarceration and abdication.[10]

Other motives for supporting the queen's cause were not quite so altruistic. The Hamilton interest, in the absence of their head, the duke of Chatelherault, was maintained not by his sons, one of whom, the earl of Arran, was insane, while the others were either dead or inept, but by his half-brother John, archbishop of St Andrews, and Gavin, commendator of Kilwinning.[11] Self-interest was foremost, for Chatelherault was undeniably heir to Mary, if not to her son James.[12] Nevertheless, complications over the subsequent succession may have allowed other prominent Marian supporters, including the earls of Argyll, Eglinton and Huntly, reversionary rights to the crown.[13] Political considerations were not, however, restricted to this issue and animosity towards the Regent Moray was an equally strong motive for opposing his authority and supporting the queen's cause. The Hamiltons were implacably hostile and were joined in this feeling not only by their fellow kinsmen but also by allies related by blood and marriage. Hamilton influence was particularly strong among churchmen — Hamiltons held the commendation of Arbroath, Kilwinning and Paisley — while James Hamilton, the reformed bishop of Argyll, preferred to follow the lead given by the Archbishop of St Andrews rather than offer his support to the protestant cause.[14]

Religious affiliation, if not a paramount consideration, was nevertheless important in determining loyalties. The earls of Atholl, Caithness, Cassilis, Crawford, Eglinton and Montrose were devout catholics and were politically committed to the queen, even if Atholl briefly flirted with Moray in 1567 and 1569.[15] The earl of Sutherland, a Gordon, was related to both Huntly and Caithness whose lead he undoubtedly followed.[16] Among lesser magnates Lord Seton was outstanding in his loyalty and one of the few who not only supported Mary at Carberry but was equally to refuse to abandon her even in 1573.[17] Of other lords prominent in the queen's cause, zealous catholics included Lords Borthwick, Carlyle, Ross and Somerville, although the last-named supported the political aims of the Reformation.[18] In this respect the bishops might have been expected to present a united front, but in the event religious affiliation did not necessarily predetermine choice of loyalty. The majority of the bishops did, nevertheless, remain nominally catholic even if two of the most stalwart, James Beaton, archbishop of Glasgow, and William Chisholm, bishop of Dunblane, had chosen exile rather than promote active opposition in Scotland.[19] Of those who chose to remain, the only two predominantly motivated by religious considerations were Robert Crichton of Dunkeld and John Leslie, bishop of Ross; others may have been guided by their beliefs, but family ties were probably of more immediate concern.[20] Of those who remained nominally catholic, the position of John Hamilton, archbishop of St Andrews, was as predictable as that of William Gordon, bishop of Aberdeen, who was a great-uncle of the earl of Huntly.[21] Family connections also influenced Patrick Hepburn, bishop of Moray, who, although remaining Catholic, was never active in promoting religious beliefs and concentrated rather on the fortunes of his kin who through their close association with Bothwell remained true to the Marian faction.[22]

Such allegiance was equally to the fore among the reformed bishops, with four out of the six supporting the queen's cause. James Hamilton, the reformed bishop of Argyll, understandably followed the family lead, while Alexander Gordon, the conformist bishop of Galloway, likewise chose to support the stand taken by his uncle, George Gordon, fifth earl of Huntly.[23] In a similar manner Archibald Campbell, fifth earl of Argyll, through kinship, was not only able to ensure the loyalty of the protestant bishop of Brechin, Alexander Campbell, but through territorial power was likewise to claim the support of the reformed bishop of the Isles, John Carswell, for the Marian cause.[24] Of the reformed bishops only Adam Bothwell, bishop of Orkney, who had officiated at Mary's marriage to the earl of Bothwell, but subsequently crowned James VI, and Robert Stewart, bishop of Caithness, who had close family ties with both the earl of Lennox and the infant king, felt able to combine their political ambitions with their protestant allegiance.[25]

If episcopal support for Mary's party was predominantly in the queen's favour, their example, with the exception of a handful of canons of cathedrals and collegiate churches, was not generally followed by other clergy, who in any case were unlikely to be found in arms for either party.[26]

Despite the numerical advantage enjoyed by the Marian faction in the sphere of episcopal support, moral rather than political backing was as much as they could offer. Several of the bishops, including Hepburn and John Hamilton were, however, also commendators of Scone and Paisley respectively, and as such had material advantages to offer to the party which they chose to sustain.[27] Other commendators, for personal rather than religious reasons, were equally positive towards the queen's cause; the Hamilton commendators, Claud and Gavin, respectively held Paisley and Kilwinning, while other commendators swayed by family allegiance included Edward Maxwell of Dundrennan and Alexander Seton of Pluscarden.[28] By the nature of their appointment commendators were unlikely to be influenced by religious considerations, Gilbert Brown, commendator of New Abbey, providing a solitary exception to this.[29] Even the most committed Marian had to be wary, for commendators were vulnerable, being dependent upon crown patronage for the retention of a commendatorship with the existing family group. This in itself may have been sufficient to restrain commendators from exhibiting too much enthusiasm for a queen who could not effectively exercise such patronage.

Faced with these restraints and the recognition that religious commitment alone would not procure a sufficient following, Mary ultimately relied upon attracting support from the other side of the religious spectrum. Personal affinity and previous friendship appear to have been the principal motives for such allegiance, both being adequately demonstrated in the case of the protestant earl of Argyll.[30] If hostility towards Moray made this decision all the easier, loyalty to the queen undoubtedly counted for more to the earl of Rothes than his staunch religious principles.[31] Other zealous protestants who adhered to the queen's cause for personal reasons included her undoubted friends Lords Livingston and Fleming, who were outstanding in their loyalty. Fleming had close ties with the Hamiltons and one of his sisters was one of the queen's Marys, of whom another was married to Livingston.[32] Two other staunch allies — Lords Boyd and Herries — were equally active in the protestant cause, as were other Marian supporters such as Lord Crichton of Sanquhar and Lords Hay of Yester, Ogilvie of Airlie, Home and Maxwell.[33]

Support for Mary among landed proprietors was not to be paralleled among townspeople, although some burghs were undoubtedly influenced in their attitudes by interests of neighbouring magnates and lairds. As few burghs were, however, directly involved in the conflict allegiances had seldom to be turned into action and few burgesses appear to have become directly involved in the struggle.[34] At Langside only a handful of burgesses appeared on behalf of the queen, but Edinburgh and Glasgow both supplied citizens for the regent's forces.[35] The burgesses of Stirling proved equally loyal during the raid by the Marians on Stirling which led to the death of the Regent Lennox.[36] The reaction of the inhabitants of Edinburgh to the occupation of the burgh by Kirkcaldy of Grange during 1571–3 provided more divided loyalties. Reasons for supporting the Marian party varied, some cowed into submission, others bent on financial gain and an uncertain number genuinely motivated by their support of the queen's cause.[37] At its peak as many as six hundred supporters may have actively aided the queen, and at least four hundred and seventy of these have been positively identified as against one hundred and fifty allied with the king's party.[38] A further analysis of these figures does, however, reveal that while craftsmen, especially those of the meaner sort, played a significant part in the town's support for the queen, the merchants, with the possible exception of maltmen merchants who stood to gain by supplying the Marians in the castle, were more inclined to view the king's cause with favour.[39] Edinburgh was, however, an exceptional case and cannot be taken to represent the general standpoint of Scottish burgesses.

Faced with such massive support for the queen's party, the task of the king's supporters led by the Regent Moray was far from easy. If the unity which had characterised the confederate lords proved illusory, others, nevertheless, remained implacably opposed to the queen's cause. Among the earls, Atholl, Morton, Glencairn, Mar and Menteith were motivated partly by political ambition and to a lesser extent, with the possible exception of the zealous Glencairn, by their commitment to protestantism.[40] Similar considerations motivated some of the lesser magnates, who included among their number Lords Ochiltree, Ruthven, Lindsay and Sempill, while others such as Cathcart, Innermeath and St John were equally sympathetic to the king's cause.[41] Lairds of similar persuasion were apparently more numerous in areas such as Fife and

Angus and the Mearns in which protestantism was deep-seated, a standpoint demonstrated by Sir Thomas Maule of Panmure.[42] Other lairds were less influenced by religious persuasion and were more motivated by the hope of clinging to public office, an attitude shared by lay commendators of religious houses such as Robert Richardson of St Mary's Isle, who was Treasurer.[43] Of the bishops, Adam Bothwell, the reformed bishop of Orkney, who had married Mary to his namesake the earl of Bothwell, but had equivocally officiated at the coronation of James VI, remained firmly committed to the king.[44] So too did Robert Stewart, the reformed bishop of Caithness and commendator of the priory of St Andrews, brother of the earl of Lennox and great-uncle of the young monarch.[45]

If in theory the queen's party possessed an obvious advantage over its rivals, it lacked in practice the resolution to further its cause by taking to arms. In this respect custody of the queen gave Moray and his supporters a tactical and psychological advantage over their opponents. Indeed, by mid-September 1567 compromise between the two parties seemed a distinct possibility: Argyll and Huntly, among others, had offered their allegiance to the king; Bothwell's supporters had surrendered Dunbar; while in the south-west bondsmen of Huntly had renounced their allegiance to the Gordons.[46] As support for the Hamilton initiative for the appointment of a regency council receded, conciliation between the two contesting parties appeared likely and indeed seemed to have been practically achieved at a well-attended parliament in December 1567.[47]

This unity was, however, shown to be illusory when less than six months later, on 2 May 1568, Mary escaped and the situation was subsequently transformed.[48] Conciliation was at an end and remarkably, within the space of only eleven days, some five to six thousand Marian supporters from throughout the south of Scotland had assembled in arms.[49] Inevitably much of this support came from central and western Scotland in which Hamilton influence, and that of their allies, the earls of Cassilis and Eglinton, was strongest.[50] If in consequence Ayrshire was to produce the most significant turn-out, both Lanarkshire and Renfrewshire also rose to the occasion.[51] From further afield the Lothians responded well, although East Lothian, geographically further from Langside than either West or Midlothian, turned out in the largest numbers, presumably because of the influence of the Hepburns and Lord Seton in that area.[52] Equally significant, however, were the small numbers in attendance from central lowland Scotland, comprising

Stirlingshire and Clackmannan, in which the influence of the Erskine family headed by the earl of Mar prevented the raising of any significant force.[53] Likewise Fife, which was under the control of families such as Lyndsay of Byres, who steadfastly supported the king, nevertheless provided a sizeable number of lairds, including eight from the family of Balfour, who were prepared to champion the queen's cause.[54]

The motive for such a large turn-out must remain uncertain as personal convictions cannot readily be assessed. Even if some had advance knowledge of Mary's escape, the vast majority must have rallied spontaneously to her cause. Religious allegiance may have been uppermost, and support from some adherents for catholic survival in some parts of the country has frequently been underestimated. Loyalty to a queen whose previous misdeeds had been overshadowed by her treatment at the hands of an unpopular regent may also have contributed to the size of the opposition to the king's party. In the event neither of these criteria was paramount, and family allegiance may have counted for much more than the personal predilictions of those who physically supported the queen by their presence in her army.[55] If the size of her forces appeared to favour the queen's army, initial tactics were equally propitious, for the decision to head for Dumbarton, then held by Lord Fleming, to await reinforcements from the north, was a wise move.[56]

Moray was holding a justice ayre in Glasgow when he heard of Mary's escape.[57] His dilemma was immediate; should he stage a tactical retreat, which might mean ruin for his party, or should he risk all in a quick battle? The latter view prevailed and proclamations were issued calling his supporters to arms.[58] Immediate assistance came from Renfrewshire and the Lennox, but support from Lothian and the Mearns quickly followed, bringing his forces to a strength of some 4000 men.[58] There were with him the earls of Morton, Mar, Glencairn, Menteith, the Master of Graham, Lords Hume, Lyndsay, Ruthven, Sempill, Ochiltree and Cathcart.[60] In addition the lairds of Bargany, Blackquharn, Drumlanrig, Cesford, Luss, Buchanan, Tullibardine, Pitcur, Grange, Lochleven, Lethington and Sir James Balfour gave their support.[61] Mar had despatched cannon from Stirling; Edinburgh provided hagbutters and the royal archers, while some six hundred Glaswegians also joined the regent's forces.[62] As there was some uncertainty about the strategy which would be deployed by the queen's army, Moray drew up his army outside the Gallowgate port of Glasgow, which lay straight across the enemy's line of march if it chose the north side of the Clyde for its route.[63] On the other hand interception would be equally possible if the south side of the river was preferred. In the event the latter plan was followed and Moray's forces were rapidly deployed in the direction of the queen's army, using carts to transport their cannon.[64]

The queen's army, which had apparently decided to engage the regent's forces if intercepted, in the hope similar to Moray's that a quick victory would confirm their ascendancy, marched from Hamilton to Rutherglen via Cambuslang and Blantyre before branching off in a north-westerly direction, which would take their forces to high ground in the neighbourhood of their adversary.[65] Moray, who was equally determined to secure this vantage point speedily, crossed the Clyde by the old bridge of Glasgow into the village of Bridgend, now Gorbals, which placed him on a direct route for Langside, an objective which he quickly attained.[66] This manoeuvre undoubtedly shaped the course of the battle and ensured a crushing victory over the queen and her supporters. In the event the decision of the Marians to fight rather than detour to the south proved to have been misguided.[67]

The greatest mistake was not, however, the Marians' determination to fight, but rather that of the queen to flee. Had she remained in Scotland, her forces joined by the expected reinforcements, might have regrouped, but flight left her supporters at a total loss.[68] The triumphant Moray, on the other hand, was able to consolidate his position by touring the south-west and Tweeddale, both of which had proved fruitful recruiting grounds for the Marian party.[69] In Dumfriesshire, the presence of Lord Crichton of Sanquhar and John Maxwell, Lord Herries, both converts to the queen's cause, had ensured substantial support for the Marians, an enthusiasm which spilled over into the neighbouring shires of Kirkcudbright and Wigtown; but while a few of the leaders, such as Lord Maxwell, nephew of Lord Herries, were ardent catholics, the overwhelming number of adherents appear to have been of protestant persuasion.[70] So too in Tweeddale where associates of Sir Thomas Ker of Ferniehirst, the son-in-law of Kirkcaldy of Grange, were protestant and devoted Marians, as were other borderers such as Lord Home, a late adherent who was thereafter one of her staunchest supporters, even if few of his kinsmen chose to follow his example.[71] Sir Walter Scott of Branxholm and Buccleuch appears to have been somewhat more successful in attracting his kinsmen into the queen's service.[72] However, all these families were divided in their loyalties and a show of strength by Moray was sufficient to ensure general quiescence. Nevertheless, the regent, whose complex character did not endear him to even his own cohorts, was unable to command wide support at his parliament held in July–August 1568, at which only four earls, nine Lords, two bishops and nine commendators were present.[73] Threats and bribes were used to alter the situation and subsequently detach Hamilton supporters from their former allegiance. Even Lord Fleming, it was rumoured, would have defected had he been able to obtain the priory of Whithorn in return for surrendering the castle of Dumbarton. Avarice and self-interest clearly had the edge over personal loyalty.[74]

Moray's success was not, however, unchallenged as many of his opponents remained in arms. Aberdeenshire, dominated by Huntly and his Gordon kinsmen, was hardly surprisingly staunchly Marian, so much so that an alternative royal administration functioned from time to time under the direction of Huntly, who although not nominally a catholic, held sway in an area in which the old faith still attracted an impressive following.[75]

Gordon influence was not confined to Aberdeenshire, but extended to and beyond the Moray Firth. The earl of Sutherland was a Gordon as was the queen's principal supporter in the north, Adam Gordon of Auchindoun, a native of Banffshire.[76] In the period following Langside, Huntly commanded the support of some two to five thousand men in Angus and Fife while Argyll and Lord Fleming threatened Glasgow with 1500 troops.[77] In East Lothian the Hepburns held sway while in central Scotland, Hamilton castle, seized by the regent after Langside, was re-captured for the family interests.[78]

Supporters of the queen still hoped for Mary's restoration, but as the 'trial' initiated by Elizabeth proceeded, doubts and indecision began to arise even amongst her most devoted supporters.[79] If the decision announced on 10 January 1570 proved inconclusive in terms of Mary's guilt or innocence, the practical outcome of retaining their queen in England while Moray was allowed to return to Scotland effectively ruined the Marian cause.[80] If for some months after the decision had been made known opposition to the regent continued, a large number of Marian supporters submitted to his authority during the course of April, while in the following month Argyll and Huntly also entered into obedience.[81] It is clear that with the exception of the Hamiltons, few if any wished to push matters to the point of confrontation. Only a renewed crisis could precipitate further action, yet if such a situation developed, the queen's party was still sufficiently strong to rise again in support of her cause.

That crisis was, in the event, precipitated by the queen's supporters

themselves when the regent Moray was murdered, with the approval of
John Hamilton, archbishop of St Andrews, at Linlithgow in January
1570 by James Hamilton of Bothwellhaugh.[82] Almost immediately the
queen's party erupted into action with operations in the north, west and
central Scotland conducted by Huntly, Argyll and the Hamiltons
respectively.[83] The five months' vacancy in the regency following Moray's
death not only brought desertions from the king's party, but also
allowed the jubilant Hamiltons to demonstrate their support by
assembling at Glasgow with 140 horse and 80 harquebusiers on 17
February.[84] The former Marian supporters returned to the fold and new
adherents, including Maitland of Lethington, took up her cause.[85]
Maitland, subsequently charged by Moray in September 1569 with
complicity in the murder of Darnley and placed in the custody of
Kirkcaldy of Grange, persuaded his keeper to declare his support for
the queen and turn Edinburgh castle into a Marian stronghold.[86] Despite
such a show of strength support for the queen was, however,
conditional, for even the most committed Marian increasingly thought
of Mary's restoration in terms of joint sovereignty with her son.[87] If in
retrospect this hope may appear fanciful, the tide of support in mid-
1570 blinded Mary's adherents to the realities of English politics,
which in turn unwittingly boosted the Marian cause by foisting the earl
of Lennox upon the Scots as their new regent in July 1570.[88]

If the appointment of an Anglophile regent attracted some further
support for the Marian cause, the ageing and ailing regent quickly
showed that resistance to his authority was not to be tolerated. A series
of successful military operations, mounted with English assistance,
recaptured Brechin which had been the scene of much fighting.[89] Doune
castle, some Maxwell strongholds in the south-west and Paisley all fell
to the regent's forces, but the real prize was the successful storming by
Crawford of Jordanhill of Dumbarton castle in April 1571,[90] an event
which proved to be the turning point of the war, for within its walls
Archbishop Hamilton was apprehended and subsequently hanged at
Stirling for his part in the assassination of the regent Moray.[91]

Nevertheless, the Marian party apparently continued to flourish.
Kirkcaldy of Grange dominated Edinburgh, causing John Knox to leave
his charge at St Giles for the safety of St Andrews.[92] The Marians,
including Huntly, worshipped there and heard John Craig preach, even
if their real concern in holding St Giles was military, rather than
spiritual.[93] Contemporaneously Angus and the Mearns continued to be

dominated by Huntly, Lord Herries retained control in the south-west, and Hamilton influence was still maintained in central Scotland.[94] With such a following it is scarcely surprising that the Marians for a time threatened to constitute an alternative government, a move which found expression in the holding of a parliament in Edinburgh in June 1571 as a riposte to that of the regent in the previous month.[95] Whereas Lennox's gathering had been a hole in the corner affair in the Canongate with members creeping to and from its meetings to avoid personal injury since even there they were threatened by the castle's artillery, the Marian parliament, graced by the presence of the regalia, had maintained a dignity denied to its counterpart.[96] Yet this 'creeping parliament' was not without significance as it took steps to forfeit the dead archbishop, his nephew Gavin Hamilton, commendator of Kilwinning and the three Maitland brothers.[97] If in practice little came of this, the threat of forfeiture apparently brought several influential Marians to heel and three earls — Argyll, Cassilis and Eglinton — and several lords, who had apparently been convinced of the queen's guilt, entered into the king's allegiance.[98] Their fears were not unfounded, for in parliament in August Chatelherault, Huntly, four bishops and numerous lairds were forfeited.[99] In hope of retrieving a situation which was turning against the queen's party, whose achilles heel continued to be not only Mary's enforced captivity but also the niggling doubts that Mary's delinquencies were only too real, Kirkcaldy of Grange decided to strike at the king's party by attacking Stirling in September 1571. In the event little was achieved, but Lennox was killed in one of the confused skirmishes which characterised the episode.[100]

If Lennox's regency had intensified the civil war, the appointment of his successor, the earl of Mar, served to defuse the confrontation. His regency, which lasted until his death in October 1572, was characterised by attempts at conciliation which led to several magnates coming over to the king's side, some assuaged by bribery, but others through the growing realisation of the futility of the continuing struggle.[101] Yet not all felt this way and in some quarters, particularly but not exclusively in the Edinburgh area, Marian activity continued unabated. In the north-east, Huntly's brother, Gordon of Auchindoun defeated Forbes, the king's lieutenant in the north, first at Tullyangus and then at the Craibstone near Aberdeen.[102] Thereafter the queen's writ was enforced and ministers were ordered to pray for her.[103] In the south-west, Herries and Lochinvar were in arms and in the Borders, Ferniehurst only narrowly failed to take Jedburgh.[104] If the queen's party was undermined during Mar's regency, he singularly failed to end the civil war, a task which fell to his successor, the earl of Morton.

The new regent was a very different man from his predecessor. Conciliation and appeasement were not in his nature. Like Lennox before him he was an anglophile, but on this occasion it did not cost him support and the king's party retained the loyalty of those won over by Mar. His election as regent in November 1572 was made by a fairly representative convention, even if the bishops, with the exception of Adam Bothwell, bishop of Orkney, Robert Stewart, bishop of Caithness and John Douglas, archbishop of St Andrews, were conspicuous by their absence.[105] Not so the commendators who included in their number some who had been active Marians.[106] With this support behind him, Morton was in a strong position to bring pressure to bear upon the remaining Marian adherents, many of whom had reconsidered their position in the light of the Massacre of St Bartholomew's Day in August 1572.[107] Fear of the implementation of the forfeitures already decreed may also have swayed some towards reconciliation with Morton in a pacification effected at Perth on 23 February 1573.[108] Such defections enabled the king's party to reoccupy Edinburgh and with English assistance to reduce the castle.[109] Sir William Kirkcaldy and a few of his principal supporters were executed, Maitland of Lethington only escaping a similar fate by dying, perhaps by his own hand, shortly after the capture of the castle. Otherwise the castilians were allowed to depart in peace.[110] Such magnanimity paid handsome dividends; the civil war was effectively at an end and with it the party which had hitherto championed the queen's cause.

The most important factor in determining the outcome of the struggle lay in the attitude of the landed classes to the contending parties, but other interested parties had nevertheless some part to play. Support for the queen was surprisingly strong among the burgesses, some of whom may have found the war profitable, while others were influenced by their allegiances through family connection with landed proprietors. Churchmen who enjoyed high office tended to be influenced by similar considerations, while the lesser clergy held aloof from the struggle. In terms of the professional classes, however, top-notch administrators appear to have favoured the king's party, leaving their less gifted colleagues to seek possible advancement through support of the queen.[111]

Considerations amongst such influential classes which led to support for either the king or the queen were both multifarious and complex. It is difficult to pin-point the reasons why any individual or group made their choice but it is clear that religious issues were a secondary concern. Catholics were certainly more likely to side with the queen and few opposed her, but protestants were much more widely divided, constitutional loyalty to the sovereign being accounted by many as of greater import than the religious beliefs of a queen who had shown herself only too willing to make concessions to her protestant subjects. Aided by such attitudes and the overwhelming support accorded at times to the queen's cause, the Marian party's failure in its objectives and its ultimate defeat may at first appear surprising;[112] but the reasons are not far to seek.

First and foremost is the absence of the queen herself. Without a ruler who could be restored to her throne, the campaign mounted by her supporters was doomed. Mary by fleeing in 1568 made the final scenario inevitable. The charade was only kept alive by Elizabeth's apparently genuine belief that Mary could be restored, if the appropriate conditions could be found.[113] As late as 1570 this remained a possibility, but by 1571 that option had almost disappeared. The publication of an indictment by Elizabeth against her cousin not only met general acceptance in England, but also in Scotland where doubts about Mary's character, which even her supporters had always harboured, seemed to have been fully justified.[114] Unease about the legality of her deposition was largely allayed, and disquiet over the massacre of St Bartholomew's Eve heightened opposition to a queen with French connections. Her friends at home were no less suspect, and suspicions as to the real intentions of the Hamiltons if the queen was restored had always occasioned some unease. And it was this very family's downfall, precipitated by the capture of Dumbarton castle and the subsequent execution of John Hamilton, archbishop of St Andrews, which marked the beginning of the end for the queen's cause. In the aftermath of these events the attack on Stirling and the death of Lennox backfired, for the expedition's failure, coupled with the fortuitous death of an unpopular regent, not only allayed the opposition of those who had questioned the political wisdom of persevering with a regency, but equally weakened the case for the queen's personal reinstatement. Subsequent regents enjoyed more popular backing in their efforts to end the civil war, and with this in mind it is hard to escape the conclusion that one of the most important factors in determining the fortunes of war and support for the contending parties lay in the character of the regents themselves. Moray and Mar had managed to maintain a degree of conciliation and if

Lennox's policies broke this mould, Morton despite his similar anglo-phile tendencies was able to turn his friendship with England into the determining factor which brought the Marian civil wars to an end. In truth, however, the outcome had been decided five years earlier following the battle of Langside, when Mary decided to flee south. Her motto 'In my end is my beginning' on this occasion turned out to be singularly unprophetic, for most assuredly the beginning of a new chapter in her life marked the end of her career as queen of Scots.

NOTES

1. R. Pitcairn (ed.), *Historical memoirs of the reign of Mary Queen of Scots, and a portion of the reign of King James the Sixth. By [John 7th] Lord Herries* (Bannatyne Club, 1836), 92–5; T. Thomson (ed.), *Memoirs of his own life. By Sir James Melville of Halhill, MDXLIX–MDXCIII. From the Original Manuscript* (Bannatyne Club, 1827), 182–5; T. Thomson and D. Laing (edd.), *The History of the Kirk of Scotland. By Mr David Calderwood, some time minister of Crailing* (Wodrow Society, 8 vols., 1842–9), ii, 362–5.
2. Melville, *Memoirs*, 23–6.
3. ibid., 253–6; Calderwood, *History*, iii, 281–5.
4. Herries, *Memoirs*, 92–3; Melville, *Memoirs*, 182; Calderwood, *History*, ii, 361.
5. ibid., ii, 361–2, 364; Herries, *Memoirs*, 92; T. Thomson (ed.), *A diurnal of remarkable occurrents that have passed within the country of Scotland since the death of King James the Fourth till the year MDLXXV* (Bannatyne Club, 1833), 111.
6. Herries, *Memoirs*, 92; Calderwood, *History*, ii, 362; J. Bain and others (edd.), *Calendar of the State Papers Relating to Scotland and Mary Queen of Scots 1547–1603* [*CSP Scot.*] (13 vols, Edinburgh, 1898–1969), ii, no. 523.
7. ibid., ii, 364–5; *Diurnal of Occurrents*, 114–15.
8. ibid., 118–19; Herries, *Memoirs*, 97, 99; Calderwood, *History*, ii, 372–7, 384.
9. ibid., ii, 387, 404; Melville, *Memoirs*, 195–6; *CSP Scot.*, ii, nos. 536, 548, 589.
10. Melville, *Memoirs*, 184; Calderwood, *History*, ii, 364, 386–7; *Diurnal of Occurrents*, 119.
11. Melville, *Memoirs*, 195–6; Sir J. Balfour Paul, *The Scots Peerage* (9 vols, Edinburgh, 1904–14), iv, 36, 366–70.
12. G. Donaldson, *All the Queen's Men*, 91–2; the author is deeply indebted to this work.
13. ibid., 92; *CSP Scot.*, iii, 54.

14. I. B. Cowan and D. E. Easson, *Medieval Religious Houses: Scotland* (London, 1976), 65, 67, 69; J. Dowden, *The Bishops of Scotland* (Glasgow, 1912), 391.

15. Donaldson, *All the Queen's Men*, 93–5; *Scots Peerage*, i, 444–5; ii, 338–40, 471–3; iii, 29–30, 440–1; vi, 226–8.

16. ibid., viii, 343–4; Donaldson, *All the Queen's Men*, 94.

17. Herries, *Memoirs*, 92–3, 102, *Calendar of the State Papers Relating to Scotland 1509-1603*, ed. M. J. Thorpe (2 vols. London, 1858), i, 316, 372.

18. Herries, *Memoirs*, 102; *Scots Peerage*, ii, 110–12, 388–9; vii, 252–4; vii, 20–2; Donaldson, *All the Queen's Men*, 97–8.

19. ibid., 99–100; Dowden, *Bishops*, 207–8, 349–52.

20. ibid., 91–3; 229–31; Herries, *Memoirs*, 139.

21. Dowden, *Bishops*, 43–4, 141–3; Herries, *Memoirs*, 133.

22. ibid., 139; Dowden, *Bishops*, 171–2.

23. ibid., 391; *Scots Peerage*, iv, 539–41; G. Donaldson, *Reformed by Bishop* (Edinburgh, 1987), 1–18; Dowden, *Bishops*, 891; R. Keith, *History of the Affairs of Church and State in Scotland* (3 vols, Spottiswoode Society, 1850), ii, 809.

24. 'John Carswell, Superintendent of Argyll', in J. Kirk, *Patterns of Reform* (Edinburgh, 1989), 280–304; R. Keith, *An Historical Catalogue of the Scottish Bishops*, ed. M. Russel (Edinburgh, 1824), 166.

25. Donaldson, *Reformed by Bishop*, 53–67.

26. Donaldson, *All the Queen's Men*, 114–15.

27. Dowden, *Scottish Bishops*, 43–5, 171–2.

28. Cowan and Easson, *Medieval Religious Houses: Scotland*, 61, 64–5, 69, 74–5.

29. *Diurnal of Occurrents*, 136; *The Register of the Privy Council of Scotland* [RPC], edd. J. H. Burton and others (Edinburgh, 1877–), first series, iv, 773–4.

30. *Scots Peerage*, i, 340–2.

31. ibid., vii, 292–3; *CSP Scot.*, iv, 543.

32. *Scots Peerage*, v, 439–42; viii, 540–5.

33. W. Fraser, *The Book of Carlaverock* (2 vols., Edinburgh, 1873), i, 497–569; *Scots Peerage*, i, 119–20; iii, 229–30; iv, 409–13, 460–3; v, 155–63; viii, 438–42.

34. Donaldson, *All the Queen's Men*, 113–14.

35. A. M. Scott, *The Battle of Langside MDLXVIII* (Glasgow, 1885), 13; Calderwood, *History*, ii, 414; R. Keith, *The History of the Affairs of Church and State in Scotland* (3 vols, Spottiswoode Society, 1835), ii, 806.

36. *Diurnal of Occurrents*, 247–9.

37. Lynch, *Edinburgh and the Reformation*, 125–48.

38. ibid., 294–362.

39. ibid., 204–6.

40. Herries, *Memoirs*, 93, 102.

41. ibid., 102; *Scots Peerage*, v, 5–6; vii, 386–7; *RPC*, first series, i, 537–8.

42. Donaldson, *All the Queen's Men*, 106, 109–10; Herries, *Memoirs*, 102.
43. Herries, *Memoirs*, 138; *The Exchequer Rolls of Scotland*, ed. J. Stuart and others (Edinburgh, 1878–1908), xix, 374; *Registrum Secreti Sigilli Regum Scotorum*, ed. M. Livingstone, and others (Edinburgh, 1908–), v, nos. 279, 3098; *RPC*, first series, 1, 637–8.
44. Calderwood, *History*, ii, 357–8, 384; G. Donaldson, *Reformed by Bishop*, 19–51.
45. ibid., 53–67.
46. Donaldson, *All the Queen's Men*, 86–7; *CSP Scot*, ii, no. 619; Calderwood, *History*, ii, 387; Keith, *History*, ii, 756–7.
47. T. Thomson and C. Innes (edd.), *The Acts of the Parliaments of Scotland* (13 vols., Edinburgh, 1814–75), iii, 3–4.
48. Calderwood, *History*, ii, 403–4; Melville, *Memoirs*, 199; Herries, *Memoirs*, 101.
49. ibid., 102; Calderwood, *History*, ii, 414; Melville, *Memoirs*, 200.
50. Herries, *Memoirs*, 102; *Diurnal of Occurrents*, 129–30.
51. Donaldson, *All the Queen's Men*, 101–4.
52. ibid., 104–5.
53. ibid., 105–6; *Diurnal of Occurrents*, 130.
54. Herries, *Memoirs*, 101 (cf. 102), 130, 135, 139; Donaldson, *All the Queen's Men*, 106; *Scots Peerage*, v, 399–400.
55. Calderwood, *History*, ii, 414–15; Herries, *Memoirs*, 102.
56. Melville, *Memoirs*, 200; Calderwood, *History*, ii, 414; Herries, *Memoirs*, 102, 120.
57. Melville, *Memoirs*, 199; *Diurnal of Occurrents*, 128–9.
58. Calderwood, *History*, ii, 404–12.
59. ibid., ii, 405, 414.
60. ibid., ii, 414–15; Herries, *Memoirs*, 102.
61. Calderwood, *History*, ii, 414–15; Herries, *Memoirs*, 102; Melville, *Memoirs*, 200.
62. Scott, *Battle of Langside*, 13; Keith, *History*, ii, 806; Calderwood, *History*, ii, 415.
63. ibid., ii, 414.
64. ibid., ii, 414–16.
65. Scott, *Battle of Langside*, 18–22; Contemporary accounts of the battle are found in the appendix, 87–98.
66. ibid., 23–4; Herries, *Memoirs*, 102.
67. Scott, *Battle of Langside*, 35–46; Melville, *Memoirs*, 200.
68. Herries, *Memoirs*, 103; Calderwood, *History*, ii, 416.
69. ibid., ii, 417; Herries, *Memoirs*, 105–6.
70. ibid., 102; *Diurnal of Occurrents*, 130; Donaldson, *All the Queen's Men*, 98, 108–9; *Scots Peerage*, iii, 229–30; vi, 482–84; *CSP Scot.*, ii, no. 650.
71. Herries, *Memoirs*, 139–44; *Scots Peerage*, v, 62–72; Melville, *Memoirs*, 201, 226, 254; Calderwood, *History*, ii, 505; Donaldson, *All the Queen's Men*, 108.
72. ibid., 108; Herries, *Memoirs*, 139–41.

73. *APS*, iii, 45–9; *Diurnal of Occurrents*, 135.

74. ibid., 136, 153; *APS*, iii, 47, 49, 55; *CSP Scot.*, iii, no. 53; *Transactions of the Dumfriesshire and Galloway Natural History and Antiquarian Society* (1862–), Series 3, xxvii, 147.

75. Herries, *Memoirs*, 105; Calderwood, *History*, ii, 487–8; *Diurnal of Occurrents*, 143–4.

76. *Scots Peerage*, iv, 24–5, 537–41.

77. *Diurnal of Occurrents*, 143–5; *CSP Scot.*, ii, no. 775; cf. Herries, *Memoirs*, 105, in which Argyll's forces are estimated at 600.

78. Herries, *Memoirs*, 105; *CSP Scot.*, ii, nos. 836, 937.

79. Calderwood, *History*, ii, 428–76; Melville, *Memoirs*, 208–12; G. Donaldson, *The First Trial of Mary queen of Scots* (London, 1969), p. 135.

80. Calderwood, *History*, ii, 471–2.

81. ibid., ii, 486–8.

82. ibid., ii, 510–11; *Diurnal of Occurrents*, 156.

83. Herries, *Memoirs*, 127; Richard Bannatyne, *Memorials of Transactions in Scotland, AD MDLXIX–MDLXXIII* (Bannatyne Club, 1836), 47–8.

84. *Diurnal of Occurrents*, 160; Calderwood, *History*, ii, 528–9; *CSP Scot.*, iii, no. 130.

85. Herries, *Memoirs*, 121–4, 135; Calderwood, *History*, ii, 544, 546.

86. Melville, *Memoirs*, 216, 220; *Diurnal of Occurrents*, 202.

87. Calderwood, *History*, ii, 547–50.

88. ibid., ii, 567–8; *Diurnal of Occurrents*, 180.

89. ibid., 182–4; Calderwood, *History*, iii, 7–9; Melville, *Memoirs*, 229–30.

90. Calderwood, *History*, iii, 10–12, 32, 54–8; *Diurnal of Occurrents*, 202–3.

91. Calderwood, *History*, ii, 58–9; *Diurnal of Occurrents,* 203.

92. ibid., 211; Calderwood, *History*, iii, 72–3; Herries, *Memoirs*, 135; Bannatyne, *Memorials*, 255.

93. ibid., 119.

94. *Diurnal of Occurrents*, 254; *CSP Scot.*, iii, nos. 427, 608, 666.

95. Calderwood, *History*, iii, 78, 91; *Diurnal of Occurrents*, 216.

96. ibid., iii, 78, 91–6; *Diurnal of Occurrents*, 214, 220–1.

97. ibid., 214; Calderwood, *History*, iii, 78; Herries, *Memoirs*, 136.

98. *Diurnal of Occurrents*, 246.

99. ibid., 245–6; Calderwood, *History*, 137.

100. ibid., iii, 139–41; Melville, *Memoirs*, 240–2; *Diurnal of Occurrents*, 247–9.

101. ibid., 249; Melville, *Memoirs*, 243; Calderwood, *History*, iii, 141, 230.

102. *Diurnal of Occurrents*, 251, 255, 264; Bannatyne, *Memorials*, 194, 212–3; A. and H. Taylor (edd.), *The House of Forbes* (Third Spalding Club, 1937), 88–92; *The Historie and Life of James the Scot MDLXVI–MDXCVI* (Bannatyne Club, 1825), 96–7; Calderwood, *History*, iii, 153–4.

103. ibid., iii, 166; *Diurnal of Occurrents*, 253.

104. ibid., 257; *CSP Scot.*, iv, 77; Calderwood, iii, 255.

105. ibid., iii, 230, 242–3; *APS*, iii, 77–81.

106. ibid., 77.
107. Donaldson, *All the Queen's Men*, 116, 125.
108. Calderwood, *History*, iii, 261–71.
109. ibid., iii, 281–7.
110. Melville, *Memoirs*, 253–5.
111. Donaldson, *All the Queen's Men*, 114–15.
112. ibid., 115–16.
113. Herries, *Memoirs*, 103–4; Antonia Fraser, *Mary Queen of Scots* (London, 1969), 419.
114. ibid., 424–5; Donaldson, *First Trial of Mary Queen of Scots*, 220–1.

6

AN ARMY SENT FROM GOD:
SCOTS AT WAR IN IRELAND, 1642-9

Raymond Gillespie

On 24 October 1641 Lord Edward Chichester, one of the largest landowners in Ulster, wrote to the king, Charles I, who was then in Edinburgh, telling him that the principal native Irish lords of Ulster had risen in rebellion two days earlier.[1] The king received the letter on 28 October. He immediately informed the Scottish parliament and asked them for aid in suppressing the rising if it could not be contained by a local settler force. Such aid was slow to be provided. It was not until 15 April 1642 that Robert Munro, together with a force of 2,896 Scottish soldiers, landed at Carrickfergus in county Antrim. Later, on 4 August, the commander of the force, Alexander Leslie, recently created earl of Leven, landed. He was accompanied by most of the rest of the force, bringing it to over 10,000 men, the strength of the force stipulated in an agreement between the parliaments of England and Scotland. While the main outlines of the treaty had been agreed in January 1642 the treaty was not finally concluded before the army landed. The remainder of the army and the artillery train arrived in late August or early September. Both Leven and Munro were practical military men. Munro had considerable military experience with the Swedish army in Germany, and Leven was also well versed in continental warfare. Leven had also been one of the key figures in the Covenanter's army during the Bishops' Wars.

The organisation, recruitment and finance of the force sent to Ulster, and also their religion, have been analysed by a generation of scholars and most recently and comprehensively by David Stevenson.[2] The approach of these works has been to examine the events of the 1640s in Ulster from the perspective of Scotland and the Scottish force and in the context of a particular set of assumptions about Ulster-Scottish relationships before the 1640s. This has given rise to the assumption that because Ulster had been extensively settled by Scots, as part of early seventeenth century informal colonisation and official plantation, that there was a 'community of interest' between the early settlers and the newly arrived Scots army. As David Stevenson has put it, 'Scotland was ready to intervene, if necessary, to protect "her" Ulster plantation'. Again Edward Furgol has explained the rapid expansion of presbyterianism in the Ulster of the 1640s as arising from the presence of Scots presbyterians in Ulster before the outbreak of the war.[3] To counterbalance this Scottish perspective this essay is an attempt to look at the Scottish army in Ulster in the 1640s through the eyes of the settler population of Ulster.

One view of Scottish involvement in Ulster during the 1640s is that it was the natural reaction of the Scottish parliament to the peril of Scots abroad. This was the explanation offered by many of those from outside settler society in Ulster. The anonymous, but native Irish, author of the *Aphromisical Discovery*, written in the 1650s, noted that settlers fled to Scotland at the outbreak of the rising

> desiring their countrymen and alliance to assist them against the Irish who thrived so far in Scotland that they came to Ireland in great multitudes and Munro sent by General Lesley as chief commander of the expedition.

According to the writer they seized Carrickfergus and 'would admit no English'. Again the two Catholic clergy who were the authors of the *Commentarius Rinuccinianus* in the 1650s referred to the Scottish forces as relieving their Ulster brothers.[4] This type of explanation tends to ignore the developments within both Ulster and Scottish society from the establishment of the Ulster plantation in 1608 to the outbreak of war in 1641.

I

One way of revealing the changes in the perception of Scotland's role in Ulster is to compare the Scottish military intervention of 1608 with that of 1642. In April 1608 a native Irish Donegal landowner, Sir Cahir O'Doherty, rebelled after being insulted by the governor of Londonderry, Sir George Paulet. Within six days of the rising the Irish lord deputy had written to the Scottish privy council asking for measures to be taken on the west coast of Scotland to ensure that the trouble was contained in Ulster. However, as the O'Doherty rising spread, the London administration ordered that 200 Scots were to be levied for service in Ireland. On 20 June the force mustered in Ayr and set sail. In the event it arrived too late to be of any use in suppressing the rising, which collapsed at the end of June. In mid-September the force was disbanded but it had been demonstrated, as the order for disbandment put it, that a scourge of the Irish was available 'from Scotland as well as from England'.[5] A generation later, in 1642, there was to be no such enthusiasm for intervention in Ireland and the intervention of Scottish forces was not an ad hoc affair arranged in a few weeks but was governed by a treaty negotiated between two sovereign parliaments.

The necessity for a treaty governing the actions of the Scottish forces in Ulster was dictated by a development of the 1630s: Charles I's attempted constitutional revolution in the three kingdoms. During the 1630s the lord deputy, Thomas Wentworth, earl of Strafford, had attempted to transform Ireland from being an entity with the structures of a sovereign kingdom, but governed by a colonial administration often more interested in personal profit than royal rights, into a distinct kingdom with all the structures of a kingdom operating at peak efficiency to the advantage of the crown. In the process he had alienated most of the ruling elite of Ireland, who played no small part in his eventual impeachment and execution.[6] Wentworth's attempt to restore royal authority in Ireland had one important side effect — it had raised an extremely important constitutional issue which had not hitherto been discussed at any length. The question concerned the relationship of the crown of Ireland, as created by the act for the kingly title of 1541, to that of England, and the relationship of the other Irish institutions of government, such as parliament, to their English counterparts. The central question was whether the English parliament had the right to legislate for Ireland.

The answers to at least some of these questions were provided by events in Scotland during the late 1630s. The Covenant and the treaty concluding the Bishops' Wars established firmly the fact Scotland was an independent sovereign kingdom and that Ireland was a dependency of the English crown. Thus any intervention by Scots in an English problem required a legal instrument. It was this constitutional consideration which was paramount in the 1642 treaty negotiations.[7] Thus the treaty sought to regulate not the details of army life but the relations between the Scots and English parliaments over intervention in Ulster.

The Scots agreed to provide and arm 10,000 men who were to be paid at English rates by the English parliament. They were to be given the two Ulster towns of Coleraine and Carrickfergus as bases. England was to supply 600 horse for the force. There were agreements as to the notice to be given for withdrawal or disbanding. Significantly it was provided that the Scottish force was to remain distinct and not to be quartered with other soldiers.[8] The most significant omission, which was to cause considerable difficulty later, was the failure to relate this force to the existing settler force, or British as they termed themselves, in Ireland. The instructions given by the Scottish parliament to the earls of Lothian and Lindsay, who were negotiating the treaty, were that the commander was to take orders from the king or the king's representative

in that free and honourable way which the general or commander of one army sent from a free kingdom for assisting of another ought to do.[9]

The Scottish commander might receive instructions from the king's representative in Ireland, the lord deputy, and relay them to his men. The question remained over the position of the commander of the Irish army, the earl of Ormond, and his relationship with the Scots army. In particular it was unclear who was to be the overall commander of the four separate forces acting in Ulster. This problem was complicated by the fact that the commander of one force, Lord Conway, was also Marshal of the Irish army and had fought on the king's side during the Bishops' Wars.[10] When Robert Munro arrived, his position was at best confused. His commission was from the king, he was paid by the Westminster parliament and the matter dealt with through the Scottish privy council. He had to use his own judgement as to whose orders he would accept. In August 1643, for example, he refused to leave Ulster to assist with the war in Leinster, although he was ordered to do so by the Irish privy council.[11]

There was one other political factor which Munro had to deal with. When he landed the treaty had not yet been agreed between the various parties. When the news of the outbreak of rebellion reached Charles I at Edinburgh on 28 October 1641 the king, in a speech, hoped the Scots would offer him support in suppressing the rising. The Scots failed to do this, offering their help only if the English parliament requested it, since Ireland was an English dependency, and only if they could spare the resources themselves.[12] On 3 November the English parliament accepted the offer under the clause in the treaty which had ended the Bishops' wars, that each kingdom would help the other against rebels. The decision was not a unanimous one by any means, and it was 13 November 1641 before the Commons and Lords agreed. Negotiations between commissioners of the two kingdoms did not begin until 3

December. By early January 1642 the main outlines of the treaty had been decided on. However, the Scots held out for greater concessions, including the port of Londonderry, which they did not get. From the Scottish perspective a certain urgency was injected into the proceedings in early January 1642 when it was rumoured that the earl of Antrim, a Macdonnell and sworn enemy of one of the treaty negotiators, the earl of Argyll, was active with the Highlander Coll Ciottagh. From then on there were complaints of the slowness of the proceedings. In the event the treaty was not approved by the Lords and Commons until 7 July 1642, but even then the king wanted changes. It was not until mid-1643 that the treaty was formally sent to the Scottish privy council and it was not ratified by the Scottish parliament until July 1644. The king never agreed to the treaty.

There is one other significant difference between the events of 1608 and those of 1642. One of the factors which weighed heavily in the decision to send the Scots troops to Ulster as part of the force to crush O'Doherty's rising was a letter sent on 9 May 1608 from Sir Thomas Phillips at Coleraine to the Edinburgh government, urging the despatch of 500 troops from Scotland for the defence of Ulster, and ending rather melodramatically 'haste, haste, haste'.[13] In 1641–2 the position was rather different. The British forces in Ulster certainly petitioned both London and Edinburgh for aid, but it was aid in the form of arms and supplies rather than a relief force. Indeed by the time Munro's force arrived, the war in Ulster appeared to be over and the insurgents on the edge of defeat. Only the arrival of Owen Roe O'Neill in July 1642 prevented the surrender of the native Irish forces. When Munro's army did arrive the various elements in Ulster did not call on it for military assistance. On 27 April, within twelve days of Munro's arrival, the mayor of Londonderry despatched a letter to him asking for supplies, but not military assistance.[14] The mayor had himself tried to obtain supplies but had failed. He presumably felt that Munro, who was in the pay of the English parliament, had a better chance of obtaining them. No supplies were forthcoming. By mid-1642 Sir Robert Stewart, commander of the settler forces in north-west Ulster, noted Munro's forces had not come that far, but added that this was quite understandable for a man who was so busy. Only when Munro's successes in east Ulster began to drive the Irish army westward did Stewart begin to complain of the pressure which was being put on his forces by Munro's activities. He asked for more arms and supplies but not assistance from Munro.[15] From the south-west of the province, which was under the command of Sir Frederick Hamilton, there was no comment at all on the activities of the Scots, since they did not impinge on Hamilton directly. It was in east Ulster, where the Scots forces were quartered, that the relationship between the Scots forces and the settlers was most tested.

Initially Munro and his forces received a guarded welcome from the British settlers in east Ulster. His arrival promised at least the prospect of supplies and arms, but when these failed to arrive, tensions began to develop and Munro's relationship with the British officers within east Ulster became strained. Most important were the difficulties of command. During the campaign of April 1642 Munro and the commander of the British forces, Viscount Conway, gave orders on alternate days.[16] Tensions also began to develop on strategy. It was the aim of the British forces to use the reinforcements which Munro's army had given them to defeat the Irish insurgents. Munro, however, was much more cautious. Only part of the Scottish force had arrived and its commander, Leslie, was still in Scotland. Munro saw his job as setting up a bridgehead which would be used by the remainder of the force when it arrived to move out into the rest of Ulster. Not surprisingly the two commanders could not agree on a role for the army in its early weeks. When the Irish rebels fled into Tyrone after an encounter with the new force in April Conway wished to pursue them and finish them off, while Munro wanted to return to Carrickfergus. The force split, but Conway, pursuing the Irish, ran out of supplies and had to return to Carrickfergus. Scottish priorities rather than settler wants also influenced Munro's decisions. The urgency with which the earl of Antrim was pursued and captured, despite the fact that he was not in rebellion, seems to have been dictated by the earl of Argyll in Scotland, who was a sworn enemy of the Macdonnell family to which Antrim belonged.[17]

Allegations of incompetence and failure to provide support for the settler forces were made against Munro. What prevented an open rift between the two groups was the possibility that Munro would have access to supplies and the belief that his appointment by the English parliament may have made him supreme commander of the forces in Ulster. By mid-1642 it was clarified that this was not the case, and that Munro's command extended only to the Scottish forces.[18] From then on the Scots army received little support from the British forces in Ulster, and there was no more than token co-operation with General Leslie when he landed in July 1642. The British forces tended to wage their own campaign, and only joined the Scots under duress or when it suited their purposes to do so. Even at the most important battle of the whole campaign, Benburb, there was little more than a token presence of British forces. The accounts of these years from the British side have few references to the Scots forces. In one account, by an officer in Sir John Clotworthy's regiment, they are described as 'the scum of that country', but he allowed that some of their officers were gentlemen.[19] There were also complaints about the activities of the Scots, with allegations by the Dublin Council that they were plundering east Ulster for their own ends and shipping large quantities of cattle back to Scotland for their own profit rather than applying their energies to fighting the enemy. It is not clear what the truth of these reports was. Certainly there are reports of the army plundering, for example at Lady O'Neill's estate at Antrim, where timber was cut down and the fishings plundered. Similarly Elizabeth Price deposed to the Dublin adminis- tration in 1643 that after being captured by the rebels she was released, and meeting Munro's force she was 'forcibly robbed and despoiled . . . of all the money and meal they had left and [the soldiers] bade them to go to the rebels and get more'. She also related how the Scots garrison at Newry had refused to give shelter to settlers who were later murdered.[20]

These difficulties were not likely to change the outcome of the war. However, the problems of the campaigning season of 1642 were to be exacerbated over the years 1643–5 and led to breaches between the Scots and the settlers over much more fundamental issues.

Two events in 1643 revealed the attitude of the Scots forces to their task and to the British forces. On 15 September a one year truce, the Cessation, was signed between the lord lieutenant, acting on the king's instructions, and the Confederate Catholics. Ten days later the Solemn League and Covenant was agreed between the English and Scottish parliaments, bringing the Scots into the 'war of the three kingdoms'. Neither event was unexpected, and there had been debate within the army during the summer about the reaction to them. To the Scots in Ulster it appeared that they should return to Scotland to fight on the parliamentary side in the war there. Charles wished the Scots to remain in Ireland to neutralise them for the campaign and directed Ormond to persuade Munro to stay there, both Ormond and the earl of Antrim being authorised to bribe him if necessary.[21] The English parliament, although initially wanting reinforcements for the campaign, were more fearful that Charles would use the opportunity of peace in Ireland to draw reinforcements for his English army from the Confederate forces, as indeed he did in the form of an Irish force under Antrim, which became part of Montrose's force in Scotland in 1644. Munro was therefore ordered to stay in Ireland and not to accept the Cessation.[22]

To order was one thing, to secure obedience another. A large proportion of the Scots force was reluctant to stay in Ulster, and problems of supply and arrears of pay did not encourage compliance with the orders from parliament. In June 1643 a delegation of officers went to Edinburgh to ask for supply but with little success. By early November the officers within the army were arguing that they should return to Scotland. On 3 February 1644 the Scottish officers met at Carrickfergus and decided that the army should leave Ireland immediately. A large, though unspecified, number did in effect desert the force in Ulster and served under Leslie in the English campaign. Three regiments also left officially. In order to stem this flow the Westminster parliament provided substantial supplies for the Scottish force.[23]

By contrast the British forces had accepted the Cessation, and hence had damned themselves in the eyes of the English parliament. London took the opportunity of an open rift between the two forces to resolve some of the outstanding problems of the Scottish army. The Adventurers, who had funded the Irish campaign in return for a promise of Irish land when peace came, were keen for a return on their investment and demanded that a commander-in-chief be appointed in Ulster, and a vigorous campaign waged against the Irish.[24] In March 1644 Lord Conway was removed as commander of the British forces in east Ulster, and Munro appointed commander-in-chief.[25] Munro, determined to exercise his new power, did two things which caused him great unpopularity, especially among the officers of the British army. First, on the morning of 14 May 1644 he seized Lord Chichester's town of Belfast, which had not been given to the Scots in the treaty. He later marched on Lisburn but retreated when it appeared that the garrison would resist. In July 1644 he attempted to enter Dundalk and Newry, which were held by Ormond.[26]

Munro's second move was the proffering of the Covenant throughout Ulster, beginning on 4 April 1644 with his own men at Carrickfergus. The Covenant spread like wildfire among the inhabitants of Ulster. However, this was not a gesture of support for Munro's actions. As has been pointed out, the arrival of the supplies for the Scottish forces, and therefore their allies, was an important incentive in the short term at least, especially as the British forces could expect no supply from

England after accepting the Cessation.[27] There was also a strong tradition within Ulster of forming mutual bonds for defence in time of crisis. In 1641, for example, the officers of Londonderry entered into a 'league' for the defence of the city. Again in 1642 Major Turner recorded that the Scots army in Ulster, being discontented about their pay, 'reflecting on the successful issue of the National Covenant of Scotland bethought themselves of making one also but they were wise enough to give it another name and therefore christened it a mutual assurance'. In 1645 the officers of the British army at a meeting in Antrim also drew up a bond, the bond of union, with an oath to hold the army together and to continue the war against the Irish.[28] The Covenant in Ulster was by no means a religious document, since even those who were sympathetic to presbyterianism refused to take it initially. On 13 May Sir James Montgomery, brother of Viscount Ards, and inclined towards presbyterianism, summoned a meeting of the British officers at Belfast to decide what their attitude to Munro and the Covenant was, but the result was inconclusive as Munro seized the town the next day.[29] Many officers did take the Covenant, but did so under pressure from their men, for to have failed to do so would have resulted in loss of control.[30] Munro's power was now at its height but was poorly based. He had alienated a substantial body of British support and he had very reluctant support thereafter. This explained, in part, why so few of the British force were with him at Benburb in 1646, only about 2,000 out of about 5,000. In the campaign against the earl Castlehaven, commander of the Confederate forces, in 1644, the British officer, Sir Theophilus Jones, and his men had to be forced to accompany Munro under threat that they would be disarmed and their supplies cut off.[31]

Munro's power in Ulster was based on the alliance of the Scots and parliament, but as this began to cool in 1645 and 1646 Munro's power base began to collapse. In December 1645 English parliamentary commissioners ordered Munro to surrender Belfast, and in the same month the united command in Ulster was abolished, so that Munro no longer had power over the British forces.[32] Munro's power was on the wane. His own force was considerably reduced by men returning to Scotland, so that by mid-1646 the force of 10,000 men from 1642 had been reduced to about 3,000. Between a third and a half of these were killed at Benburb, and most of the rest became part of the army of the Engagement. So great were the losses that the Scots, contrary to the terms of the treaty, were trying to recruit local men to their regiments.[33] Relations between Munro and the parliament worsened, especially after the battle of Benburb, which had demonstrated how ineffective the Scots forces had become through lack of supplies and men. Munro tried to repair his position by becoming involved on the fringes of a number of British royalist plots which petered out.[34] The New Scots force was disbanded in 1647 by order of the House of Commons. Munro himself remained in Ulster and was captured when Carrickfergus castle fell to Monck, the parliamentary commander, on 16 September 1648. It was significant that the fall of the castle was due to the 'great animosities between the officers of the British army and those of the Scottish army', which led to its betrayal by a number of British officers.[35]

II

It is clear from this summary of the events of the 1640s that there was little that could be described as a 'community of interest' between the Scots settlers of the early seventeenth century and the new military arrivals of the 1640s. The army under Munro remained a distinct entity and not the relievers of their distressed brothers in Ulster. They called themselves 'New Scots' to mark themselves off from the 'Old Scots' or 'British' settlers, and according to Sir John Clotworthy, an English presbyterian settler at Antrim and member of the Long parliament, some of them termed themselves 'a party'.[36] They also regarded themselves as a mercenary force, and concerns about supply and pay bound them into a body with grievances distinct from those of the settlers. So strong were those grievances even by late 1642, according to Turner, that they entered into a bond of 'mutual assistance to make themselves independent of anyone except their paymasters'.[37] Again in 1643, when there were rumours that regiments would be shipped back to Scotland, a similar bond was taken that they would not disband until paid what they were owed.

The reality that the Scots army was a mercenary force, taking orders from whoever paid them, was an important influence on the relationship between the settlers and Munro's men. The forces shaping Munro's actions were those of England or Scotland, depending on the regularity of supply, whereas the influences acting on the settlers were those of Ireland. In Ireland in 1642 the principal concern was not the balance of rights between the English king and parliament, but rather the problem of survival in the face of a native Irish rebellion. It is this which accounts for the highly regionalised pattern of Irish warfare during the 1640s. Activity by Ulster landlords as military commanders was based almost exclusively in Ulster. In Munster the same pattern emerged,

Munster landlords confined their activities as military commanders to their own province. In August 1642, for example, Lord Conway refused to march the settler troops out of Ulster to help with the war elsewhere, even though Ulster appeared fairly secure after Munro's campaign of the spring and summer. Again in 1644 and 1645 parliament ordered that an Ulster settler force of 2,000 was to be sent to Munster to help Lord Inchiquin, and to assist with the war in Connacht, but again they refused.[38] Direct appeals from Munster settlers to their Ulster counterparts were also refused. Even within Ulster the war was highly regionalised and was pursued in a series of uncoordinated campaigns. In west Ulster it was fought by the Laggan forces, by a distinct force in south-west Ulster, and by yet another force in east Ulster.[39] Each was under the command of local men who often jealously guarded their own rights of command.

A second reason making for discord between the Scots army and the settlers was that the army was perceived to be a threat to the settlers' power base. This was evident on a number of levels. In the most immediate sense the issue of command of the British forces was an extremely sensitive one. Settler commanders feared that Munro wished to subsume all military power into his hands and become the supreme military commander in Ulster. As early as January 1642, when the outlines of the treaty for sending over the force had been agreed, Sir John Clotworthy had used his position as a Westminster MP to have a resolution passed to ensure that he continued his command of the boats on Lough Neagh, which his father had held. Thus he not only controlled the most important communication route between east and west Ulster but also retained his military command.[40] Such posts in seventeenth-century Ulster were at a premium, not because men were particularly warlike, but because military commands were intimately connected with social status. Many of those who had come to Ulster in the early seventeenth century had come from what were very unpromising social backgrounds. They achieved wealth rapidly but were often denied the social recognition which landholding would have carried in England and Scotland. They attempted to underpin their new-found positions with offices of many descriptions in an effort to gain social acceptance. The result was that military commissions were seen by the Ulster settlers as more than mere commands.[41] One instance of the sensitivity which underlay appointment to commands was demonstrated in September 1642, when an attempt was made to have Sir William Stewart appointed supreme commander of the Laggan forces in west

Ulster. However, appointment of a supreme commander disrupted the local power structure whereby a number of local gentry had rotated the command between them. After protest the old system had to be restored by a commission of 15 December 1642.[42] The right to appoint officers was a contentious issue which in the 1630s Lord Deputy Wentworth had kept to himself and used as the power to reward or punish. The right of appointment, and hence of patronage, was a source of contention in 1640 between the earl of Ormond, as commander of the Irish army, and the lord lieutenant, as the king's representative.[43]

While the appointment of Munro as supreme commander was a blow to pride it also had more tangible effects. In the 1640s there were at least two kinds of commissions held by officers of the British forces in Ulster. Both Sir John Clotworthy and Lord Conway had held commissions before 1641, and these were recognised by both king and parliament. On the outbreak of war many local landlords had organised their tenants into forces to defend themselves. This position had been regularised by the king, who had granted royal commissions to Lords Clandeboy and Ards and to Sir Robert Stewart to raise regiments, effectively composed of their tenants. Initially these commissions were not recognised by parliament, and they were not supplied or paid from the Exchequer until 1 July 1642.[44] Thus these commissions interwove the position of landlord and commander. Any reduction of the military status would also be a reduction in the power of the landlord to protect his tenants and consequently a reduction in his status.

As commissions underpinned the social authority of the commanders of the British forces and set them off from the Scots, so also did the regulations on quartering set out in the treaty. The Scots were to occupy two towns only: Carrickfergus, to have a supply route to Scotland, and Coleraine, which was to give them a base to operate against the main possible threat to Scottish security, the earl of Antrim, based at Dunluce. The Scots had also asked for Londonderry, but it had not been given to them for fear of upsetting the parliamentarian London Companies, as it was part of their plantation scheme. Since towns were owned by landlords, quartering troops in them reduced the landlords' authority. This is evident in Munro's seizure of Belfast in May 1644. Belfast was a town created and controlled by the Chichester family in a way that Carrickfergus, their other town, was not. Carrickfergus was a medieval town and was also a county. It was ruled by a corporation which held all the town lands. Belfast, by contrast, was the recent creation of the Chichester family and they controlled its politics and economy. In early

June 1644, about a month after the seizure of the town, the burgesses and commoners of Belfast petitioned the sovereign, Thomas Theaker (who was also Chichester's estate agent) to allow free choice of the burgesses and commoners of the town who had previously been elected by the freemen and approved by Chichester. The burgesses were to be resident, which they had not been before, and were to be compelled to take the Covenant. Any other election was to be deemed unlawful. Theaker's reaction was to flee the town and go to Chichester, who was camped near Dublin. It was the undermining of his authority within the town of Belfast which caused Chichester more concern than the taking of the town itself.[45]

Yet another concern which created tension between the Ulster settlers and the Scots forces was the possibility of land confiscation from the settlers at the end of the war to pay the Scots forces. In the early stages of the negotiation of the treaty which regulated the Scottish intervention in Ulster, the matter of a share in the fruits of victory was raised by the Scottish privy council, which requested equal shares in any future settlement. The possibility of some sort of post-war settlement was made a reality on 11 February 1642, when a number of London citizens proposed the 'Adventurers Act' by which individuals would subscribe money towards the reconquest of Ireland and receive recompense in Irish land after the war. It received royal assent on 19 March. The Scots commissioners negotiating the treaty asked that its army should be part of the Adventurers' arrangements, but this was refused on the grounds that English soldiers going to Ireland would not be covered by the act.

The issue was again raised in 1643 when a delegation from the Scots forces in Ulster went to Scotland to demand supplies and arrears of pay. Some at least were prepared to accept payment in Ulster land if money could not be found, to which the English commissioners agreed. Others objected that Ulster land was of little use to them if they were to return to Scotland. At least some were interested enough in Ulster land to revitalise the claim in 1661 as part of the Restoration land settlement, but it was disallowed.[46] How many were interested in acquiring Ulster land as a reward for their services and settling there is unknown. Some certainly did settle there. These included Munro himself, who married the widow of Viscount Ards, although against her sons' wishes. Probably fairly few actually settled in Ulster. This does not mean that the concern of the earlier settlers should be underestimated. In many cases the settlers' titles were at best dubious, and given the financial difficulties in which many of the existing settlers found themselves, confiscation would have been easy and long defensive law suits impossible.

If there was any legacy of the Scots army in Ulster it was the establishment of presbyterianism there. Undoubtedly many of those who came from Scotland in the early seventeenth century to settle in Ulster had what can best be described as 'presbyterian leanings'. Many of their views tended to be modified by the migration process and the strongly Calvinist Church of Ireland did little to disrupt local accommodations. Such presbyterianism as did take root was regarded with suspicion by the General Assembly in Edinburgh, whose leaders in the late 1630s were worried about 'Irish innovations' being introduced into the Scottish church. Indeed when Munro established his new presbytery at Carrickfergus in 1642, the Assembly expressed concern that 'all the men who went over to that land should be in danger . . . to favour any differences from our church'.[47] There were a few in early seventeenth-century Ulster who objected to the making of arrangements with an episcopal church, the most prominent being Robert Blair at Bangor, but these were in a minority within the Ulster church as a whole. They failed to establish any of the main structures of presbyterian church government with the exception of a few sessions. It was the army which established the first presbytery of Ulster at Carrickfergus on 10 June 1642. In the summer of 1644, to ensure that the Covenant was being observed, the jurisdiction of the army presbytery was extended to the civilians in Antrim and Down.

This was a radical departure from the early seventeenth-century position. A separate structure was set up to rival that of the Anglican establishment. According to Patrick Adair, the reformation of Ireland was begun in the 1640s and 'the first means God used for this end was the sending over of the Scotch army'.[48] The immediate impact of this on the early seventeenth century settlers was dramatic. Settlers' rights, for example, to present to benefices were undermined. The Montgomery Manuscripts recorded the effect of the changes on the north Down estate of the presbyterian inclined Viscount Ards:

But alas this beautiful order appointed and settled by his lordship lasted no longer than until the Scottish army came over and put their chaplains in our churches, who having power regarded not law, equity or right to back or countenance them, they turned out legal loyal clergy who would not desert episcopacy and the service book and take the Covenant, a very bitter pill indeed to honest men.[49]

Initially the changes were relatively modest. Of the ten army chaplains, only five attended the first presbytery meeting. The careers of some of the others were not imposing. James Houston, for example, had been minister at Glasford in the presbytery of Hamilton, but had fallen into 'flagrant sin' and was deposed. He went to Ireland with the army and was permitted to preach by the presbytery of Paisley. In 1643 the Synod of Glasgow suggested that he might be readmitted, but the General Assembly reproved their actions and removed Houston from ministerial office.[50]

Relatively little is known of the character of the army as a whole, but the fact that many had fought in the Bishops' Wars might suggest that they had some awareness of the issues of religion; and Munro was described by Adair as 'very instrumental for promoting presbyterial government'.[51] There is little doubt that at least one function of the army was to introduce the 'presbyterian revolution' to the Ulster of the 1640s. Its success with such limited resources, which were not enlarged in any significant way despite repeated petitions to the General Assembly throughout the 1640s, has usually been ascribed to the presence of Scots settlers in Ulster long before the wars. Yet the Scots who were already settled there were of a rather different outlook from those who arrived with the army in the 1640s.

An understanding of the reasons for the success of the presbyterian church structures introduced by the army would require a study of the session records for the early congregations. Unfortunately few of these have survived. One survival is the session book of Templepatrick, where Sir Mungo Campbell of Lawers' regiment was based. The session book for the 1640s suggests two significant features of this early congregation. First, there was a considerable number of native Irish and English among its members, and secondly it was a congregation which was tightly integrated into the community.[52] This is a particularly important point given the localism which developed in Ulster during the 1640s as a result of the war, and the need of local communities to protect themselves, with or without their landlords. In December 1641 an Ulster officer wrote to Ormond that the men of Antrim and Down had been organised but he added:

we could not (by any means) draw them together from their own towns either to assist one another or to oppose the enemy in any other place (were the occasion never so important) where their own particular interests did not evidently press them unto it.[53]

The session was seen as much as a unit of local organisation as an expression of religious belief. It was a body which would be useful in maintaining control when the mechanisms of central government were near collapse. Certainly in the late seventeenth century the local power of the session was considerable, and there were a number of serious disputes between session and presbytery in various parts of the country before their respective rights were established.

Thus it is possible to explain the success of a presbyterian structure in the Ulster of the 1640s without recourse to the settlers of the early seventeenth century. Even if the Scots did survive from the earlier plantation — and there is little evidence of large scale continuity since many left Ulster at the outbreak of the rebellion — the sort of presbyterianism they practised was rather different to that which Munro and his chaplains advocated.[54] In the same way as the spread of the Solemn League and Covenant was bound up with the issue of supply, so the spread of the kirk session depended more on the organisation of the local community than on its theological or ethnic origins.

III

If Robert Munro expected any kind of fraternal support from the settlers in Ulster when he landed in April 1642 he was to be disappointed. Already, many of the Ulster settlers were second generation, having been born in Ireland or having come there so young as not to remember any other home. Many of the ties which had bound the earlier settlers to Scotland and England had begun to weaken. The outbreak of hostilities in the three kingdoms had forced many of the settlers to choose which war they were to fight in, and where their priorities lay. The earl of Antrim, Sir Randal Macdonnell, was still closely bound into the politics of the south-west highlands of Scotland and his actions must be understood in that context. This was a problem which Munro knew how to cope with. His dealings with the earl of Antrim were effective. Munro was less effective in dealing with the British forces composed of a 'middle nation': the men who, by their backgrounds, were apparently Scots and English, but were rapidly moving towards what the keeper of the register of the University of Glasgow in the 1660s was to describe as 'scoto-hibernicus' and 'anglo-hibernicus'.[55] What these men were developing in Ulster was a rather different type of society to that of England or Scotland. Thus the standards which these men used to judge their actions were not those of the royalist or parliamentarian in England. Their concerns were more parochial. They had to defend what had been developed over almost half a century against threats from both the native Irish rebels and confiscation by the English parliament. They were dependant on the king for their wealth and status, and had only recently acquired their lands directly from him rather than by inheritance. It was this political reality which Munro failed to understand. He was a military commander sent to Ulster in confusing circumstances. He was usually reluctant to act without instructions, either from his nominal paymasters in London or his actual paymasters in Edinburgh. The result was that he was caught up in a complex political game and ended up being condemned from all sides and isolated and powerless in a situation he did not really understand.

It was not only in the realm of politics that Munro was confused. His experience of the warfare of the 'military revolution' of continental Europe with the set piece battle was of little use to him in Ireland. Munro was disappointed with his Ulster military experience. Within a few weeks of landing in Ulster Munro wrote: 'it will be a war in my judgement very strange for the whole march I never had any alarm given us being quartered in the fields untrenched'.[56] The native Irish preferred a guerilla type warfare with occasional sallies against enemy troops rather than set piece battles. In terms of artillery, many of the heavy cannon which Munro had brought were to prove useless in this type of situation, and totally unsuitable for transporting over the rugged Irish terrain.[57] Thus Munro was not even to have the consolation of a spectacular victory on the battlefield because the one engagement for which he was trained, the battle of Benburb, came too late. His forces were depleted and short of supplies, his men too weak to push a pike according to one account. Munro had to flee the battlefield leaving his wig behind him.[58]

The danger of interpreting the experience of the Scots army in Ulster from the perspective of England or Scotland is clear. Those who expected to find in early seventeenth-century Ireland the politics or religious problems of some other part of the British Isles writ small were asking for trouble. The settlers were no longer Scots or English in Ireland, but already in an embryonic form, Scots-Irish or Anglo-Irish. They had their own solutions to their problems, and to misread the signs was to court disaster, as Munro discovered to his cost.[59]

NOTES

1. PRO SP 63/261/25, 26; for the context R. Gillespie, 'The end of an era: the outbreak of the 1641 rising in Ulster' in C. Brady, R. Gillespie (eds.), *Natives and Newcomers: essays on the making of Irish colonial society, 1534–1641* (Dublin, 1986), 191–213.

2. D. Stevenson, *Scottish Covenanters and Irish Confederates* (Belfast, 1981); E. M. Furgol, 'The Military and Ministers as Agents of Presbyterian Imperialism in England and Ireland, 1640–48' in J. Dwyer, R. A. Mason, A. Murdoch (eds.), *New Perspectives on the Politics and Culture of Early Modern Scotland* (Edinburgh, 1982), 95–115; H. Hazlett, 'A History of the Military Forces operating in Ireland, 1641–9', Ph.D thesis, Queens University Belfast, 1938.

3. Stevenson, *Scottish Covenanters and Irish Confederates*, 295; Furgol, 'The Military and Ministers', 103–5, 110–11.

4. S. Kavanagh (ed.), *Commentarius Rinuccinianus* (Dublin, 1932), i, 329; J. T. Gilbert (ed.), *A Contemporary History of Affairs in Ireland* (Dublin, 1879), i, 23.

5. *Register of the Privy Council of Scotland [RPC] 1607–10*, 106, 497–8, 508, 511–12, 519–21; *Calendar of State Papers Relating to Ireland [CSPI] 1608–10*, 10, 22, 448.

6. H. Kearney, *Strafford in Ireland* (Manchester, 1959); T. Ranger, 'Strafford in Ireland: a re-evaluation' in T. Aston (ed.), *Crisis in Europe, 1560–1660* (London, 1965), 271–94; M. Perceval Maxwell, 'Protestant Faction, the Impeachment of Strafford and the Origins of the Irish Civil War', *Canadian Jnl. of History*, xvi (1982), 235–55.

7. D. Stevenson, *The Scottish Revolution, 1637–44* (Newton Abbot, 1973), 151–61, 214–43; *Calendar of State Papers, Domestic [CSPD] 1641–3*, 184.

8. The text of the treaty is printed in Stevenson, *Scottish Covenanters and Irish Confederates*, 315–18.

9. Stevenson, *Scottish Covenanters and Irish Confederates*, 317.

10. Bodleian Library, Oxford [Bodl.] Carte Ms 16, 299; Historical Manuscripts Commission [HMC], *Ormond Mss.*, n.s. i, 124, 193; Thomas Carte, *History of the Life of James, First Duke of Ormond* (2nd edn, Oxford, 1851), v, 504.

11. Bodl. Carte Ms 6, 299; Carte Ms 3, 457.

12. This description of the negotiations is based on Stevenson, *Scottish Covenanters and Irish Confederates*, 43–65.

13. *RPC 1607–10*, 504–5.

14. Gilbert, *Contemporary History*, i, 424.

15. J. Hogan (ed.), *Letters and Papers relating to the Irish Rebellion* (Dublin, 1936), 45–51.

16. The campaign is described in Stevenson, *Scottish Covenanters and Irish Confederates*, 105, 117–20.

17. E. Hogan (ed.), *A History of the War in Ireland* (Dublin, 1873), 25.

18. Hogan, *Letters and Papers*, 99–100; HMC, *Ormond Mss.*, n.s. i, 124, 131, 193, 218; Carte, *History of the Life of James, First Duke of Ormond*, ii, 486.
19. Hogan, *History of the War in Ireland*, 50.
20. Carte, *History of the Life of James, First Duke of Ormond*, i, 311; HMC, *Ormond Mss.*, n.s. i, 144; *CSPI 1632–47*, 417; Trinity College, Dublin, Ms 836, 105.
21. Carte, *History of the Life of James, First Duke of Ormond*, vi, 5–6, 33, 530; Gilbert, *Contemporary History*, i, 90; Stevenson, *Scottish Covenanters and Irish Confederates*, 165–70.
22. Gilbert, *Contemporary History*, i, 550–1; Charles McNeill (ed.), *The Tanner Letters* (Dublin, 1943), 163–4; *CSPD 1641–3*, 564.
23. Carte, *History of the Life of James, First Duke of Ormond*, v, 504; vi, 46, 52; Hogan, *Letters and Papers*, 185–6; Bodl. Carte Ms 8, 10; National Library of Scotland [NLS], Advocates Ms 33.4.8., 50–7, 69–70.
24. McNeill, *Tanner Letters*, 171.
25. McNeill, *Tanner Letters*, 165.
26. Hogan, *Letters and Papers*, 185–6.
27. M. Perceval Maxwell, 'The Adoption of the Solemn League and Covenant by the Scots in Ulster', *Scotia*, ii (1978), 1–18.
28. *A True Copy of a Letter Sent From Doe Castle From an Irish Rebel to Dunkirk* (London, 1643); J. Turner, *A Memoir of his own Life and Times* (Edinburgh, 1829), 24–5; P. Adair, *A True Narrative of the Rise and Progress of the Presbyterian Church in Ireland*, ed. W. D. Killen (Belfast, 1866), 127.
29. Stevenson, *Scottish Covenanters and Irish Confederates*, 161.
30. Bodl. Carte Ms 10, 201, 205, 325, 395.
31. Bodl. Carte Ms 11, 322, 336.
32. *CSPI 1632–47*, 558–61; McNeill, *Tanner Letters*, 203–6.
33. Hogan, *History of the War in Ireland*, 50. Estimates of the size of the army at various times are given in Stevenson, *Scottish Covenanters and Irish Confederates*.
34. Stevenson, *Scottish Covenanters and Irish Confederates*, 240–64.
35. Hogan, *History of the War in Ireland*, 64–5.
36. Bodl. Carte Ms 3, 325–7.
37. Turner, *Memoirs*, 24–5.
38. *CSPD 1644–5*, 200, 294; HMC, *Egmont Mss*, i, 467.
39. Gilbert, *Contemporary History*, i, 26.
40. J. S. Reid, *History of the Presbyterian Church in Ireland* (Belfast, 1867), i, 367.
41. R. Gillespie, *Colonial Ulster* (Cork, 1985), 145–6.
42. HMC, *Ormond Mss*, n.s., i, 355.
43. W. Knowler (ed.), *The Earl of Strafford's Letters and Despatches* (London, 1799), i, 138, 142; HMC, *Ormond Mss*, n.s., i, 286–94.
44. Stevenson, *Scottish Covenanters and Irish Confederates*, 51–2.
45. R. Gillespie, 'Urban Oligarchies and Popular Protest in the early Seventeenth Century: Two Ulster Examples', *Retrospect* (1982), 54–7.

46. K. Bottigheimer, *English Money and Irish Land* (Oxford, 1971); H. Hazlett, 'The Recruitment and Organisation of the Scottish Forces in Ulster', in H. A. Cronne, T. W. Moody, D. B. Quinn (eds.), *Essays in British and Irish History in Honour of James Eadie Todd* (London, 1949), 115–16; NLS Advocates Ms 33.4.8., 16–23, 30–5; Stevenson, *Scottish Covenanters and Irish Confederates*, 56–7; *CSPI 1660-2*, 383. It was argued in 1645 that the reason the Scots in Ulster were so ineffective was that they did not have land there: McNeill, *Tanner Letters*, 181–2.

47. M. J. Westerkamp, *Triumph of the Laity* (Oxford, 1988), 40–2; D. Stevenson, 'The Radical Party in the Kirk, 1637–45', *Jnl. of Ecclesiastical History*, xxv (1974), 137, 143, 147, 148, 151.

48. Adair, *A True Narrative*, 93–5.

49. G. Hill (ed.), *The Montgomery Manuscripts* (Belfast, 1869), 127. On Montgomery's background, M. Perceval Maxwell, 'Strafford, the Ulster Scots and the Covenant', *Irish Historical Studies*, xviii (1972–3), 544–5; Reid, *History of the Presbyterian Church*, i, 374–5, 394–5.

50. Reid, *History of the Presbyterian Church*, i, 392–3, Adair, *A True Narrative*, 124–5.

51. Adair, *A True Narrative*, 88–9, 124–5, 150.

52. PRONI CR4/12B/1. Selections from the session book are in W. T. Latimer, 'The Old Session Book of Templepatrick Presbyterian Church', *Jnl. Royal Society of Antiquaries of Ireland*, xxv (1895), 162–75, 259–72. For more detail R. Gillespie, 'The Presbyterian Revolution in Ulster, 1660–1690' in W. J. Sheils, *The Church, Ireland and the Irish, Studies in Church History xxv* (Oxford, 1989), 159–70.

53. Bodl. Carte Ms 2, 203.

54. R. Gillespie, 'Landed Society and the Interregnum in Ireland and Scotland', in R. Mitchison, P. Roebuck (eds.), *Economy and Society in Scotland and Ireland, 1500-1939* (Edinburgh, 1988), 39.

55. R. Gillespie, 'The Making of the Montgomery Manuscripts', *Familia* ii (1986), 23–9; B. Cunningham, R. Gillespie, 'An Ulster Settler and his Irish Manuscripts', *Eiqse*, xxi (1986), 34–6.

56. Gilbert, *Contemporary History*, i, 421, 423.

57. Stevenson, *Scottish Covenanters and Irish Confederates*, 109.

58. G. A. Hayes McCoy, *Irish Battles* (London, 1969), 174–99.

59. Owen Roe's experience, in many ways similar to Munro's, is described in Raymond Gillespie, '"Master in the art militarie": Owen Roe O'Neill', in Gerard O'Brien (ed.), *Nine Ulster Lives* (Belfast, forthcoming).

7

FROM SCOTTISH LORDS TO BRITISH OFFICERS: STATE BUILDING, ELITE INTEGRATION AND THE ARMY IN THE SEVENTEENTH CENTURY

Keith M. Brown

The origin of the modern nation state in Western Europe in the course of the sixteenth and seventeenth centuries is one of the most important and enduring developments of the period. The most obvious examples are probably France, England, and Sweden and Denmark. What of Scotland? There nationhood had been established by force of arms around the unifying symbol of the crown as early as the fourteenth century, but while the personal and ideological power of the Scottish monarchy now appears to be an unquestioned fact of medieval and even early modern Scottish history, there is little doubt that Scotland was lagging behind in state development before the union of the crowns in 1603.[1] It is easy to exaggerate the extent to which Scotland had already travelled down that road because of the overwhelming impact of the regal union on the government of the kingdom, an impact which seems to confer inevitability on the developments in government after 1603. King James VI was probably more responsible than most for creating the impression in his little joke about swords and pens that Scotland was not so very different from England. The truth was that it was only in the last seven years before union that he finally found himself able to dominate Scottish politics, and he did so as a personal ruler, not through the agencies of a state apparatus. Certainly there was something to build on following the achievements of the mid-1590s when noble factionalism markedly declined and the nobility indicated a willingness to surrender areas of personal justice to the state, and when the church was set on an Erastian course. However, it could all so easily have fallen apart had James lost his touch, or if he had fallen victim to assassination, or if Prince Henry proved to be a troublesome heir (after all the last Scottish king to have an adult male heir was James III!). The instability in France after the death of Henry IV and Louis XIII ought to encourage a more cautious assessment of James VI's achievements than is often the case. But of course James did become king of England, and what might have been merely episodic became instead foundations of statehood.

One of those foundations was the crown's success — spurred on, it has to be said, by the church's increasingly punitive attitude to crime — in winning acceptance of the idea that justice was a state function, not a matter for private vengeance. When parliament conceded this in 1598 it sanctioned an important step towards a state monopoly of violence, a crucial prerequisite for any nation-state. What the debate over the bloodfeud had done was turn the minds of the political elite around to accepting the idea that only the king acting as a divinely appointed magistrate had the right to exert force in the interests of justice, just as political violence used without royal sanction had for long been accepted as treasonous. At an ideological level at least, force had already become a royal monopoly, and violence was now the last resort of traitors and criminals.[2] Just how far the degree of available force or violence can be equated with power has been a debatable point since Plato set Thrasymachus up for Socrates to demolish, but the most influential political thinkers of the sixteenth and seventeenth centuries, Machiavelli, Hobbes and Spinoza, all placed great emphasis on coercive power as a fundamental basis to political order.[3] Of course, if force was all that mattered, Scottish kings before 1603 were virtually powerless, and their repeated triumphs in the face of such a dire lack of direct control over violence is an indication of the importance of other factors, primarily ideological, in evaluating power. In spite of having no army, militia or police, and being wholly dependent on the nobility to provide those functions out of their own resources — and the nobility did exert a near monopoly over the agencies of force in medieval Scotland — Scottish kings were remarkably successful in defeating international and domestic enemies.

Yet in an age when kingship became increasingly equated with success in war — and here it is worth recalling Machiavelli's commonplace dictum that 'war is the only art expected of a ruler' — James VI was described by one typically martial (and no doubt macho) Spanish commentator as a king who 'is very timid and hates war'.[4] In a Spaniard the barely concealed contempt was understandable, but so was James VI's caution given his military resources. James might have thought of war as an expensive waste of money, and he had an understandable concern about assassination, but he did successfully take the field with his soldiers on six occasions between 1587–94 in order to subdue rebellions (and he probably had more experience of military campaigns than any English monarch since Henry VII!). However, on all these occasions his political options were limited by his military weakness. When in the later 1590s his neurosis about the English succession led him to contemplate fighting for his cause, the true nature of Scotland's Lilliputian military resources became painfully apparent. The country had not been at war in earnest with a foreign enemy since the 1540s when the inadequacies of the common host in the context of modern warfare had been woefully exposed. In fact James's vision of leading a Scottish conquest had touches of the Don Quixote to it. His nobility were even more riven by feuds than Scottish lords usually were, and one of the motives behind the royal campaign against feuding was to facilitate war preparations. Even more worrying was the government's decision to abandon wappinschaws in 1599 because of the lack of cooperation in the localities. Scotland might have been an armed society, but it was not suitably armed for war. This was recognised by the crown, which on the one hand was trying desperately to reduce the private use of weapons, and on the other was endeavouring to encourage the importation of more arms. This business the burghs with good commercial foresight 'altogidder refuisit' to take on hand. Consequently in July 1599 it was contracted out as a private monopoly to Sir Michael Balfour of Burleigh who agreed to import suitable equipment for 2,000 horsemen and 8,000 footmen. However, the entire exercise floundered amidst a sea of public obstructiveness and dissent which ranged from the willingness of government officials to accept 'frivolous reasons' for excepting people from the act, to efforts to impose customs rates on the merchandise Balfour brought in from Flanders, and to the simple logistics of distribution.[5] Behind this lay a general feeling that it was all unnecessary as everyone was fairly certain that the succession issue was in the bag. Even if it was not there was no guarantee that the Scots would have gone to war in support of the king's dynastic ambitions, a lesson James III had learned over a century before when parliament refused to sanction support for military adventuring in France.[6]

James VI did not need an army to capture the English throne, which was just as well. The King of Scots had no army and no likelihood of ever having one unless parliament and, in particular, the nobility thought it necessary. Consequently there was little aggressive warfare before 1603. But after 1603 James VI and I found that he was elevated from command of a handful of under-paid palace guards to control of what

was, by Scottish standards, the impressive military inheritance of
Tudor England.[7] By the end of the seventeenth century the contrast
with the Scottish crown's military power before 1603 is staggering, for
both William II and Queen Anne commanded vast armies with which
they could wage wars on the continent, police their kingdoms, and
exploit the patronage stakes. And here one encounters something of a
paradox. Scottish kings after 1603 now had available to them greater
force than any of their ancestors had ever enjoyed. But what was
rapidly becoming a state monopoly of violence was controlled largely
from outside Scotland by the British crown and the English parliament.
Where then does this leave the Scottish state?

    That a monopoly of violence, or something approximating to it, was
acquired by the Scottish crown after 1603 is obscured by James VI's
skill in not needing to use it, and Charles I's ineptitude when he did try
to operate in a British dimension by calling in English force to try to
subdue Scotland in 1638.[8] The brief illusion of a nation in arms
defending itself against the violence of the embryonic British state
which the Army of the Covenant created between 1638–51 was blown
away at the battles of Dunbar and Worcester. Oliver Cromwell proved
what had been possible since 1603, that a London based executive
could subdue and rule Scotland by force alone, a point which Andrew
Fletcher of Saltoun repeatedly made in his *A Discourse concerning
Militias and Standing Armies*, published in 1697.[9] The very fact that
this force was in reality in the hand of a British executive rather than a
truly Scottish one poses problems when one comes to look for the
elusive Scottish state. Seventeenth century English historians have
little trouble in applying the 'nation state' concept to England in spite of
the fact that the *state* never acquired the same prominence in the
political vocabulary of Englishmen as it did in France. In England
violence had become a state monopoly, but arguably not a crown
monopoly, over the course of the sixteenth century, and it was the
question of who controlled that monopoly which was the fundamental
constitutional issue in England from the reign of Charles I until 1688.[10]
But the Scottish state never did come into being, partly because the
executive was hi-jacked by London in 1603, and partly because the
control of force lay outside the kingdom. To look for what a Scottish
state might have been like is therefore extremely difficult. Only during
the 1640s was political decision making and military force centred in
Scotland, but the very special circumstances of that decade make it a

murky window in which to peer for the clues to a counterfactual reconstruction of a possible Scottish state.[11]

As has already been indicated, Scotland experienced a fairly limited amount of warfare during the course of the sixteenth century. Since war was perhaps the greatest catalyst to state power in early modern Europe — 'the biggest industry in Europe'[12] — it is perhaps not surprising that there was little in the way of a state structure by 1603. In the seventeenth century war became much more prominent in Scottish affairs. Most obviously the mid century Wars of the Three Kingdoms militarised Scottish society to an extent unknown since the fourteenth century, possibly even more so. But even before then Scotland had experienced being dragged along in the wake of English foreign policy in the commercially ruinous wars against France and Spain in the latter half of the 1620s. After the Restoration a similar pattern emerged in the Anglo-Dutch Wars of the 1660s and 1670s, and after 1689 Scotland found herself a reluctant participant in a European struggle which had equally little to do with her own direct national interests, but which was in the interests of the governing elite of an emergent British state.

Naturally this resulted in a greater military establishment in Scotland and in greater numbers of Scots being employed by British governments to fight their wars. Until the outbreak of the First Bishops' War in 1639 the impact of war on Scotland was largely economic, both in the ruined trade with France, and in the increase in taxation which Charles I demanded, and got, to pay for his Anglo-centric foreign policy. Scotland continued to have no army, but Scottish troops were levied under contract by the crown in much the same way as Scottish regiments were employed by continental states. In effect the Scots were mercenaries working for the English crown.[13] The Covenanting wars changed this dramatically, as Scottish society was maintained on a war footing for over a decade at a cost in human and material resources which Scotland could ill afford. Exhaustion was inevitable even without the added strain of civil war in 1644–5 and the defeats inflicted by Cromwell after 1647. Following the final crushing blow at Worcester in 1651 Scotland had to endure military occupation for the next nine years. Yet in some respects the war had already projected the military into the centre of Scottish government and society, and the Covenanting revolution itself was founded on force in 1638. In 1660 the New Model Army marched away, and in 1663 the nobility forced Charles II to put his faith in an aristocratically dominated militia rather than in a standing army. The militia might have been 'the crucial underpinning of Stewart power in late seventeenth-century Scotland',[14] but the mid-century wars left an enduring legacy in the militarisation of government,[15] a point which was underlined by the role of old soldiers like the earls of Rothes, Middleton and Crawford in its personnel. Although opinion in Scotland and England was very much against the retention of a standing army after 1660, a permanent army had in fact arrived to stay, and even the modest Restoration army of 2,946 men at its peak in 1688, while small by Covenanting standards, was a considerable increase on the fifty border guards James VI had had at his disposal in the early 1600s.[16] After 1689 the long wars with France ensured the army's permanency in the emerging British state, and its role in protecting the interests of the state against foreign and domestic enemies made that permanency increasingly acceptable to the political elite of the new state.

That political elite was, even at the end of the seventeenth century, still predominantly aristocratic, even if that aristocracy had been forced to adjust itself to changing conditions in order to retain its grip of political power. Traditionally the Scottish nobility has been seen even as late as the early modern period as something of a warrior aristocracy, addicted to private violence and deriving their power from the military potential of their following. Recent research has moderated the anarchic picture this has often conjured up, but the reality of violence at the heart of Scottish lordship remains.[17] As long as that was the case the nobility clearly were unable to fulfil the very crucial role military elites play in creating a state structure.[18] However, towards the end of the sixteenth century aristocratic attitudes to lordship began to change under pressure from Renaissance civil education, Calvinist religion, and crown assertiveness. There was no question of noblemen being forced to change, for as has been argued already it was they who controlled the means to exert force, not the king. However, they were persuaded that the use of private violence in the pursuit of justice was no longer civilised, Christian, or respectful of royal authority.[19] The result was a dramatic decline in bloodfeuds, and with it the erosion of lordship as it had been exercised in Scotland since time immemorial. Without violence to act as a catalyst binding men together the nobleman gradually changed his role from that of lord to patron, while deference replaced dependancy. Yet the physical and ideological control of force did not immediately flow from the nobility to the crown. That process took most of the seventeenth century to complete, and was not irreversable until the Covenanting wars, when the Covenanting government harnassed its own aristocratic influence in the localities to a nascent national state structure.[20]

What the mid-century carnage revealed about attitudes to violence was what Sir George Clark has called the '*etatisation* of war'.[21] Scottish social and political elites might have decided that they could no longer sanction private violence, but they were enthusiastic about the use of state violence to crush dissent, much more enthusiastic than their sixteenth century ancestors, who had largely avoided religious persecution and had steered clear of executions for even the most blatant acts of treason. It has been argued that the civil war also showed just how superficial the layer of civil society was in Scotland. This is too harsh, for on the whole the violence of the wars was channelled through public institutions or ideologies, not private ones, although the division between the two was a very thin one. Besides, in the seventeenth century civil society largely accepted the legitimisation of violence in war, and it approved the growth in state power in response to the demands of war. Ultimately the beneficiaries of these changes were the nobility, who provided a ready made officer class for the new and greatly enlarged armies.[22]

Unlike the French nobility, for whom nobility itself was almost perceived as a military profession, that in Scotland was bound up with the wider role of lordship. Even so, war held considerable attractions for an elite whose ideological foundations lay in military service and in a violent honour code.[23] Renouncing feuding was relatively easy because the crown had neither the intention nor the means to swoop in and assume control of force; instead there was something of a stalemate in which the nobility retained most of the physical control of violence while the crown acquired recognition of its exclusive right to exert force. When Charles I blundered into Scotland with an English army, the nobility fused the two in the Covenanting government which they dominated. Once again the nation was mobilised under its aristocratic leaders to resist English invasion, and Robert Baillie recorded that 'In all the land we appointed noblemen and gentlemen for commanders'.[24] As late as 1644, when the Army of the Solemn League and Covenant marched into England, the peerage were prominent among the officers. Of the thirty-one colonelcies of horse and foot, thirteen were held by earls (including Leven), five by lords and three by sons of peers.[25] Yet the very fact that noblemen were appointed to military commands signified a crucial change in the conduct of war. Clearly the old feudal host with its amateur methods and its basis in the private, centrifugal control of force was no longer acceptable as the foundation of the kingdom's defence. Noblemen therefore raised regiments not retinues, their localities were defended by militias not convocations of dependants, they served on war committees rather than holding informal counsel with their friends and neighbours. These new military structures continued to be dominated by the nobility, but they enhanced the power of the state rather than of localised lordship. A form of lordship still operated, but it was being forced into new moulds. Thus in 1639 the earl of Eglinton still raised support from his locality to follow him in defence of the Covenant, but he did so as colonel of the shire, and he expected the state to pay him 21,050 merks in expenses for arming and feeding his men.[26] The lords were therefore forced to adapt to the role of officers in an army in which noble birth still counted for a great deal, but in which lordship was no longer the sole basis of authority. Robert Baillie recorded his own fears about the viability of a Scottish army under the command of the professional mercenary Alexander Leslie:

> We were feared that emulation among our Nobles might have done harme, when they should be mett in the fields; bot such was the wisdome and authoritie of that old, little, crooked souldier, that all, with ane incredible submission, from the beginning to the end, gave over themselves to be guided by him, as if he had been Great Solyman.[27]

By the reign of James VII the nobility had come to accept the discipline and hierarchy of the army, largely because they themselves had successfully 'colonised' its command structure, thus completing the aristocracization of the officer elite. Naturally there was some resistance to this, and in 1689, for example, the earl of Crawford complained to the earl of Melville that as a mere captain of an independent company of horse he 'must obey the meanest field officer'.[28] Crawford made it clear that the problem was not obeying orders, but obeying the orders of men who were not themselves noblemen. However, the important point was that Crawford recognised the fact that he had to obey his military superiors whatever their social background. Ultimately it was the success of the nobility in penetrating the officer elite which had the dual effect of keeping the army subservient to the interests of the aristocracy while maintaining the military ethos of the nobility.[29]

One gets some idea of this process in operation by looking for example at the house of Ross, a west Renfrewshire family of modest wealth and even more modest political clout. During the 1640s Robert,

9th Lord Ross, sat on the committee of war for Edinburgh and was colonel for the shires of Ayr and Renfrew, offices in which he was succeeded by his heir, William, 10th Lord Ross, in 1648. After the Restoration his son, George, 11th Lord Ross, was a commissioner for the Ayr and Renfrew Militia, was granted a captain's commission in one of the new troops of horse in 1674, was a lieutenant-colonel of the guards by 1677, and participated in the campaign against the Covenanters two years later. William, 12th Lord Ross, served the crown under Claverhouse in 1680–6, and his younger brother became colonel of the 5th Irish Regiment of Dragoons, reaching the rank of lieutenant-general in the British army by 1712. The Ross family thus moved from holding military command by virtue of a form of quasi-lordship during the Wars of the Three Kingdoms, to office in the para-military police force that constituted the Restoration army, to a command in the professional army of the British state.[30]

Yet while the wars of the 1640s and 1650s were a new experience for many noblemen, the martial tradition which had been fostered for so long by the bloodfeud and in the aristocratic honour code had already been channelled into mercenary service before then. In the years 1625–42 the privy council authorised the raising of 47,110 men for foreign mercenary service. Here was a reservoir of military talent which could provide a professional stiffening to any Scottish army, as indeed happened after 1638. The most obvious example is, of course, Alexander Leslie, 1st Earl of Leven, who appears to have been the kind of apolitical mercenary soldier so essential in the early stages of state building. But the army Leven commanded in 1644 was, in spite of the large number of noblemen commanding regiments, dominated by veterans of continental wars with social backgrounds below the peerage. All the general officers fell into this category, as did eleven of the thirty-one colonelcies (including Leven), twenty-four of the twenty-nine lieutenant-colonelcies, and twenty-three of the twenty-nine majors. It was these men who really made the Covenanting armies so successful in its early stages.[31] Scottish officers could be found serving in most European countries throughout the seventeenth century. Sweden was perhaps the most popular employer with Scottish soldiers during the first half of the century, and Alexander, 11th Lord Forbes, who returned to Scotland in 1643 to take command of the army in Ireland, was a lieutenant-general in the Swedish army and had fought under Gustav Adolph. So too had the 1st earl of Forth and the 1st earl of Eythvin, while the Munro kindred could number three generals, eight colonels, five lieutenant-colonels, eleven majors, and over thirty captains in the famous Swedish king's service.[32] Almost as common was service in the Dutch army. Walter, 1st Lord Buccleuch, took over a regiment to fight for the States General in 1604, and his son, Walter, 1st Earl of Buccleuch, followed in his footsteps in 1627. Particularly in the later years of the century William of Orange's Dutch army proved to be a springboard for a number of Scottish soldiers, like Sir David Colyear and Sir Thomas Livingston, to gain entrance into the upper ranks of Scottish society.[33] France was a less important employer of Scots mercenaries than in the medieval period, but careers could still be made there. George Douglas, later 1st earl of Dumbarton, began his military career in French service in 1647 at the age of eleven, and remained in French employment for over twenty years until in 1661 he brought his entire regiment, the Royal Scots, into the British army (although Charles then leased it back to Louis XIV).[34]

In addition to providing the raw material for a standing army, the experience of common service to continental employers allowed an early opportunity for something like a British military elite to develop its own identity. Even in the sixteenth century the common threat that Scottish and English protestants saw in the likely wake of a Spanish victory in the Netherlands had persuaded both governments to cooperate in sending men to fight alongside the Dutch, and in 1597 Scots and English fought together under Maurice of Nassau. Charles I too sent British armies to France and Germany, although in the latter case the effect of Scottish 'red-shanks' on English troops was allegedly to lead them 'to fall into any tumult or mischief' they could devise.[35] The Anglo-Dutch Brigade is the best example of this kind of co-operation, although it is perhaps a little naive to say, as J. W. Fortescue did, that 'English and Scots already loved to fight side by side'. Certainly national tensions remained, and when the Anglo-Dutch war broke out in 1665 the English officers refused to take an oath of allegiance to the States General and took their men home, while the Scottish officers remained loyal to their Dutch paymasters and saw no need to identify with an English cause.[36]

Not surprisingly, mercenary careers were most likely to appeal to poor noblemen, or to younger sons of noblemen for whom the military life offered some possibility of retaining their social status. For a few it even provided a route to wealth and entitlement.[37] This, of course, was not unique to Scotland; Monluc, Wallenstein and Marlborough all came from what might be conveniently described as the lesser nobility of their respective countries.[38] Behind this surge into military occupations lay powerful economic pressures. Up until the early seventeenth century most noble families had been able to set up successful cadet branches or to provide careers for younger sons relatively easily. Even after noble families were approaching the point of saturation in their local land colonization, towards the end of the fifteenth century,[39] opportunities continued to exist in the church. In the later sixteenth century the secularisation of church lands, the growing business potential of the legal profession, and after 1603 the increased patronage of the crown, all helped to maintain noble kindreds with the minimum of economic and social debasement among their junior ranks. However, by the third decade of union there was no more church land to go around, and the crown was soon to initiate moves to recover some of those lands already distributed; royal patronage was drying up due to economies and the fact that the Scots were increasingly unpopular in London; the legal profession was consolidating around established legal dynasties able to freeze out new-comers; merchant wealth was such that penurious younger sons could not possibly compete with the urban elite; and with the decline in feuding, noblemen were less inclined to support large retinues. In addition, noble finances in general were less secure than they had been for centuries. Military service at home or abroad was therefore one means by which an over-bloated and financially precarious nobility might avoid slipping into a kind of petty, debased nobility. This is not to say that an army career was always decided by push factors, for the military life continued to attract noblemen for more positive reasons, chiefly because it met their expectations of a martial nobility in a way that civil society no longer did, and because of the sheer excitement of war.[40]

The seventeenth century therefore saw a growing number of Scottish noblemen seeking service abroad or, especially after 1660, pursuing commissions in the forces of the British Crown. Archibald, 7th Earl of Argyll, joined the Spanish army in 1617 partly to avoid his creditors and partly as a result of his conversion to Roman Catholicism. Hard up debtors like the 11th Lord Forbes, the 2nd earl of Lothian, and the 1st earl of Buccleuch all kept themselves afloat by periods of foreign military service, and the landless and impoverished 2nd Lord St Colme, the 14th earl of Crawford, and the *de jure* 9th Lord Sommerville could do nothing else but sell their swords abroad. This continued after 1660, but now the small standing army in Scotland provided limited opportunities at home. At the peak of his career in the army George, 3rd

Earl of Linlithgow, was drawing pensions worth £900 p.a., and in 1684 he sold the colonelcy of his regiment in exchange for the office of lord justice general and an annual pension of £500.[41] After 1689 war was almost continuous, a development which had the effect of puting up the value of military office as political prejudices against a standing army declined and the long-term investment value in a military career increased.[42] The financial advantages of military office were pointed out in a desperate letter in January 1692 from James, Earl of Angus, to his father, the 2nd marquis of Douglas. Angus wrote from Utrecht about how his father's concern to shield his only son from the dangers of the battlefield had made him the laughing stock of the army and the court. Furthermore, by missing the last campaign during which Lieutenant-General Douglas had died he had lost out on the opportunity of being given command of the guards regiment, 'a post more honourable and lucrative than any I can expect to gett in many years to come'. Particularly in view of what Angus described as 'the low circumstances of our family', he thought he ought to pay heed to those who advised him that 'the making of a campaign will be the surest way to gett some part of his majestys good graces'. Unfortunately, Angus was killed at the Battle of Steinkirk later that year.[43] The number of younger sons in military careers was even greater, and William Drummond, George Douglas, George Hamilton, and Charles Murray were all younger sons who had very successful careers in the army.[44]

All of these younger sons were themselves able to acquire titles as a result of military service to the crown, and in fact the seventeenth century saw the greatest number of new peers being created for military service since the fourteenth century. For the crown this had advantages as it represented a non-pecuniary form of reward, while for soldiers on the fringes of noble society it allowed them to gain entrance to the social elite. Charles I began this trend as ennoblement provided him with a cheap means of attracting support from skilled soldiers during the civil war. Patrick Ruthven, for example, was the second son of a minor laird who had served in the Swedish army from 1615–36 before returning home to hold Edinburgh Castle for the king against the Covenanters in 1640, having been created Lord Ruthven of Ettrick the year before. His continued military service included a command at the battle of Edgehill and ultimately the rank of field marshall, and he was rewarded with the Scottish earldom of Forth in 1642 and the English title of earl of Brentforth two years later. In much the same way James King of Birness and Dudwick moved from the Swedish army to the royalist army and the title of Lord Eythvin in 1642. Others who fought for the crown and were rewarded with entry to the peerage were Angus MacDonald of Glengarry, 1st Lord MacDonell and Aros, one of Montrose's lieutenants, and the former Covenanters turned royalists, the commoner John Middleton, 1st Earl of Middleton and David Leslie, 1st Earl of Newark, the fifth son of the impoverished Lord Lindores.[45] These last three had to wait until after the Restoration for their rewards, but while Charles II did remember his and his father's old soldiers, his reign was a leaner period in terms of ennoblement for military service. There were exceptions, notably the 1st earl of Dumbarton in 1675, and John Churchill's first title was in the Scottish peerage as Lord Churchill of Eyemouth.[46] However, James VII made up for this, creating the 1st earl of Dunmore, 1st Viscount Strathallan and 1st Viscount Dundee all in 1686.[47] William II was also generous with titles for his officers, and the 1690s and 1700s saw the officer elite become the most 'upwardly mobile' group in British society. George Hamilton was created 1st earl of Orkney in 1696, having fought for the king in Ireland and in Flanders, and having attained the rank of brigadier-general of foot. In the same year William also created Thomas Livingston, his commander-in-chief in Scotland, Viscount Teviot. William also rewarded Sir David Colyear in 1703 with the title of earl of Portmore. Portmore, who was born in Brabant of Scots parents, perhaps provides the best example of the Scots mercenary family on the make. His grandfather rose from obscure origins to a captaincy in the Dutch army, his father became a regimental colonel, an English baronet and a Scottish landowner, while Portmore himself rose to the rank of general in the British army and married an English duchess.[48]

Such patronage gave the crown a dual leverage over soldiers who wanted to become noblemen and noblemen who needed jobs in the army. It therefore helped create a greater dependency on the king, or at least, given the events of 1688–9, on the crown and the emergent British state.[49] Of course Scottish noblemen had always sought crown patronage, and even before the outbreak of revolution in 1637 they had become much more accustomed to pandering to the crown's desire for flattery in order to get it. Boot-licking was certainly not invented after the Restoration, but noblemen after 1660 did manage to turn it into something of an art, and the pursuit of military commissions provided new opportunities for practising it. In January 1680 William, Earl of Menteith, wrote to the earl of Montrose begging him to ask the duke of York for a command in the army as 'ther is nothing on earth that I love so weill as to be in a just war for my King and Prince'. More importantly, perhaps, Menteith needed money and was in reality selling his sword to the crown, but it no doubt helped to be able to believe that in doing so he would be fulfilling a noble occupation and performing a noble service to his Prince.[50] While Menteith was able to find a local broker to take up his suit, the control of military patronage, especially after 1689, lay in London, largely with English politicians. It was therefore to Treasurer Godolphin that the earl of Leven applied for command of the army in Scotland when Lieutenant-General Ramsay died in September 1705, an application which Godolphin passed on to Marlborough and which was ultimately successful.[51] Apart from causing an undue amount of absenteeism within the Scottish army as officers hung around the court hoping to curry favour,[52] such dominance of military patronage by London had the effect of drawing the aristocratic officer elite even further into the British establishment.

In 1688–9 that establishment was shown to be more than simply a court interest, but the Scottish aristocratic officers demonstrated a marked tendency to remain loyal to James VII. At a lower level too there was considerable dissatisfaction with the revolution, and Scottish regiments played a prominent part in the mutinies of 1689.[53] There were some minor scares about the loyalty of officers after the revolution, for example in March 1689 when a younger son of the earl of Hartfell and his brother officers in the Royal Regiment of Foot were arrested, and in May 1692 the former officers, the earls of Newburgh, Middleton, and Dunmore were all involved in treasonable plotting. Not surprisingly, the politicians were vigilant in keeping their eye on military loyalty, just in case. After all, the army had been disloyal to the king in 1688–9! On 7 May 1689 William II wrote to Melville authorising him to purge the army of 'Officers and Soldiers whose fidelity to Us and our Government We have no just cause to have confidence in'.[54] Similarly in an intelligence report prepared in December 1704 by General Ramsay on his own officers, Ramsay submitted his opinion on all the higher officer elite. The duke of Argyll and his troop of guards was, he thought, completely loyal, as was Crawford's troop of horse grenadiers. However, Colonel John Stewart of the guard regiment was suspect since he 'did vote wrang in the succession, but says he was abused in his vote, which I am ready to believe'. Less forgivable was the earl of Mar who 'has appeared in this Parliament against every thing proposed by her Majestie's ministers and therefore in my opinion is not to be trusted with his regiment nor the Castle of Stirling'.[55]

One consequence of this combination of patronage and professionalism was that noble officers increasingly found themselves employed in repressive actions against opponents of the crown.[56] While the army certainly was used politically by the crown in England, particularly at the Oxford Parliament in 1681, that in Scotland was even 'rougher' in its treatment of dissidents. Lauderdale's willingness to make 'illegal' use of it was one cause of the considerable hostility expressed in the House of Commons in 1673–4 in the *Address Against Lauderdale*.[57] Noblemen like the earls of Linlithgow, Strathmore and Winton were all active in suppressing conventicles, overseeing the operations of the Highland Host and in the campaigns against Covenanting rebels either as officers in the regular army or in the militia.[58] The Restoration governments had a quasi-military flavour to them, providing a continuity to the militarisation of the nobility which the civil wars had encouraged. John Middleton, who had begun his career as a teenage pikeman in Hepburn's regiment a few years before the outbreak of revolution in 1637, was appointed to the command of the Scottish army in 1660–3; John, 1st Duke of Rothes, who had fought on the Worcester campaign, was appointed general of the forces in Scotland in 1666; the 3rd earl of Linlithgow's first command was as colonel of the Stirlingshire regiment at the siege of Newcastle in 1644, and he went on to become commander-in-chief of the army in Scotland in 1667–9.[59] In addition to the small army, local militias provided the crown with important patronage in the localities, although here the freedom to exploit that patronage was limited by the constraints imposed by local elites. In 1668 the commissioners for Ayrshire and Renfrewshire were headed by the local nobility, lords Montgomery, Crichton, Cathcart, Bargany and Cochrane, while the captaincies of troops were held by the earls of Eglinton and Cassillis and the master of Cochrane.[60] At the revolution too the new government was very dependant on the co-operation of the local nobility, and thirteen independent troops of horse and eight independent companies of foot were raised in 1689, twelve of these by peers or their sons.[61]

This ensnarement of the nobility in the military apparatus of the state was accelerated after 1689, when William II's wars increased the size of the army and the government machinery required to administer it. Furthermore, after the revolution the distinctiveness of the Scottish army began to disappear and Scots increasingly were being drawn into what was already a British army. The deliberate mixing of nationalities in an army was in fact a characteristic of the period, and one seen to have positive advantages. In 1630 the Spanish marquis of Aytona had commented that 'there is no surer strength than that of foreign soldiers',[62] but the kind of multi-national armies of the Spanish and Austrian Hapsburgs did not create a sense of common national identity within the state they served, whatever other benefits may have accrued to their political masters. While an English-dominated government might have regarded Scottish and Irish troops as foreign, and therefore more dispensable, there was, however, little doubt that an integrated British army was already in the making before 1707. Thus when the size of the army was debated in the House of Commons in 1699 it was argued that it should be restricted to 'his Majesty's natural born subjects' which meant the disbandment of the Huguenot regiments, but not the Scots or Irish.[63] In theory the Scottish, English and Irish armies were independent before 1707, with separate establishments, little exchange of officers, and only their common loyalty to the king uniting them. Yet even at this stage it was common for Scottish regiments to be placed on the English establishment when sent overseas to fight,[64] and there were other small moves towards a single British army such as the adoption in 1679 by the Scots of the *Abridgement of English Military Doctrine*.[65]

Turning to the military elite, one finds a growing amount of integration towards the end of the century. Robert Harley's motion in the House of Commons in November 1693 that 'the English foot might be commanded by a native of their Majesties dominions' was aimed at Count Solmes, who was blamed for the high casualties at Steinkirk, but it implied an acceptance of Scottish or Irish officers.[66] This is not surprising given the gradual assimilation of Scottish officers into the British army. In 1661 the only Scottish nobleman with a command in the English army was Andrew, Lord Jedburgh, who was colonel of his own regiment, and throughout Charles II's reign only a handful of Scots were granted commissions in the English army.[67] Under James VII the process was accelerated, and when the king assembled his army on Hounslow Heath in June 1686 the Scots were well represented. The earl of Dumbarton was one of the three lieutenant-generals, there were no Scottish brigadier-generals, Colonel Hugh Mackay was one of the three major-generals, Colonel Robert Ramsay was one of the two adjutant generals, and three of the twenty-six colonelcies were held by Scots (Dumbarton, Arran and Sir James Douglas).[68]

However, it was under William II that the process of integration became much more noticeable, both in the careers of individual officers and in the overall character of the officer elite. John, 8th Lord

Elphinstone, began his military career with the army in Scotland under Charles II, he disagreed with James VII's policies and entered Dutch service, returned home with William of Orange, and then served as a captain in the British forces in Flanders until his retiral in 1696.[69] John, 19th Earl of Crawford, began his military career by raising his own regiment of foot in 1694. Four years later he was appointed lieutenant-colonel of the Scots Troop of the Life Guards, was colonel of the Scots Troop of the Grenadier Guards by 1704, brigadier-general of the Forces in Scotland in 1704, was a major-general with the army in Spain by 1707, and he was appointed a lieutenant-general in 1710.[70] Even more spectacularly John, 2nd Earl of Stair, entered the army as a volunteer in 1692, fighting at Steinkirk, he held a string of regimental colonelcies under Marlborough and fought in most of his major campaigns before going on to become commander-in-chief of the allied army in Flanders in 1742 and commander-in-chief of the army in Great Britain in 1744–5.[71] Stair, and his colleague John, 2nd Duke of Argyll, demonstrated that individual Scots could go all the way in the new British army which technically came into being in 1707 when the English army simply swallowed up the Scottish army. Yet on the eve of the parliamentary union, Scots already held 10% of the regimental colonelcies in the army, and were providing a disproprtionate number of the rank and file, a fact recognised by both Andrew Fletcher of Saltoun and Daniel Defoe.[72] At the Battle of Blenheim on 13 March 1704, of the sixteen regimental colonelcies in Marlborough's army, only seven were held by Englishmen, five by Scots and four by Irishmen. Marlborough's general staff clearly reflected the British complexion of the army; of his four lieutenant-generals one was Scottish (the earl of Orkney) and one Irish, of his three major-generals one was Scottish (Charles Ross), of his eight brigadier-generals three were Scots (James Ferguson, Archibald Row and Lord John Hay) and three were Irish, and of his seven majors of brigade two were Scots (Alexander Irwin and Patrick Gordon) and one was Irish.[73] Opportunities for Scots increased after 1707, helped by the huge increase in the number of commissions and the rapid rate of promotion brought about by the war. During the first half of the eighteenth century 25% of all regimental offices in the British army went to Scots, and the Scots captured 20% of all colonelcies between 1714 and the end of the Seven Years War.[74]

Naturally there were problems with this process of integration. National loyalties complicated the issues for soldiers, slowing down the process by which the military aristocracy was being subjected to state authority.[75] Charles I's friend, James, 3rd Marquis of Hamilton, recognised this in 1639 when he wrote that 'nothing can grieve me more in this world than to be sent in any hostile manner against my friends, kindred and country'.[76] But the localised world of friends, kinsmen and even country was being broken down over the course of the seventeenth century, and the civil wars did as much as anything else to hasten that disintegration. Hamilton had already experienced the problems of leading a British army in Germany in 1631, where it was reported that the English troops 'do not like serving under a Scottish commander', even as Anglicized a courtier as Hamilton. He, it seems, antagonised his men still further by insisting that they beat the Scottish march. In 1647 he encountered similar hostility when he was unable to arouse much local help for his Engagement Army in the north of England.[77] Hamilton himself was allegedly as racist as the English in his attitudes, and when he heard that Cromwell was attacking his English ally Langsdale at a critical point in the Preston campaign, he commented 'Let them alone, the English troops are but killing one another'.[78] His attitude was mirrored in that of Cromwell himself, who purged some 300 Scottish officers from his New Model Army. Cromwell found it hard to conceal his dislike for his Scottish allies, and told the earl of Manchester that 'I could as soon draw my sword against them as any in the King's army'.[79] In fact, throughout the civil wars the military alliance between the Covenanters and the English parliament was strained severely by national interests, and one gets the feeling that both sides were happiest once religious and political issues could be laid aside after 1647 and an old fashioned Anglo-Scottish war could get under way.[80]

Military cooperation between these allies was at its most strained when it came to the behaviour of Scottish troops in England. Thus the English commissioners on the 'Committee of Both Kingdoms with the Scottish Army' complained that 'The [Scottish] soldiers so often plundered, spoiled and wasted their parts that little is left besides the earth which they could not carry away with them'. Complaints of this nature continued after 1660, and in 1667 five companies of Lord George Douglas's regiment was accused of having 'abused shamefully' the people of Rye while awaiting embarkation for France. Again, in 1672 Sir William Lockhart's regiment caused considerable discontent in Newcastle because of their 'somewhat intemperate' behaviour, and because their presence aroused memories of the Scottish occupations of 1642 and 1644.[81] For their part the Scots had no great wish to see English troops in Scotland, and in 1667 General Dalziel wrote to

Lauderdale on the subject of English help in putting down unrest, commenting 'From inglis assistens mightay God deliver us'.[82] Even after 1688 tensions remained. Naturally the London-based government gave preference to its English regiments, and Scottish officers at times had to fight a rear-guard action against inequitable cuts in their troop strength. This quarrel was at its most bitter when regiments were disbanded after the Peace of Ryswick in 1697. Colonel Archibald Row angrily complained to the earl of Annandale about the unfair treatment of Scottish officers, and about English disregard for the precedence of Scottish regiments over their own, and Viscount Teviot also wrote dejectedly to Annandale, commenting that 'All goos to pot'![83]

What helped ease integration was that it was not only proceeding at one level. Thus the duke of Hamilton may have been a Scot, but he was also earl of Cambridge, he had been, briefly, to Oxford, he had an English wife, and he was one of the great figures of the English court. The captain of Charles II's Life Guards from 1650–70 was Sir James Livingston of Kinnaird, 1st Earl of Newburgh, a gentleman of Charles I's bedchamber, and the husband of the eldest daugher of the earl of Suffolk. James VII's commander-in-chief in Scotland, the earl of Dumbarton, was married to a daughter of Robert Wheatly of Bracknell. Colonel Charles Murray, 1st Earl of Dunmore, had an English mother, he was born at Knowsley, was master of the horse to Princess Anne and the duchess of York, later Queen Mary, and he himself married the heiress of a Hertfordshire gentleman. This same level of social integration among the officer elite continued after 1689. John, 2nd Duke of Argyll, already had an army career under Marlborough before 1707, and rose to be commander-in-chief of the army by 1742. In addition he had an English mother, two English wives, a string of English titles and offices, and he died at his home at Sudbrooke in Surrey in 1743. The 1st earl of Orkney fought in most of the major campaigns of William II and Marlborough and became a field marshall in 1736, the year before his death. He was married in London in 1695 to a former mistress of the king, Elizabeth Villiers, daughter of Sir Edward Villiers and sister of the 1st earl of Jersey, from 1710 he sat in the House of Lords as a representative peer, and his residence was at Cliveden near Maidenhead. Nor was integration confined to England, and the Hamiltons of Abercorn provide an example of a Scottish family with a very strong military tradition who did extremely well in Ireland. Here then was a whole mesh of inter-connected lines of integrative relations of which the army was only part of a whole.[84]

However, the military elite was more committed to the British state than the nobility in general. One of the common complaints of the English House of Commons during the reign of Queen Anne was over the role of 'placemen' in supporting the crown there, and prominent among these were military officers.[85] Not surprisingly, one finds the same tendency to support the court by officers in the Scottish parliament. This can clearly be demonstrated in the union debates of 1707. Of the nineteen military officers in the parliament in January 1707, eighteen supported the union, and of the twenty-seven peers who were either serving officers, who had held commissions since 1688, or whose eldest sons were officers, twenty-one supported the union.[86] No doubt patronage played its part in this, and those wishing to continue with a successful army career would have to think carefully about voting against the government. Yet to explain attitudes to the union simply on the grounds of material self-interest is more than a little crude. As members of a British military elite loyal to the British crown, experienced in warfare against the enemies of the emerging British state, and functioning within an institution, the army, which was already British in its organization and career mobility, they would be very unlikely to vote against a union of parliaments, particularly when national security (which was a British and not merely an English argument) was so fundamental to the union case.

The fact that something like a third of the peers in parliament in 1707 were in one way or another linked to the British military establishment demonstrates just how important the army had become to the aristocracy. Back in 1603 only a very small handful of Scottish noblemen had experience of what could realistically be described as military service, but in 1707 thirty-three of the noblemen in parliament had served or were serving in the post-restoration armies. The aristocratic officer had become a familiar sight in Scotland as the inheritor of the military tradition which had for so long been associated with nobility. With the demise of lordship during the course of the seventeenth century, that tradition could only be fostered in the army. There Scottish officers found themselves being integrated into a British military elite committed to the defence of the crown and to a view of the world shaped by the interests of a British state.

APPENDIX

Military Careers of Members of Parliament and the Union Debates, 1707

Serving Officers (all MPs)

Bennet, William, conjunct muster-master-general of the   pro-union
    Forces in Scotland (12 Aug. 1706).
Campbell, James, younger of Ardkinglass   pro-union
    brigadier in Scots Troop of Life Guards (20 May 1704).
Campbell, John, 2nd Duke of Argyll   pro-union
    first commission 1694, colonel of H.M.'s Troop of Life
    Guards of Horse in Scotland (21 July 1703) and major-general
    of the Forces (1 June 1706). Appointed colonel of H.R.M.
    the Prince of Denmark's Regiment of Foot on 24 Feb. 1707,
    lieutenant-general 1709, c-in-c Scotland 1712, and c-in-c of
    the Forces 1742. Brother of Islay (see below).
Cunningham, William 11th Earl of Glencairn,   pro-union
    first commission 1692, captain in Maitland's foot
    (19 April 1700). Appointed colonel of the foot, 27 Aug.
    1707. Eldest son, William Lord Kilmaurs was lieutenant-colonel
    of Strathnaver's foot (16 Sept. 1703).
Dalrymple, William of Glenmuir,   pro-union
    conjunct muster-master-general of the Forces in Scotland
    (12 Aug. 1706). Son of earl of Stair (see below).
Erskine, David, 9th Earl of Buchan,   anti-union
    first commission 1690 and capt. of a company of foot in
    Blackness Castle (31 May 1706).
Erskine, John, 6th Earl of Mar,   pro-union
    first commission 1702, captain of a company in Edinburgh
    Castle (25 Aug. 1702). Jacobite commander in 1715.
Erskine, John (Stirling burgh),   pro-union
    lieutenant-colonel and military governor of Dumbarton Castle,
    (25 Aug. 1702).
Forbes, William 13th Lord Forbes,   pro-union
    first commission 1689, lieutenant-colonel of Scots Troop of
    Life Guards (4 May 1704).
Fraser, Charles, 4th Lord Fraser,   pro-union
    first commission 1702, lieutenant-colonel of foot
    (20 March 1703). Retired 1712.
Grant, Alexander, younger of Grant,   pro-union
    colonel of Grant's foot (4 March 1706).
Johnston, Sir John of Westraw,   pro-union
    lieutenant-colonel of foot (29 March 1703).
Ker, William, 2nd Marquis of Lothian,   pro-union
    first commission 1689, colonel of a regiment of dragoons
    (renewed 11 Sept. 1703) and lieutenant-general of the horse

in Portugal (1 Jan. 1707). Appointed colonel of 3rd Foot
Guards 25 April 1707. Two sons in the army.

Lindsay, John, 19th Earl of Crawford,   pro-union
    first commission 1694, colonel of Scots Troop of Grenadier
    Guards (4 May 1704) and major-general of the Forces in Spain
    (1 Jan. 1707). Appointed lieutenant-general 1710.

Melville, David, 2nd Earl of Melville and 3rd Earl of Leven,   pro-union
    first commission 1688, c-in-c of the forces in Scotland
    (2 March 1706). Eldest son George, Lord Balgonie, an ensign
    in Maitland's foot, and son Alexander may already have been
    in the army.

Pollok, Sir Robert of that Ilk, major in Hyndford's Dragoons.   pro-union

Ramsay, William, 8th Earl of Dalhousie,   pro-union
    first commission 1693, lieutenant-colonel of Scots Foot
    Guards (29 Jan. 1704). Died in Spain 1710. Brother James
    also in the army.

Sandilands, James, 7th Lord Torphichen,   pro-union
    captain of grenadiers in Mar's Foot (3 Aug. 1702).
    Appointed major in 1712.

Scott, Henry, 1st Earl of Deloraine,   pro-union
    first commission 1702, colonel of Deloraine's Irish foot
    (1 March 1704). Appointed brigadier-general 1710 and
    major-general by 1730.

Possible Serving Officers (all MPs)

Balfour, Henry of Denboug,   anti-union
    described as a major c.1707.

Campbell, Archibald, 1st Earl of Islay,   pro-union
    first commission probably c.1705. Appointed colonel of
    Alnut's foot 6 March 1708. Brother of Argyll.

Colville, John, 6th Lord Colville,   anti-union
    an ensign at Malplaquet in 1709 but unclear when joined army.

MacLeod, Daniel (Tain burgh),   pro-union
    described as a captain c.1707.

Ogilvy, Patrick of Lonmay (Cullen burgh),   pro-union
    described as a colonel c.1707.

Oliphant, Patrick, 8th Lord Oliphant,   anti-union
    captain in Royal Regiment of Foot 3 Nov. 1708 but possible
    army career before then.

Sempill, Francis, 9th Lord Sempill,   anti-union
    captain in Carmichael's Dragoons in 1711 but possible army
    career before then.

Other Military Connections (peers only)

Carmichael, John, 1st Earl of Hyndford,   pro-union
    colonel of Carmichael's Dragoons 1694–7, and again 1703–6
    when resigned command to his son James, Lord Carmichael.

Dalrymple, John, 1st Earl of Stair,   pro-union
     no military career. Eldest son John served under William II
     from 1692, colonel of Scots Greys 24 Aug. 1706. Son William
     a muster-master-general, see above.

Douglas, James, 2nd Duke of Queensberry,   pro-union
     first commission 1685, colonel of Scots Troop of Life Guards
     1688, resigned 1694.

Elphinstone, John, 8th Lord Elphinstone,   pro-union
     first commission 1674, captain in Maitland's foot 1693,
     retired 1694. Eldest son Charles served with Grant's foot in
     Flanders and was wounded in 1708.

Fraser, William, 2nd Lord Fraser,   anti-union
     had been a captain of a company of foot in 1681.

Gordon, John, 15th Earl of Sutherland,   pro-union
     colonel of Strathnaver's Foot 1689, retired 1696. Eldest son
     William Lord Strathnaver was colonel of Strathnaver's foot
     1703–10.

Hamilton, Charles, 2nd Earl of Selkirk,   anti-union
     colonel of 4th Dragoon Guards 1688 and accompanied William II
     to Ireland and Flanders.

Hamilton, James, 4th Duke of Hamilton,   anti-union
     first commission 1685, colonel of Royal Regiment of Horse and
     colonel of all the horse 1688. Military career ended by
     1688 revolution.

Hamilton, James, 6th Earl of Abercorn,   pro-union
     possibly held a commission under James VII, but served under
     William II during 1690 Irish campaign.

Hamilton, John, 2nd Lord Belhaven,   anti-union
     captain of an independent troop of Scots horse in 1689 and
     fought at Killiecrankie.

Hamilton, William, 3rd Lord Bargany,   anti-union
     captain of Bargany's foot in 1689.

Hay, John, 2nd Marquis of Tweedale,   pro-union
     served in 1685 campaign against Argyll, captain of an
     independent troop of horse in 1689. Son John was a
     brigadier-general under Marlborough but died in 1706.
     Son William also in the army, and was a brigadier-general
     by 1710.

Hume, Patrick, 1st Earl of Marchmont,   pro-union
     no military record. Eldest son Patrick Lord Polwarth's
     first commission was in 1688, colonel of dragoons in 1704,
     and appointed colonel of Lothian's Dragoons 28 April 1707.

Johnston, William, 1st Earl of Annandale,   anti-union
     captain of a troop under Claverhouse and of an independent
     troop in 1689.

Lindsay, Colin, 3rd Earl of Balcarres,   pro-union
     fought at Southwald in 1672, captain in King's Own Royal

Regiment of Scots Horse 1683. Military career ended by
1688 revolution. Eldest son Alexander served in Flanders
and son Colin, Lord Cumberland was a captain of dragoons c.1707.

Livingston, William, 3rd Viscount Kilsyth,   anti-union
    lieutenant-colonel of Royal Scots Dragoons 1688. Military
    career ended by 1688 revolution.

Murray, Charles, 1st Earl of Dunmore,   pro-union
    first commission 1678, colonel of Royal Scots Dragoons 1686.
    Military career ended by 1688 revolution. Eldest son James,
    Viscount Fincastle, a captain in Macartney's Foot until death
    in 1704. Son John, Viscount Fincastle, joined army in 1704
    and fought at Blenheim. Son Robert joined in 1705. Brother
    of Atholl.

Murray, John, 1st Duke of Atholl,   anti-union
    first commission 1682, colonel of Murray's foot 1694–7.
    Eldest son John a colonel by 1707 under Marlborough and son
    William joined army in 1707. Brother of Dunmore, and two
    other brothers in army.

Primrose, Archibald, 1st Earl of Rosebery,   pro-union
    served as a mercenary in the Imperial Army in Hungary in 1680.

Ross, William, 12th Lord Ross,   pro-union
    first commission 1678, major in Claverhouse's Horse 1686,
    but retired 1686.

Summary of peers only

	pro- union	anti- union
Serving Officers	11	1
Peers who had served as officers since 1688 and/or whose sons were in the army c.1707	10	5
Total	21	6
Total peers in parliament	47	23

Voting record is taken from P. W. J. Riley, *The Union of Scotland and
England* (Manchester, 1978), Appendix A.

NOTES

1. On nationhood and medieval kingship, see A. Grant, *Independence and
   Nationhood: Scotland 1306–1469* (London, 1984); G. W. S. Barrow,
   Robert Bruce (Edinburgh, 1976). Of course J. Robertson is quite right to
   point out that 'all the ideological pride and sophistication of that Declaration
   [Arbroath] could not disguise the reality that Scotland was a community

by arms alone': J. Robertson, *The Scottish Enlightenment and the Militia Issue* (Edinburgh, 1985), 3. For the early modern period see J. M. Wormald, *Court, Kirk and Community: Scotland 1470–1625* (London, 1981); G. Donaldson, *Scotland, James V–James VII* (Edinburgh, 1971). M. Lee, *John Maitland of Thirlstane and the Foundations of Stewart Despotism in Scotland* (Princeton, 1959), and M. Lee, *Government by Pen* (Urbana, 1980) lean most towards the idea that the crown was developing a state apparatus before 1603. V. G. Kiernan, *State and Society in Europe 1550–1650* (Oxford, 1980), 133, thought that Scotland lacked the ingredients which would have allowed it to evolve into a nation state without the catalyst of the regal union. See too V. G. Kiernan, 'State and Nation in Western Europe', *Past and Present*, 31 (1965), 20–38, where he argues that 'it was the State that came first and fashioned the mould for the nation', something which was plainly not true for Scotland. For some comments on Scottish nationhood and the origins of the British state see A. D. Smith, 'State-Making and Nation-Building' in J. A. Hall (ed.), *States in History* (Oxford, 1986), 245–6.

2. K. M. Brown, *Bloodfeud in Scotland, 1573–1625: Violence, Justice and Politics in an Early Modern Society* (Edinburgh, 1986). For some discussion of the usage of *violence, force* and *power* see G. Sorel, *Reflections on Violence*, tr. T. E. Hulme and J. Roth (Collier-Macmillan, 1961), 175, where force is identified with the establishment of and obedience to legitimate authority, while violence is directed against it. H. Arendt, *On Violence* (Allan Lane, 1970), 42, contrasts violence with power. L. J. Macfarlane, *Violence and the State* (London, 1974), 41–52, takes the view that violence is the illegitimate imposition of force on another person, while force is legitimately imposed. Throughout I have employed these terms rather loosely, but my own understanding of them is closest to MacFarlane.

3. For Plato, see A. P. D'Entreves, *The Notion of the State* (Oxford, 1967). J. H. Shennan, *The Origins of the Modern European State 1450–1725* (London, 1974), 107–11, makes this point about Hobbes and Spinoza. For the monopoly thesis which largely grows out of this view of state power see N. Elias, *State Formation and Civilisation* (Oxford, 1982), 104ff, and O. Hintze, 'Military Organization and the Organization of the State' in O. Hintze, *The Historical Essays of Otto Hintze* (Oxford, 1975). Hintze argues that 'All state organization was originally military organization, organization for war'. For further discussion of the extent to which the military is instrumental in the creation and development of the state see M. Mann, 'The Autonomous Power of the State: Its Origins, Mechanisms and Results' in Hall, *States and History*, 109–36, and M. Mann, *The Sources of Social Power, vol. I: A History of Power from the Beginnings to 1760 AD* (Cambridge, 1986); S. Andrzejwski, *Military Organization and Society* (London, 1957); M. Feld, *The Structure of Violence: Armed Forces as Social Systems* (Beverly Hills, 1977);; A. Vagts, *A History of Militarism: Civilian and Military* (New York, 1959); J. A. Hall, 'War and the Rise of the West' in M. Shaw and C. Creighton

(eds.), *The Sociology of War and Peace* (London, 1986); M. Janowitz, *Military Conflict: Essays in the Institutional Analysis of War and Peace* (Beverly Hills, 1975); B. Abrahamson, *Military Professionalization and Political Power* (1971); S. E. Finer, *The Man on Horseback: the Role of the Military in Politics* (London, 1962).

4. Quoted in P. Anderson, *Lineages of the Absolutist State* (Oxford, 1979), 32. The full sentence is 'A prince should have no other thought or aim than war, nor acquire mastery in anything except war, its organization and discipline; for war is the only art expected of a ruler'. M. A. S. Hume (ed.), *Calendar of Letters and State Papers. Spanish. Elizabeth* (London, 1892–9), iv, 604.

5. On the armed society, wappinshaws and arms control see *Bloodfeud*, 21–2, 246–52. For Balfour's monopoly see T. Thomson and C. Innes (eds.), *The Acts of the Parliaments of Scotland* (12 vols, Edinburgh, 1814–75), iv, 168–9, 190–1; J. H. Burton and others (eds.), *The Register of the Privy Council of Scotland* (14 vols, Edinburgh, 1877–98), vi, 365, 466, 515–16 and *passim* for customer resistance. The requirements laid down for an earl, lord or baron were that all had to own a corslet of proof, a head-piece, vanbraces, teslets and a Spanish pike. Every earl was to have twenty stands of arms for his household, every lord ten, and every baron one per fifteen chalders of victual his lands annually produced. Gentlemen worth 300 merks annual rent were to be armed with a corslet and pike, or a musket and head-piece. Townsmen worth £500 p.a. were to be furnished with a corslet, pike, halbert and two-handed sword, or a musket and head-piece. Presumably Balfour lost a good deal of money on the enterprise. In 1625 Sir Patrick Hume of Polwarth complained to Sir Robert Kerr that Scotland had never been 'In worse equippage both for hors and armes', and that 'There is not a craftsman to make a steel bonnet in al the land lyke as quhen theys wes no smyth in Israel', D. Laing (ed.), *Correspondence of Sir Robert Kerr, first Earl of Ancrum and his Son William, third Earl of Lothian* (2 vols, Edinburgh, 1975), ii, 482.

6. N. Macdougall, *James III: A Political Study* (Edinburgh, 1982), 92–8.

7. For the Elizabethan army, see C. G. Cruikshank, *Elizabeth's Army* (Oxford, 1966), where he argues that England could not afford this level of military expense; L. Boynton, *The Elizabethan Militia 1558–1638* (London, 1967). Both the army and the militia were far from satisfactory when compared with France or Spain, but the military power they represented was still vastly greater than that of Scotland.

8. James did use English naval power to extend crown control of the western islands and highlands: Lee, *Government by Pen*, 77. The disaster of the Bishops' Wars was largely due to the quarrel between Charles I and his English Parliament; his military strategy of crushing Scottish dissent with English or Irish aid was sound enough. During the 1640s the Scots were well aware of the need for closer union with England in order to ensure some control over the English army and thus improve their security from arbitrary rule: C. L. Hamilton, 'Anglo-Scottish militia negotiations, March–April 1646', *SHR*, xliii (1963), 86–8. Later seventeenth century

governments were prepared to employ similar tactics and, for example, in 1677 and 1679 Charles II mobilised troops in England and Ireland to help put down the Covenanters, while English troops were again put on alert in 1707 during the union debates: J. Childs, *The Army of Charles II* (London and Toronto, 1976), 200–3; J. R. Elder, *The Highland Host of 1678* (Glasgow, 1914), 20–33; W. Fraser, *The Melvilles Earls of Melville and the Leslies Earls of Leven* (Edinburgh, 1849), ii, 211: Marlborough to Leven, 7 December 1706. Similarly Scottish regiments in the Netherlands were used in 1685 to help crush Monmouth's rebellion: C. Dalton, *English Army Lists and Commission Registers 1661–1714* (6 vols, London, 1960), ii, ix–x.

9. Robertson, *Militia*, 22–6. Fletcher also believed that both Charles II and James VII had come close to imposing arbitrary military rule on Scotland because of the combination of rule from London and a standing army. This anti-military tradition surfaced during the Restoration period itself in the 'Sanquhar Declaration' and in Renwick's 'Apologetical Declaration'.

10. H. A. Lloyd, *The State, France, and the Sixteenth Century* (London, 1983), 146–168. On the Tudor monopoly of violence see L. Stone, *Crisis of the Aristocracy 1558–1642* (Oxford, 1965), 199–270, and for doubts about it, M. E. James, *English Politics and the Concept of Honour, 1485–1642: Past and Present Supplement*, 3 (1978), 44, and K. Wrightson, *English Society, 1580–1680* (London, 1982), 130–1.

11. A history of the Covenanting state has yet to be written, but one gets the right impression of its authoritarian and more centralised workings in D. Stevenson, *The Scottish Revolution, 1637–44* (Newton Abbot, 1975); D. Stevenson, *Revolution and Counter Revolution in Scotland, 1644–51* (London, 1977); D. Stevenson (ed.), *The Government of Scotland Under the Covenanters 1637–1651*, SHS Fourth Series, 18 (Edinburgh, 1982); W. H. Makey, *The Church of the Covenant, 1637–1651* (Edinburgh, 1979).

12. V. G. Kiernan, 'Foreign Mercenaries and Absolute Monarchy', in T. Aston (ed.), *Crisis in Europe 1560–1660* (London, 1965), 131. Also Anderson, *Lineages of the Absolutist State*, 29–33, where he argues that 'Absolutist states . . . were machines built overwhelmingly for the battlefield'. However, it is worth bearing in mind the conclusion to J. R. Hale's *War and Society in Renaissance Europe, 1450–1620* (London, 1985), 252, that 'war conditioned but did not create those changes that occurred between 1450 and 1629'. This point probably has a relevance to Scotland long after 1620. See too C. Oman, *A History of War in the Sixteenth Century* (London, 1937); A. Corvisier, *Armies and Society in Europe 1494–1789* (Bloomington, Indiana and London, 1979); M. Roberts, 'The Military Revolution, 1560–1660', in M. Roberts, *Essays in Swedish History* (London, 1967), 195–225; G. Parker, 'The Military Revolution, 1560–1660 — A Myth?' in *Journal of Modern History*, xlvii (1976), 195–214; J. Childs, *Armies and Warfare in Europe, 1648–1789* (Manchester, 1982).

13. For example William, 6th Earl of Morton, raised a regiment to fight under Buckingham at La Rochelle in 1627: J. Balfour Paul (ed.), *The Scots*

Peerage (9 vols, Edinburgh, 1904–14), vi, 376; J. Ferguson (ed.), *Papers Illustrating the History of the Scots Brigade in the Services of the United Netherlands* (3 vols, Edinburgh, 1899, 1901), i, 396–405. See too the part played by Mackay's regiment as part of the British involvement in the Thirty Years War: E. A. Beller, 'The Military Expedition of Sir Charles Morgan to Germany, 1627–9', *EHR*, 43 (1928), 528–39.

14. B. Lenman, *The Jacobite Rebellions in Britain 1689–1746* (London, 1980), 284.

15. Robertson, *Militia*, 5, where he suggests that the wars helped destroy much that remained of the martial strain in Scottish society, while enhancing the quasi-military nature of the state. While agreeing with the latter point I have some doubts about the former. Of course the martial spirit was prolonged by the revival of chivalry in the later sixteenth century and the advent of the duel: A. B. Ferguson, *The Chivalrie Tradition in Renaissance England* (Cranbury, 1986); V. G. Kiernan, *The Duel in European History* (Oxford, 1988), 68–115. See also K. M. Brown, 'Gentlemen and thugs in seventeenth century Britain', *History Today*, 40 (1990), 27–32.

16. In 1667 Charles was allowed to retain two troops of lifeguards and eight companies of foot: Donaldson, *James V–James VII*, 368. By 1688 the English army had grown to 31,000, and that in Ireland to 8,938. The Scottish army was not only the smallest, but it also had the highest rate of desertion. For its size see Childs, *Army of Charles II*, 197; J. Childs, *The Army, James II and the Glorious Revolution* (Manchester, 1980), 1–4. On the Irish army see J. C. Becket, 'The Irish Armed Forces, 1660–1685' in J. Bossy and P. Jupp (eds.), *Essays Presented to Michael Roberts* (Belfast, 1976), 41–53. While the army in Scotland was almost universally derided the militia has been praised, and was probably better than its English counterpart: Childs, *Army of Charles II*, 198. It numbered some 20,000 foot and 2,000 horse. The comparatively better quality of the militia over the army is hardly surprising given the long tradition of locally based and noble led defence organization. In the highlands too local lordship remained essential to effective policing: B. Lenman, *The Jacobite clans of the Great Glen 1650–1784* (London, 1984), 28–73.

17. Wormald, *Lords and Men*; Brown, *Bloodfeud*.

18. For elites in general see T. Bottomore, *Elites and Society* (Harmondsworth, 1982), and on military elites in particular which he sees as having a modernising role in new states, 105–7. On the question of elites, class and cognitive definitions of nobility, particularly in relation to military service, see T. M. Barker, 'Armed Service and Nobility: General Features' in T. M. Barker, *Army, Aristocracy and Nobility: Essays on War, Society and Government in Austria, 1618–1780* (New York, 1982), 122–36. On the importance of the military in the development of the French state see D. C. Baxter, *Servants of the State: French Intendants of the Army 1630–70* (Urbana, 1976); C. Jones, 'The Military Revolution and the Professionalisation of the French Army under the Ancien Regime' in M. Duffy (ed.), *The Military Revolution and the State 1500–1800* (Exeter, 1980), 29–48.

Kiernan, *State and Society*, 265, argued that 'The coming of the standing army was inseparable from that of later, more fully developed absolutism'.

19. Brown, *Bloodfeud*, 'Part Three: Uprooting the Feud'. This, of course, was part of a wider European demilitarisation: see Hale, *War and Society*, 91. R. Mitchison, *Lordship to Patronage: Scotland 1603-1745* (London, 1983), sees this as the major theme of the seventeenth century, but fails to describe adequately how it occurred.

20. *Bloodfeud*, 'Conclusion', especially 270. Although the decline was a long-drawn-out one, and Robertson is right to point out that 'The end of lordship in Scotland is a subject still virtually unexplored', *Militia*, 6. Robertson too believes that the undermining of Scotland's 'martial strain' came about not as a result of government initiatives, but as a result of social pressures. I would agree with this, but would add ideological changes. For the Highlands where a localised and private violence continued to flourish, see G. A. H. McCoy, *Scots Mercenary Forces in Ireland, 1565-1603* (Dublin, 1937); D. Stevenson, *Alastair MacColla and the Highland Problem in the Sixteenth Century* (Edinburgh, 1980); P. Hopkins, *Glencoe and the end of the Highland War* (Edinburgh, 1986); and J. M. Hill, *Celtic Warfare 1595-1763* (Edinburgh, 1986), which is much less satisfying.

21. G. N. Clark, 'War as a Collision of Societies', in G. N. Clark, *War and Society in the Seventeenth Century* (Cambridge, 1958), 73-4.

22. Robertson, *Militia*, 5; Clarke, 'The Analogy of the Duel' in Clarke, *War and Society*, 29-51. H. Kamen, *European Society 1500-1700* (London, 1984), 303, has made the point that 'No modern state could wage war properly without training an officer class, and in every case the increase in military activity boosted rather than diminished the power of the traditional elite'.

23. E. Schalk, *From Valor to Pedigree. Ideas of Nobility in France in the Sixteenth and Seventeenth Centuries* (Princeton, 1986), 3-21. Thus one finds Montaigne writing that 'the proper, sole and essential life for one of the nobility in France is the life of the soldier', quoted in M. Keen, *Chivalry* (New Haven and London, 1984), 249. In fact the emphasis on the military function of nobility contrasted with the actual role the French nobility played in war: Schalk, *Valor to Pedigree*, 35. See too D. Bitton, *The French Nobility in Crisis 1560-1640* (Stanford, 1969), 25-41. Unfortunately the ideas which sustained the nobility in seventeenth-century Scotland have not yet been explored, indeed the whole subject of the nobility in that century is much less understood than the period up until 1603 and after 1707. Certainly the military role of the nobility has received little comment, although there are numerous biographies of the more important soldiers of the century. See for example, H. R. Rubinstein, *Captain Luckless, James 1st Duke of Hamilton 1606-1649* (Edinburgh, 1975); E. J. Cowan, *Montrose: For Covenant and King* (London, 1977); C. S. Terry, *The Life and Campaigns of Alexander Leslie, first Earl of Leven* (London, 1899); C. S. Terry, *John Graham of Claverhouse Viscount of Dundee 1648-1689* (London, 1905); P. Dickson, *Red John of the*

Battles: John 2nd Duke of Argyll and 1st Duke of Greenwich 1680-1743 (London, 1973); and Dalton, *Scots Army*, contains short biographies of the commanders-in-chief of the Restoration army. There are also a number of military memoirs for the period, for example, *Memoirs of His own Life and Times by Sir James Turner, 1632-1670* (Edinburgh, 1829); A. Crichton (ed.), *The Life and Diary of Lieutenant Colonel John Blackader of the Cameronian Regiment* (Edinburgh, 1824); H. Mackay, *Memoirs of the War Carried on in Scotland and Ireland* (Bannatyne Club, Edinburgh, 1833).

24. D. Laing (ed.), *The Letters and Journals of Robert Baillie* (3 vols, Edinburgh, 1841), i, 195.

25. C. S. Terry (ed.), *Papers Relating to the Army of the Solemn League and Covenant, 1643-1647*, SHS, xvi (2 vols, Edinburgh, 1917), i, xxiv–xxv. However, when the army was remodelled in 1647 the marquis of Argyll was the only peer among the fifteen colonels. For a detailed analysis of the covenanting armies, see E. M. Furgol, *A Regimental History of the Covenanting Armies 1639-1651* (Edinburgh, 1990).

26. W. Fraser, *Memorials of the Montgomeries Earls of Eglinton* (Edinburgh, 1859), ii, 291.

27. Baillie, *Letters and Journals*, i, 213-14. Leslie's commission of May 1639 gave him full command over the army and its officers 'of what qualitie, degrei or estait so ever they be', Fraser, *Melvilles*, 162–4. See too Terry, *Army*, 3–12 for the 'Articles and Ordinances of War' which clearly reflected a hierarchy in which authority was wholly derived from military office.

28. *Letters and State Papers Chiefly addressed to George, Earl of Melville Secretary of State for Scotland 1689-91* (Bannatyne Club, Edinburgh, 1843), 138–9.

29. This point is made in Childs, *The Army, James II and the Glorious Revolution*, 27–8: 'The old distinctions between "gentlemen" officers and professionals was fast disappearing'. See too I. Roy, 'The Profession of Arms' in W. Prest (ed.), *The Professions in Early Modern England* (London, 1987), 181–219. In a European context this was a process which had been going on since the creation of a French standing army in the later fifteenth century: Keen, *Chivalry*, 243, 247. 'It was no longer enough for a man to be noble and entitled to the arms that his ancestor had borne in battle for him to call himself a warrior. If a man claimed to be a soldier, he must belong to some identifiable martial unit, otherwise he was not a soldier. Thus the conception of an estate of knighthood, with a general commission to uphold justice and protect the weak, was being pared down into the conception of the officer whose business it is to fight the King's enemies'. In exchange the crown was forced to allow 'the indulgence of noble aspirations, including, of course, the martial aspirations of nobility'. Hence, 'Martially, the officer and gentleman of the post-medieval period felt, and was encouraged to feel, much the same sort of pride in service to his king as the knight had taken in the service of his natural lord and his order'.

30. *Scots Peerage*, viii, 256-60.

31. I. R. Bartlett, 'Scottish mercenaries in Europe, 1570-1640: A Study in

attitudes and politics', in *Scottish Tradition*, xiii (1984-5), 15-24; Terry, *Leven*, 15, contrasts Leven, the professional soldier who was obedient to the state with Cromwell, the amateur soldier who saw the army as a means to dominate the state. This idea that mercenaries/professionals were creatures of the state surfaces more sinisterly in the careers of Thomas Dalziel and William Drummond, whose harsh treatment of Covenanters under Restoration governments was blamed on their service in Russia. Barker has argued that in Britain there was no role for the foreign military entrepreneur and mercenary who was 'a mainstay of the centralised bureaucratic state which began to appear in the sixteenth and seventeenth centuries in the form of monarchical Absolutism': T. M. Barker, 'Absolutism and Military Entrepreneurship: Hapsburg Models', in Barker, *Army, Aristocracy, Monarchy*, 1. See too Kiernan, 'Mercenaries and Monarchy', 117-40; M. Howard, *War in European History* (Oxford, 1976); Roy, 'The Profession of Arms'. For the influence of the Dutch army in generating military professionalism, M. D. Feld, 'Middle-Class Society and the Rise of Military Professionalism: the Dutch Army 1589-1609', in Feld, *The Structure of Violence*, 169-203, and for the Anglo-Dutch Brigade, Childs, *The Army, James II and the Glorious Revolution*, 84-5.

32. For Forbes, *Scots Peerage*, iv, 62; for Forth, *ibid.*, iv, 103-5; for Ethyvin, *ibid.*, iii, 591-3; for the Munros, Dalton, *Scots Army*, 35. For the Scots in Swedish service, see P. Dukes, 'The Leslie Family in the Swedish Period (1630-5) of the Thirty Years War', in *European Studies Review*, xii, No. 4 (1982).

33. For Buccleuch, W. Fraser, *The Scotts of Buccleuch* (Edinburgh, 1828), i, 235-6, 253-9. For Colyear, *Scots Peerage*, vii, 88-93; and Livingston, *ibid.*, viii, 374-6; and see Ferguson, *Scots Brigade*, for other Scottish noblemen in Dutch service.

34. For Dumbarton, *Scots Peerage*, iii, 216-17 and Dalton, *Scots Army*, 67-9. Also of interest is C. T. Atkinson, 'Charles II's Regiments in France, 1672-1678', *Journal of the Society for Army Historical Research [JSAHS]*, 24 (1946), 53-65. Another nobleman in French employ was James, 9th Lord Sommerville, who spent three years in Louis XIII's guards before going on to serve in the Venetian army, and finally putting his skills to use for the Covenanters in 1639: *Scots Peerage*, viii, 28-9. In addition one finds Alexander, 2nd Lord Spynie, and Donald Mackay of Strathnaver both fighting under Christian IV of Denmark and later joining Charles I in the civil war: *Scots Peerage*, i, 346-51; vii, 167-8. For eastern Europe see J. W. Barnhill and P. Dukes, 'North-east Scots in Muscovy in the seventeenth century', *Northern Scotland*, i, No. 1 (1972); P. Dukes, 'Problems concerning the departure of Scottish soldiers from seventeenth century Muscovy', in T. C. Smout (ed.), *Scotland and Europe 1200-1850* (Edinburgh, 1986). Obviously Scots mercenaries would have preferred service at home, but there were simply not enough opportunities before 1638, or again between 1660-89; see the letter by Patrick Gordon of Auchleuchries in 1669: Dukes, 'Departure of Scottish soldiers', 147.

35. C. Barnett, *Britain and her Army, 1509-1970* (London, 1970), 53; Beller, 'Expedition', 533.

36. J. W. Fortescue, *A History of the British Army* (13 vols, London, 1910–30), i, 160, 296–7. However, following the Indulgence of 1687 the Scots officers demanded that command of the brigade be taken out of the king's hands and be transferred to trustworthy 'British' officers: Childs, *The Army, James II and the Glorious Revolution*, 129–30. The Netherlands was not the only place where Scots and English professional officers fought together; one finds this for example in Denmark in 1626–7: Fortescue, *British Army*, 173–9. See too Charles II's grant to the earl of Castlemaine allowing him to raise men in England, Scotland or Ireland for service with any prince or state in friendship with him: Childs, *Army of Charles II*, 173.

37. Bottomore, *Elites and Society*, 106, believes that new armies in the contemporary world are also 'one of the most effective channels of upward social mobility'.

38. See Vagts, *History of Militarism* (New York, 1959), 47, on this theme.

39. Grant, *Independence and Nationhood*, 120–43. Contrast this with the unsettled conditions in the later sixteenth century: Brown, *Bloodfeud*, 65–80.

40. For a general discussion of this in a European context see Vagts, *Militarism*, 49–52, where he argues that the new standing armies of the period were created 'for the employment and sustenance of a feudal class which could not make a living otherwise'. This is probably too negative, and is based on an exaggerated idea of noble impoverishment in the sixteenth and seventeenth centuries. However Keen, *Chivalry*, 244–5, also draws attention to the economic factors which pushed lesser noblemen in fifteenth century France into the army. For the underlying economic problems of the Scottish nobility see K. M. Brown, 'Noble Indebtedness in Scotland between the Reformation and the Revolution', *Historical Research*, 60 (1989), 60–75, and K. M. Brown, 'Aristocratic Finances and the Origins of the Scottish Revolution', *EHR*, civ (1989), 46–87. Apart from the dangers of being killed, maimed or taken prisoner, a military career was often financially precarious; see e.g., G. S. Thomson, 'A Scots officer in the Low Countries, 1714', *SHR*, 27 (1948), 65–70.

41. For Argyll, *Scots Peerage*, i, 346–51; Forbes was in the Swedish army: *ibid.*, iv, 62; for Lothian, *ibid.*, v, 448–73; Buccleuch fought for the States general: Fraser, *Buccleuch*, i, 253–9; St. Colme was in Swedish service: *Scots Peerage*, vii, 395; as was Crawford, *ibid.*, iii, 33–4; Sommerville was in France and then Venice: *ibid.*, viii, 28–9; for Linlithgow, *ibid.*, v, 447; Dalton, *Scots Army*, 29–34. However, governments were notoriously obstructive when it came to paying for military service; see for example the difficulties the Buccleuchs experienced in the Netherlands: Ferguson, *Scots Brigade*, i, 256–69, 378–95.

42. J. Holmes, 'Introduction: Post-Revolution Britain and the Historian', in J. Holmes, *Britain After the Glorious Revolution* (London, 1969), 5; J. H. Plumb, *The Growth of Political Stability in England 1675–1725* (Harmondsworth, 1973), 125–6; A. Bruce, *The Purchase System in the*

British Army, 1660-1870 (London, 1980); R. E. Scouller, 'Purchase of commissions and promotions', *JSAHR*, 62 (1984), 217-226. There was also a huge increase in the size of the army from 23,000 in 1688 to 120,000 in 1706-11, bringing with it an increase in the number of officers from around 300 to something like 4,000. After 1712 the system of half pay greatly increased the stability of a military career: S. Holmes, *Augustan England: Professions, State and Society, 1680-1730* (London, 1982), 241-2, 265-6.

43. W. Fraser, *The Douglas Book: Memoirs of the House of Douglas and Angus* (Edinburgh, 1885), iv, 382-6.

44. Drummond (Strathallan) was the son of Lord Maderty: *Scots Peerage*, viii, 217-22; Douglas (Dumbarton) of the marquis of Douglas: *ibid.*, iii, 216-17; Hamilton (Orkney) of the duchess of Hamilton: *ibid.*, vi, 578-80; Murray (Dunmore) of the marquis of Atholl: *ibid.*, iii, 383-5. See too I. Grimble, *Chief of Mackay* (London, 1965), which demonstrates the economic pressures on a highland chief which forced him to take up arms on the continent under Charles I.

45. For Forth, *Scots Peerage*, iv, 103-5; for Eythvin, *ibid.*, iii, 591-3; for MacDonell, *ibid.*, v, 562-5; for Middleton, *ibid.*, vi, 183-5; for Newark, *ibid.*, vi, 440-2. General Alexander Hamilton was not raised to the peerage, but it is an interesting comment on the period that while his father, the 1st earl of Haddington, made his fortune in law and as a government official, his eldest son was killed when the magazine in his castle exploded and his younger son became a soldier in the Swedish army: *ibid.*, 366-8.

46. For Dumbarton, *Scots Peerage*, iii, 216-17; for Churchill, *ibid.*, ii, 532.

47. For Dunmore, *Scots Peerage*, iii, 383-5; for Strathallan, *ibid.*, viii, 217-22; for Dundee, *ibid.*, iii, 324-31.

48. Holmes, *Augustan England*, 262-74; for Orkney, *Scots Peerage*, vi, 578-80; for Teviot, *ibid.*, viii, 374-6; for Portmore, *ibid.*, 88-93.

49. Clark has seen in the vast growth of military patronage in the seventeenth century a major contribution to what he has called the institutionalisation of war: Clark, 'War as an Institution', in Clark, *War and Society*, 1-28.

50. W. Fraser, *The Red Book of Menteith* (Edinburgh, 1880), ii, 177-9. For similar letters see *Leven and Melville Papers*, 61, 256.

51. Fraser, *Melville and Leven*, ii, 189-94. Even more cloying was the earl of Crawford's letter to Godolphin in January 1706 reminding him of 'the assurance I had of your assistance in my favors on the first promotione of the green ribbon': *Report of the Historical Manuscripts Commission on the Laing Manuscripts preserved in Edinburgh University* (London, 1914, 1925), ii, 125.

52. Childs, *The Army, James II and the Glorious Revolution*, 39.

53. Childs, *The Army, James II and the Glorious Revolution*, 25-6, 180-4; Dalton, *Army Lists*, ii, 210-20; C. D. Ellestad, 'The mutinies of 1689', *JSAHR*, 53 (1975), 4-21. Of the noble officers in the army Lord Livingston, the commander of the Scots Troop of the Life Guards, was imprisoned in 1689 for his suspected Jacobitism, and William, Earl of Buchan, the

guidon of the troop, died in Stirling Castle in 1695 for his loyalty to James. In the Royal Regiment of Horse Colonel John Graham, Viscount Dundee, was killed at Killiecrankie, and James, 2nd Earl of Ogilvy, Colin, 3rd Earl of Balcarres, and Lord William Douglas along with at least two other non-noble captains were all Jacobites. The colonel of the Royal Regiment of Dragoons, Charles, Earl of Dunmore, and at least two of his six captains were loyal to James. There were no noblemen in Buchan's or Wachop's regiments of foot, but both colonels were Jacobites. Of the general officers James, Earl of Arran, a brigadier-general, and his brother Charles, Earl of Selkirk, colonel of the horse, were both opposed to the revolution. Lord William Murray, who held a captain's commission, was also pro-James. The only Scottish colonel to support William of Orange was Colonel James Douglas of the Scots Foot Guards, and the only nobleman in that regiment, Lord Carnwath, was also pro-William. The other noble officer to desert James VII was James, Earl of Drumlanrig, Dundee's lieutenant-colonel, who switched sides on 24 November 1688 after dining with the king.

54. *Scots Peerage*, i, 263; Dalton, *Army Lists*, ii, xxii (for 1692 plot); *Leven and Melville Papers*, 434.

55. *HMC Laing*, ii, 92–3. Even in the lower ranks the level of ideological awareness appears to have been higher in Scottish and Irish regiments than in English ones, which showed a more 'professional' attitude: R. E. Scouller, *The Armies of Queen Anne* (Oxford, 1966), 290–1. However, there is no evidence of Scottish regiments being stiffened with English contingents as occurred in Ireland after Colonel Blood's 1663 conspiracy: J. C. Beckett, 'The Irish Armed Forces, 1660–1685', in J. Bossy and P. Jupp (eds.), *Essays presented to Michael Roberts* (Belfast, 1976), 44–5.

56. Childs, *The Army, James II and the Glorious Revolution*, 94, highlights this effect of professionalism in England. The army had by then come a long way from its early days in the 1660s when it was little more than 'a weak and often poorly run police force': Childs, *Army of Charles II*, 14.

57. J. Childs, 'The army and the Oxford parliament of 1681', *EHR*, 94 (1979), 580–7; Childs, *The Army, James II and the Glorious Revolution*, 111–12; Elder, *Highland Host*, 109–18; Donaldson, *James V–James VII*, 367.

58. For Linlithgow, *Scots Peerage*, v, 447, and for his son who was also in the army, *ibid.*, 448–9; for Strathmore, *ibid.*, viii, 301–2; for Winton, *ibid.*, viii, 601–2.

59. For Middleton, *Scots Peerage*, vi, 183–5; Dalton, *Scots Army*, 5–10; see too A. C. Biscoe, *The Earls of Middleton, Lords of Clermont and Fettercairn* (London, 1876), 11–133; for Rothes, *Scots Peerage*, viii, 299–301; Dalton, *Scots Army*, 11–16; for Linlithgow, *Scots Peerage*, v, 147; Dalton, *Scots Army*, 29–34.

60. Fraser, *Eglinton*, ii, 329–31. During the 1640s committees of war had been forced to recognise the same restraints. However, what is unclear is how strong the loyalty between lord and man now was. In the early seventeenth century the military governors of France still controlled enormous patronage in their localities, but they were unable to translate it

into political muscle in rebellion. In effect the governor was little more than a conduit for royal patronage, their clientage networks having little of the personal loyalty of lordship: R. H. Harding, *Anatomy of a Power Elite: The Provincial Governors of Early Modern France* (New Haven, 1978), 202–4.

61. Dalton, *Army Lists*, iii, 38, 85–98. Raising regiments for the crown was of course one good way of getting a colonelcy, assuming one could get the regiment put on the government pay-roll, and it was seen as an expression of loyalty. For example, in the 1680s the earl of Mar raised what became the Scots Fusiliers: *ibid.*, v, 626.

62. G. Parker, *The Army of Flanders and the Spanish Road 1567–1659* (Cambridge, 1972), 27–35.

63. H. Horowitz, *Parliament, Policy and Politics in the reign of William III* (Manchester, 1977), 249. At the Battle of the Boyne William's army had been composed of English, Irish, Scottish, Dutch, Danish, Swedish, Prussian and French Huguenot troops. By 1699 the three highest paid officers in the English army were all naturalised foreigners, the duke of Schomberg, the earl of Portland and the earl of Grantham: G. Davies, 'The reduction of the army after the Peace of Ryswick, 1697', *JSAHR*, 28 (1950), 16, note 5.

64. Childs, *Army of Charles II*, 46, 196; Scouller, *Armies of Anne*, 83.

65. Childs, *Army of Charles II*, 64. However, it was a Scot, Sir James Turner, who was 'the principal British military theorist of the period', Turner having written *Pallas Armata: Military Essays of the Ancient Greek, Roman and Modern Art of War* in 1683. In addition, Viscount Teviot wrote the *Exercise of the Foot, with the Evolution according to the Words of Command etc* in 1693: Childs, *Army of Charles II*, 63; *Scots Peerage*, viii, 374–6. Military integration is briefly discussed in B. Levack, *The Formation of the British State: England, Scotland, and the Union 1603–1707* (Oxford, 1987), 188–9.

66. Horowitz, *Parliament, Policy and Politics*, 106–7. While race clearly was a problem, religion was more likely to create prejudices at this time, as was the case in the affair of the Portsmouth Captains: E. J. Priestly, 'The Portsmouth Captains', *JSAHR*, 153–64; J. Miller, 'Catholic officers in the later Stuart army' in *EHR*, lxxxxviii (1973), 35–53.

67. Dalton, *Army Lists*, i. Jedburgh's regiment was later incorporated into the Tangier Regiment of which he was the colonel until his death in action in Tangier in 1663. Among the few who did get English commands under Charles were the earls of Middleton and Dumbarton. With only some 200–300 military commissions available, the Scots had little hope of competing with the English for places in their own army: Holmes, *Augustan England*, 240.

68. Dalton, *Army Lists*, ii, 89–92.

69. *Scots Peerage*, iii, 542–3. Henry, 3rd Lord Cardross, received the colonelcy of a regiment of dragoons as well as being given a seat on the privy council and the office of general of the mint: *Scots Peerage*, ii, 36–7. Others of William's officers then serving in the Dutch army were Major-General

Hugh Mackay, who was later killed at Steinkirk, and Colonel David Colyear (Portmore), 'one of the best foot officers in the world': Dalton, *Army Lists*, ii, xxix.

70. *Scots Peerage*, iii, 38.
71. *Ibid.*, viii, 151–2.
72. Dalton, *Army Lists*, v, 1–12; H. F. Johnston, 'The Scots army in the reign of Anne', *T.R.H.S.*, fifth series, 3 (1953), 1–2.
73. Dalton, *Army Lists*, v, part ii. At Malplaquet in 1709 there were twenty-five general officers, of whom ten were Scots and three Irish: *ibid.*, 297–357.
74. Scouller, *Armies of Anne*, 1–79; J. Hayes, 'Scottish Officers in the British Army, 1714-63', *SHR*, xxxviii (1958), 385–7; I. F. Burton and A. N. Newman, 'Promotion in the Eighteenth-Century Army' in *EHR*, lxxviii (1963). The absence of a military academy may have retarded the evolution of a self-conscious awareness of their identity among the officer elite, although in the early eighteenth century the Life Guards did briefly fulfil this role in a very limited way: Childs, *Armies and Warfare*, 94–5.
75. Clark, 'War and the European Community', in Clark, *War and Society*, 97–8, argues the general case for this process.
76. Rubinstein, *Luckless*, 113.
77. Rubinstein, *Luckless*, 31, 200. Another Scottish commander, General Mackay, was more understanding in 1689 and after Killiecrankie he commended his English regiments as 'very well inclined and ready for their Majesties service, as all the English forces which served with me this yeare have showen themselves': Mackay, *Memoirs*, 267.
78. Rubinstein, *Luckless*, 207.
79. R. Ashton, *The English Civil War, Conservatism and Revolution 1603–1649* (London, 1979), 231 and 409, note 36; C. H. Firth, *Cromwell's Army* (London, 1902), 47; C. Hill, *God's Englishman: Oliver Cromwell and the English Revolution* (Harmondsworth, 1975), 74. Religion was the ostensible difference between Cromwell and the Scots, but the undertones of racism are fairly obvious. However, on the dismissal of the Scots officers see M. A. Kishlansky, *The Rise of the New Model Army* (Cambridge, 1979), 49 and 301, note 111, where he shows that many of them wanted to leave. The royalist army contained sixteen Scottish officers, including Patrick Ruthven, 1st Earl of Forth, the c-in-c 1642-4: P. R. Newman, *Royalist Officers in England and Wales 1642–1660* (New York and London, 1981).
80. See for example, C. Mulligan, 'The Scottish Alliance and the Committee of Both Kingdoms', *Historical Studies*, xiv (1970), 175–8.
81. Mulligan, 'Scottish Alliance', 178; Childs, *Army of Charles II*, 216; Dalton, *Scots Army*, 32. Childs admits that racial reasons probably explain why the Scots and Irish soldiers had the worst reputations for misbehaviour in England: *The Army, James II and the Glorious Revolution*, 99. See too E. M. Furgol, 'The Military and Ministers as Agents of Presbyterian Imperialism in England and Ireland, 1640-1648', in J. Dwyer, R. A. Mason, A. Murdoch (eds.), *New Perspectives on the Politics and Culture of*

Early Modern Scotland (Edinburgh, 1982), 95–111. However, this was clearly not a problem associated with Irish and Scottish soldiers alone: see L. Boyntoun, 'Martial Law and the Petition of Right', *EHR*, 79 (1964), 255–84.

82. Dalton, *Scots Army*, 49.
83. W. Fraser, *The Annandale Family Book of the Johnstones* (Edinburgh, 1894), ii, 149–50. However, Colonel Row's wrath was chiefly directed against the Scottish nobility, 'antient' and 'moderne', for failing to protect Scottish interests. In November 1689 General Mackay wrote to Lord Melville criticising the king's decision to disband some of the Scottish regiments rather than redeploying them in Ireland. 'I think strange', he wrote, 'that the English scruple so much to have Scots sent to Ireland, seeing they can imploy them as they doe other strangers, and send them away when their work is don': Mackay, *Memoirs*, 298. See too Davies, 'Reduction of the Army', 15–28.
84. For Hamilton, *Scots Peerage*, iv, 376–8; for Newburgh, *ibid.*, vi, 452–3; for Dumbarton, *ibid.*, iii, 216–17; for Dunmore, *ibid.*, iii, 383–5; for Argyll, *ibid.*, i, 368–76; for Orkney, *ibid.*, vi, 578–80. For the Abercorn Hamiltons, *ibid.*, i, 43–5, 52–7.
85. See G. S. Holmes, 'The Attack on "The Influence of the Crown" 1702–16', *BIHR*, xxxix (1966), 47–68, esp. 49 and 67; H. Horowitz, 'The Structure of Parliamentary Politics', in Holmes, *Britain After the Glorious Revolution*, 106; Holmes, *Augustan England*, 262–4, 271–2. Around 15% of the House of Commons were army officers at this time: Roy, 'Profession of Arms', 209.
86. Dalton, *Army Lists*, iii–vi and see appendix.

8

MILITIA, FENCIBLE MEN,
AND HOME DEFENCE, 1660–1797

Bruce P. Lenman

The early modern European state, according to Professor Michael Roberts, was exposed between about 1560 and 1660 to a 'Military Revolution' involving dramatic changes not only in strategy and tactics, but also in the sheer scale of warfare in Continental Europe, and in the impact of that warfare on civil society.[1] Roberts' thesis has stood up well to subsequent scholarly testing.[2] It may be that the size of single field armies did not necessarily expand spectacularly compared with the largest armies assembled for a single campaign by some European sovereigns before 1560, but major powers like France and Spain became capable of deploying several such armies simultaneously as they fought on more than one front. Above all, the period 1560 to 1660 saw a decisive move into the era of the standing army. In the words of G. N. Clark, whose remarkable volume on *The Seventeenth Century*, originally published in 1929, anticipated so much of modern scholarship:

> One after another the princes began to keep standing forces, and by the time of the wars of Louis XIV it was normal for a sovereign to have an army in the winter and in time of peace.[3]

Thus the early modern warfare state was born, carrying a formidable military apparatus on what was usually an inadequate and inefficient fiscal base. Though money-saving procedures were rapidly evolved, such as paying off a significant number of private soldiers in peacetime, and keeping only the officer cadres, some on half-pay, these early modern European armies could pose horrendous problems for their paymasters. A situation calling for a scale of mobilisation out of the ordinary could strain the resources of a state to breaking point, and if such mobilisation was achieved and proved successful, there was always the nightmare possibility that the successful military machine might turn into an uncontrollable or irremovable juggernaut, simply because the ruling class who ran the state could not face the political or monetary price of demobilisation. It was crucial to the long-term success of the American Revolution that Americans managed to demobilise the armies they had created to win their independence from Westminster's army. The bright promise of the early French Revolution was, on the other hand, blighted by the incubus of the army establishment originally created to repel the invasion of the 'Predatory Powers': Austria and Prussia. Only that lucky event in French history — Napoleon's Russian campaign of 1812 — finally rid the French of most of the Grande Armée by involuntary demobilisation, and set up the fall of the megalomaniac dictator who commanded it.

The British Isles can scarcely be said to have participated in the mainstream of the 'Military Revolution'. The standing armed forces of James VI and I were risible by Continental standards. Those of Charles I were not much better, and it is a fact that civil war finally broke out in England in March 1642 over the question of control of the militia, the only numerically significant body of armed men in the realm.[4] In the end, the groups of politicians at Westminster who claimed (rather unconvincingly in the absence of a monarch) to be a parliament, reluctantly raised professional armies capable of winning their struggle with Charles I, only to find themselves caught after victory by the insoluble problem of an army which they could not dispense with, for both financial and political reasons. Much the most important development during the series of ad-hoc decisions which restored Charles II to his English and Irish thrones in 1660 was the passage by the Convention Parliament in England in the spring of 'An Act for the Speedy Provision of Money for Disbanding and Paying Off the Forces of this Kingdom both by Land and Sea'. With full arrears, the cost of this exercise was £835,819–8s–10d. The representatives of the ruling classes assembled in the Convention Parliament regarded the taxation needed to raise the necessary money as a necessary but bitter pill. In fact, they only voted taxes capable of raising £560,000, and Charles II had to provide the balance of nearly £376,000 out of his own pocket. He was wise to stump up, for nothing pleased the conservative Englishmen who restored him to his thrones better than the experience of not having to raise the £55,000 per month which had latterly been needed to sustain the army of the Cromwellian Protectorate.[5]

Scotland in 1660 had at least no such comparable problem when it recovered its old identity and institutions with the collapse of the Commonwealth regime which had incorporated all three kingdoms of the British Isles in one body politic. The unprecedented Covenanting standing armies raised to fight the Bishops' Wars, the War of the Three Kingdoms, the Second Civil War and the final Anglo-Scottish conflict of 1650–51 had all been stood down in the end by a series of shattering defeats, starting with those inflicted on the armies of the Estates by Montrose and Alasdair MacColla in 1644–45, and then going through the rout of the Engagers' army at Preston to the defeat at Dunbar, and the final disasters of Worcester and Inverkeithing. There was a standing army in Scotland in 1660, technically the army of the Commonwealth, but in fact the remains of an English army of occupation, most of which had marched south with General George Monck. It is clear from an undated petition of 1660 to Charles II from 'The Noblemen, Gentlemen and Burgesses of Scotland, met at London' that the speedy removal of these troops was regarded as profoundly desirable by the Scottish political nation. The petition urged 'that Your Majestie employ such of Your Scots subjects as You sall think fit for securing of the garisons and the peace of the kingdome'. This should certainly not be construed as a request for the creation of a substantial Scottish national standing army. A massive reduction in the permanent military presence in Scotland was universally desired, and the most astute of the London Scots, John Maitland, earl (later duke) of Lauderdale, had no difficulty in persuading Charles II that the four great Cromwellian citadels in Scotland — Ayr, Perth, Inverness and Leith — should be disposed of and slighted since the royal government could not garrison them and did not want them to be available for anyone else. There was delay in removing two regiments of foot and a troop of horse, which units remained in Scotland under the command of Major General Sir Thomas Morgan, mostly in the Leith citadel, until the spring of 1662. The explanation for this delay was that in the spring of 1661 there were still £30,000 of arrears due to English troops in Scotland outstanding. The Scots parliament appealed to Charles II to deal with this matter which, in due course, he did sufficiently generously for the last English units in Scotland to depart for service in Portugal in the spring of 1662 in good heart.[6]

The Restoration regime in Scotland then and then only had to face up to the question of what sort and scale of military establishment it deemed necessary. It was, of course, a very conservative regime, utterly dominated by the only fully self-conscious social class in the hierarchical society of orders which was early modern Scotland. That self-conscious class was the nobility, thanks to whom it is possible to talk about the class obsessions and interests of a regime under which, in the classic phrase of Gordon Donaldson, 'Office and power lay with the nobles, some of them the very men who had been active against Charles I'.[7] If Walter Makey be right, the nobility had suffered relative loss of economic and social clout in the first half of the seventeenth century.[8] From the period of their Engagement with Charles I in 1647–48, they had been reacting compulsively against that relative decline in their social weight (indeed, only class paranoia of a fairly extreme kind can explain the solidarity of the aristocracy behind a policy stamped with such egregious political and military folly as the Engagement). The Restoration regime in Scotland was therefore a rightist backlash by an angry, greedy nobility which had suffered acutely from the fines and taxation of the Cromwellian occupation which they had done so much to pull down on their own heads. Low taxation tends to be, in real terms, the first priority of such regimes. This can lead to problems, because they are often also committed to expensive military establishments. Napoleon, who stopped the French Revolution dead in its tracks, was driven to an endless search for new frontiers of plunder for his military power-base. President Ronald Reagan, by cutting taxes irresponsibly low whilst spending prodigally on arms, created an appalling fiscal crisis for the United States. Restoration Scotland had no such in-built dilemma. The aristocracy identified the power of a standing army, as it did the power of a clerical élite, with subversive radicalism.

For the clergy, the nobility proposed a diet of the most grovelling erastianism. When James Sharp made his rapid transition from presbyter to archibishop in 1661, he was almost certainly engaging in a damage-limitation exercise and, with the passage of the outrageous Act of Supremacy in 1669, he should perhaps have resigned in the face of such evidence of the relentless extremism of the regime's anti-clericalism.[9] For the standing army, the nobles proposed and implemented an equally drastic regimen: fiscal starvation designed to ensure that Scotland maintained more the ghost than the face of a standing army. The Earl of Middleton, the professional soldier who briefly dominated Scottish politics in the early years of the Restoration, naturally hoped for a permanent military establishment of some size, and had persuaded Charles II to support the idea of 'an Establishment much greater than Scotland ever knew'. In fact, Middleton, whose post as General of all Scottish forces raised or to be raised was totally unprecedented and unnecessary, was an upstart with little affinity or backing among the older Scots nobility. By 1663, he was tottering towards his political downfall, outmanoeuvred by his arch-rival Lauderdale. The latter's henchman, Sir Robert Moray, was clear that the existing standing forces in Scotland were unpopular and irrelevant. They were scarcely large, consisting of two troops of horse, one of which was called the Guards, the other being Middleton's Troop, and six companies of foot. Of course, there also had to be garrisons in the strategic royal castles of Edinburgh (of which Middleton was Captain), Stirling and Dumbarton. Moray suggested that before the Scots Parliament, whose expense and long duration was another noble grievance, was dissolved to make way for the 'good old form of Government by His Majesty's Privy Council', it should pass legislation setting up an adequate Scots Militia. The Scots Estates actually expressed a willingness in 1663 to provide Charles II by these means with 20,000 foot and 2,000 horse.[10]

They did this in an act entitled 'A Humble Tender to his Sacred Majestie of the duetie and loyaltie of his antient Kingdome of Scotland', which offered these troops 'sufficiently armed and furnished with fourty dayes provision' and spelled out, after allocating the several shires their due contingents, that the whole force would be ready 'As they shall be called for by His Majestie to march to any parte of his dominions of Scotland England or Ireland for suppressing any forraigne invasion, intestine trouble or insurrection'. The assumption was that the several contingents would be raised by local nobility. Significantly, when the administrative arrangements proposed dividing up a county, they identified the parts by the names of local magnates, referring to the Earl Marischal's part of Aberdeenshire and to 'the Earle of Seaforth and Lord Lovat their division of Inverness'. Though doubtless sincere, the offer was not, in fact, taken up by Charles II. It served what was probably always its immediate purpose by speeding-up the demise of most of the standing forces.[11]

Ironically, after Middleton resigned his post as Captain-General in Scotland and Captain of Edinburgh Castle in January 1664 and retired to England, the first of his several subsequent military appointments came on 30 June 1666 when he was appointed Lieutenant-General of all the Militia Forces in Kent during the Second Anglo-Dutch War. He died Governor of Tangier in 1673. John Leslie, seventh Earl of Rothes, who succeeded Middleton as Captain-General of the Forces in Scotland, was a politician turned policeman rather than a professional soldier. Middleton's Troop of horse was disbanded, although Rothes was allowed to raise his own troop of eighty cavalrymen in 1664. The rest of the small remaining standing force was mainly used to harass religious dissenters in the western Lowlands.

Historians have lightly used the word 'militia' about the forces which the Estates offered to raise in 1663, but it is doubtful if the Scots had the same common usage of the word as their southern neighbours. It was essentially an English concept. The *Dictionary of the Older Scottish Tongue*, edited by A. J. Aitken, Volume IV, has a definition for 'militia' in which it says, sensibly enough, 'This late 17th c. equivalent of the modern territorial army was levied proportionately from the various shires and burghs in local troops and companies'. But when the *Dictionary of the Older Scottish Tongue* examples are checked, all the early ones are references in Scots sources with an English context. The earliest reference to a Scots town militia company is in the Haddington burgh records for 1671. The Estates did not describe the forces they offered in 1663 as militia. By comparison, Volume II of the *Dictionary of the Older Scottish Tongue* has a far fuller entry under 'Fensabill— fencible' which shows how commonplace is the use of the concept of 'fencible men' in Scottish sources going way back into the medieval period and meaning 'Able for defence; fit for and liable to be called upon, for military service'. Volume IV of the *Scottish National Dictionary* reminds us that 'the usages are mostly Sc.', and starts its examples with the famous 1704 Act of the Parliament of Scotland obliging heritors and burghs to provide arms for all Protestant fencible men. Its second example is a complaint from Glasgow in 1715 about the shortage of arms for its fencible men. How wise Jack Aitken was to imply that texts making regular use of the word 'militia' are in Scotland a late seventeenth-century phenomenon. The Scots thought primarily in terms of a general obligation for all fencible men to serve the King's Majesty's interest in arms, under the command, of course, of their natural superiors.

The Scottish Militia, properly speaking, is an invention of the Restoration era. It has never found a historian for its brief era of true importance. Professor J. R. Western, who wrote a classic work on the English militia in the eighteenth century, would have been an ideal man to tackle the topic. He worked in Edinburgh University for a number of years and, indeed, completed his doctorate during this period. In a footnote in his English militia book, he said in 1965, 'I hope later to write an account of the Scottish militia at the Restoration'.[12] When he died prematurely in November 1970 at the age of 43, whilst holding a chair at Manchester, he had written two more books, one published posthumously, neither of them on the Scots militia. Both his later books were essentially surveys based on wide reading in secondary and printed primary sources. What follows in this present essay is, therefore, no more than a sketch of the more salient developments in an institution which deserves a lengthy chronicle drawing heavily on manuscript sources, in the style of Western's first monograph.[13]

It was the combination of the Second Anglo-Dutch War of 1665–67 and the Pentland Rising which gave birth to a settled militia force in Scotland. The war was unpopular in Scotland, since it served no national purpose and involved a rupture of relations with the Protestant government of a state which was Scotland's principal trading partner overseas. To maintain internal security, a force of 3,000 infantry and eight troops of cavalry were raised, with Generals Thomas Dalziel and William Drummond as first- and second-in-command. Despite these precautions, the Pentland Rising took place late in 1666. Charles II was furious and, apart from a military party led by Lord Rothes, the Scots nobility was averse to the maintenance of these forces after the outbreak of peace. Sir Robert Moray acted as honest broker between King Charles and Scotland.[14] He was careful not to suggest a complete disbanding of the professional forces but, by 6 May 1668, the Scots Privy Council was in receipt of a royal letter announcing Charles's resolve forthwith 'to setle a militia in that our auncient kingdome for the good of our service and preservation of peace ther' on the lines suggested in 1663 but 'only in the shyres which are sett doune in the inclosed list'. The qualification was vitally important.

The shires selected started with Roxburgh and Selkirk, where the Duke of Buccleuch was to be both Colonel of foot and Captain of horse (the lieutenant-colonel of foot was to be Scot of Thirlestane). Berwick followed, with the Earl of Home Colonel of foot and Home of Polwarth Captain of horse. So it went on through the three counties of the Lothians, where the Earl of Lauderdale was to be Colonel of foot in Edinburghshire (the city itself was to have the Lord Provost of Edinburgh as Colonel). Where there were two rival royalist magnates, as in Fife and Kinross, where the Earls of Rothes and Wemyss were both active, they were made conjoint Colonel of foot. The same happened in Perthshire where the Marquis of Montrose and Earl of Atholl shared office. In 'Kincardin and Earl Marshalls part of Aberdein', the Earl Marischal was Colonel of foot with his brother George as his Lieutenant-Colonel. In Argyllshire, the only named officer was Colonel the Earl of Argyll, a man actively loyal to and in favour with Charles II. In short, what was set up was a regionally selective militia commanded by magnates of known political reliability, usually with younger or cadet branches of their houses in subordinate commands. Commissioners of Excise and Justices of the Peace were to bear responsibility for the settling of the militia, which was to be armed like regular soldiers. One-third of the foot were to trail pikes, two-thirds were to be musketeers armed with matchlock muskets. The cavalry were to bear swords and pistols. Yet it was clear that it was never envisaged that these forces would operate much in large units. Division into regiments was regarded as unusual and unlikely. Nor did Charles entirely trust even these trusties. That was why he insisted on matchlocks, forbidding 'fyre armes with snap works' because most of the match in the country was in government arsenals, so he had an additional source of control.

Organising the militia proved less straightforward than expected. Nobody could agree just what was the Earl Marischal's part of Aberdeenshire, so the Privy Council suggested that a militia be settled for Aberdeenshire and Banff. Later in 1668, Council was fuming at the delays caused by those who refused to cooperate in raising and paying for men. It proposed a system of fines for recalcitrants.[15] Despite the appointment of Thomas Elphinstone of Calderhall as Muster-Master General of the Scots militia in March 1671, with instructions to oversee both the construction of muster rolls and the regular mustering of the shire militias, there were always difficulties in making the militia machinery work smoothly. That is hardly surprising. What is striking is the relative efficiency and reliability soon displayed by the militia. By November 1670, the few regular units stationed in Scotland were known to be so far in arrears with their pay that they were in real distress. Equally distressed was the Scots Privy Council when it heard that a company of foot under the command of Colonel Borthwick, stationed in the Canongate, had finally mutinied after corresponding with equally impecunious infantry companies stationed in Glasgow. Council at once wrote to the Duke of Hamilton urging him to mobilise his three militia troops in Hamilton and cooperate with the Glasgow magistrates in containing any trouble. The Edinburgh magistrates were ordered to pursue Borthwick's men with a hundred of their militia. In the event, the mutineers returned to Holyrood Abbey and laid down their arms after the Earl of Linlithgow gave promise of payment. The ringleaders very sensibly vanished, but the official enquiry found 'that the occasion and ryse of the mutiny hes bein for the want of the said pay'. At least the mutiny made the government do something about back pay, but the whole episode shows that a mean-minded ruling class was wise to rely on a militia it controlled and paid only when mustered rather than on professional soldiers whom it habitually cheated.[16]

By the start of 1672, Charles II was committed to a predatory Third Dutch War in which he was to fight as the ally of Louis XIV, whose pensioner he had become. There was such a crippling shortage of funds in England that on 2 January of that year, Charles' minister Thomas Lord Clifford carried through the long-contemplated Stop of the Exchequer, whereby he repudiated obligations to pay specified tax yields in an agreed sequence to existing government creditors. The declaration of war came in mid-March. From a Scottish point of view, it was a totally undesirable conflict and, although the London ministry could and did drag Scotland after it into the war, there could be no question of serious financial assistance from England to Scotland to help with the Scottish war effort. Indeed, in April 1673, the Scots Privy Council received a letter signed on behalf of Charles II by Lauderdale which made it clear that Charles feared intrigues between the Dutch and his disaffected Scots subjects. The royal government claimed to have 'information that our enemies, the States Generall of the United Provinces, have a design to raise troubles in that our ancient kingdome . . .' and it demanded a strict search of all ships likely to bring seditious messages, arms or agents from the United Netherlands to Scotland. This the Privy Council set out to organise.[17]

For internal police duties, the Scots militia was ideal. It was freely used to try to put down illegal conventicles held by Presbyterian dissenters, and in July 1674 the Privy Council

> . . . considering that the present standing forces are frequently imployed and diverted in quartering for public dues, and that the same may be also conveniently done by those listed in the severall shyres for the militia, doe hereby requyre and command the commissioners of the excyse and commanders of the militia in the respective shyres to obey and putt in execution all such orders as were formerley direct to the standing forces for imbringing the excyse and uther publick dewes by quartering either within these shyres to which they belong or to the shyres adjacent, they imployed therein haveing the same allowances dureing the tyme of their quartering as the standing forces had.[18]

Of course, in a time of acute religious and political conflict it proved impossible totally to isolate the militia from the tensions in the disturbed society around it. In September 1674, the Privy Council in Edinburgh was investigating a mutiny of the foot regiment of the militia commanded by the Earl of Callander. The mutiny occurred at the set place of rendezvous, Stirling. It was crushed, but with some difficulty, for the Laird of Alva was quite seriously wounded in the fracas, and it seems to have sprung from a reasoned refusal of several tenants of the Earl of Callander, who were serving in the ranks, to take the prescribed oath of allegiance to Charles II on politico-religious grounds. The men were eventually banished from Scotland.[19]

Peace had broken out with Holland in February 1674, when Charles II was forced out of the war by defeat, financial crisis and an English public opinion which, quite rightly, saw the bellicose policy of the court as a thin cover for absolutist plots at home. Scotland was spared an unpopular conflict which had greatly heightened internal tension. However, the regime in Scotland did not, in fact, ease off the increased pressure on religious dissenters which had been one of the hard-line policies adopted on the approach to the Third Dutch War. Three new troops of horse were raised in August 1674, and from the correspondence of one of the troop commanders, Lord Ross of Hawkhead, with Lauderdale, it is clear that their main function was the suppression of field conventicles. Yet the Scottish government could not significantly increase military expenditure. On the contrary, a letter from the Commissioners of the Scottish Treasury in August 1675 forced Charles II to disband the three troops of horse and Monro's Regiment. Charles tried to rescue a company of 100 picked men from among the disbanded soldiers, with a view to adding them to 'Our Regiment of Guards', but in early 1676 fiscal stringency compelled the disbanding of the Earl of Rothes' Troop of Guards. It is hardly surprising that in the face of steadily mounting disturbance in the Western shires of Lowland Scotland, Lord Lauderdale in December 1677 alerted Lord Granard, commander of Irish Army units in Ulster, that he must be prepared in a crisis to move his units across the narrow waters to the west of Scotland. The political price for such a move, recalling the genocidal invasion of Argyll by Antrim MacDonalds during Montrose's wars in the 1640s, would have been appalling.[20]

It was never paid. In 1677, Lauderdale issued the famous Bond making heritors and masters responsible for the loyalty (as defined by government) of all resident on their lands. Faced with extensive recalcitrance on the part of landowners in the disturbed western shires, Lauderdale sought for an instrument of military execution by the time-honoured procedure of quartering, and found it in that much-misunderstood body, the Highland Host of 1678. No horde of bare-arsed banditti these, but a manifestation of the organised, low-cost coercive violence which was the ultimate underpinning of Restoration Scotland. It was composed of regular troops (few of whom, in fact, even entered the target areas); the Edinburgh and Stirling militia, militia regiments from the lands of the Earls of Airlie, Mar, Moray, Perth and Strathmore; and what were described as levies of fencible men from the lands of the Marquis of Atholl and the Earl of Caithness. Atholl does seem to have cast his net wider than the two regiments of foot and two troops of horse which constituted the Perthshire militia force, for he marched with eighty-eight horse and 2,118 foot, but the county militia formed the core even of his force, and it produced the one fatal casualty suffered by the expedition: Militiaman Alexander McGregor. The additional levies were, of course, regimented for the occasion. Above the level of lieutenant, the officers drew no pay, but the regular militia rendezvous rates applied otherwise *viz: per diem* thirteen shillings Scots per horseman, six shillings per foot-soldier, a sergeant of foot one shilling and sixpence, and so on right up to the dizzy heights of a lieutenant of foot at four shillings and a corporal of horse at three. Normally the Scots Treasury allowed for ten days pay a year to cover four company and one regimental muster.

In 1678, the cost of the operation vastly exceeded this prudent figure because, on top of the troops mobilised to march west, substantial militia forces were embodied to maintain order in Midlothian, Fife and Stirling. The bulk of the units, which had mustered at Stirling on 24 January 1678, were withdrawn after five weeks, but the last of them, the Angus militia, were only stood down in Dundee early in April. They did, indeed, live at free quarters in the west, but Presbyterian historians like Wodrow, with their wild tales of plundering, looting and terror, do rather slide over the fact that these men were regimented, paid soldiers, officered by the aristocracy of, admittedly, regions different in politics, culture and religion from the one they occupied. Although probably a bad political error of judgement (for it formed the prelude to the assassination of Archbishop Sharp and the outbreak of a major rebellion), the Highland Host was an impressive display of police power, far beyond the capabilities of the 1,100-strong standing forces of Scotland in 1678.[21]

It was also provocative and, in the long run, counter-productive, for illegal conventicles increased sharply in number and the general level of subversive violence rose to a crescendo in May 1679 with the murder of

Archbishop Sharp on Magus Muir just outside St Andrews, and the subsequent defeat of John Graham of Claverhouse's cavalry and dragoons on 1 June by a vast armed conventicle at Drumclog. The standard modern history of the military in the reign of Charles II by John Childs is entitled *The Army of Charles II*, which is odd since that monarch had three armies. Needless to say, the book concentrates on his English army (hence the singular in the title) with a nominal chapter on the Scottish and Irish ones. The Scottish coverage is condensed to the point of being of little use in sorting out quite basic problems like the relationship between the militia and the standing forces in Restoration Scotland. He does spot the fact that, in the face of the rising tide of internal violence, the Scottish government started to raise additional standing forces, but he is less good at sorting out the complexities of the resulting situation.[22]

In May 1678, two companies of dragoons (of 100 men apiece) were raised by a royal warrant. September of that year saw authorisation of the raising of a regiment of foot by the Earl of Mar, a unit destined to become the Royal Scots Fusiliers, and the issue of commissions to the Earls of Home and Airlie and John Graham of Claverhouse as captains of three new troops of cavalry. Viscount Kingston had a troop of dragoons bestowed on him. Two companies of Highland infantry were also ordered to be raised 'for securing the peace of the Highlands'. The effect of all of this was roughly to double the size of the regular Scots Army, from a little over 1,000 to a figure in excess of 2,000. That force, under the command of Charles II's son, James Duke of Buccleuch and Monmouth, Captain General of the Forces in England and Scotland, proved adequate to defeat the biggest rebellion of the reign in Scotland — the rising which occupied Glasgow before being dispersed in July 1679 at Bothwell Bridge. There were proposals to raise all sorts of new units in England to help put down the Scottish rebels, but significantly they came to nothing due to lack of funds. Only four or five troops of English horse stiffened the Scots regulars at Bothwell Bridge. Monmouth's 2,000 or so professionals plus four poorly manned guns under John Slezer, the Lieutenant of Artillery for Scotland and future engraver of the *Theatrum Scotiae*, proved capable of dispersing a much larger undisciplined Covenanting rabble but, of course, the regulars were too expensive and too few for the extensive policing operations which continued to be necessary in Restoration Scotland.

The two Highland companies which had been raised in 1678 had been disbanded by 1681. Even the care of the great state castles of

Edinburgh, Dunbarton and Stirling was conducted on the most radically parsimonious basis. Thus, Sir William Purves of Woodhouslea, Solicitor-General for Scotland under Charles II, waxed indignant in his great 1681 survey of the revenues of the Scots Crown because the Crown had been paying the noble Keeper of Stirling Castle, the Earl of Mar, sums of money to help maintain the garrison. Sir William and the other senior members of the tiny royal bureaucracy thought this quite improper. He cited a 1634 ruling that

> . . . the Captaines and Keepers of the Castells haveing great fees and allowances for keeping of the same ought to have no allowance for the watchmen and souldiers . . .[24]

Charles II himself after Bothwell Bridge suggested a 'New Model' Militia in Scotland, which would have selected from the Scots militia: 5,000 foot organised in five regiments, and 500 horse divided into five troops. This select segment of the militia would, in effect, have become a standing army. Charles proposed it be half funded by the Crown and half by the country, and that to save money lieutenants be substituted for captains. He faced at once furious and united opposition from all segments of the Scottish political nation, from royalist conservatives to Whig aristocratic republicans like Andrew Fletcher of Saltoun who, with Sinclair of Stevenson and Murray of Blackbarronie, was cited before the Privy Council in 1680 for publicly opposing the militia proposals. The three lairds expounded so eloquently what they saw as the practical objections to the proposals that they were dismissed by their sympathetic hearers with a mere rebuke. Despite the presence in Scotland in 1679 and 1680–82 of James Duke of York and Albany, the future James VII, with specific instructions to try to push the new militia project through, it proved totally abortive.[25] The fact was that it violated the basic social compact on which the Restoration rested.

No sooner did James VII ascend the Scottish throne in 1685 than he was faced with a demonstration that the militia system as set up in 1668 was capable of coping with subversion in the shape of the half-baked invasion attempt by Archibald, Earl of Argyll. Argyll's campaign was designed to complement the much larger but equally unsuccessful rebellion led by the Duke of Monmouth in the West of England. Argyll ill-advisedly left many of the weapons and much of the ammunition he had obtained in Holland in an island castle exposed fatally to the guns of James' navy. To crown his miseries, Argyll found that there was little enthusiasm for his venture outwith his own Campbell country. The Privy Council promptly mobilised the militia of loyal areas against him, calling on trusties like Lord Strathmore, the Duke of Gordon, Grant of Grant, the Macintosh, Lochiel, Glengarry, the Earl of Seaforth, MacLeod of MacLeod, the Earl of Caithness and the Earl of Home. There was a more general appeal to 'all heretors and freeholders within this realm above one hundred pounds Scots of valued yearly rent' to turn out on horseback supported by their followers, but this was a pious hope. When the forces were stood down after the ignominious collapse of the rebellion, the Privy Council expressed its warm thanks 'to the severall noblemen and gentlemen, commanders of the militia underwritten'.[26]

Just in case James had not grasped the message, a secret committee of the Privy Council produced a report 'by my Lord Treasurer to his Majestie of the present state of this Kingdome since the late rebellione'. The report is signed by the Marquis of Atholl, Lord Tarbat, the Lord President Falconer, and the Lord Advocate Sir George Mackenzie. This glittering group of Restoration nobles stated as their conclusion:

> . . . the forces which his Majestie hath in this kingdome are sufficient to suppress any comotione that can aryse within it selfe, and as many as can be conveniently entertained in the kingdome. For the povertie of the natione is above what any can think, and some things are necessarie to be done for the natione by the publict stock . . . And it is certaine that if my Lord Threasurer had not had mony in the castle, the intertainment aither of horse or militia had been impossible and the enemi might have ranged at pleasure. And therefore it vere advisable and more . . . that the number of single souldiers in tyme of peace should rather be diminished than any new forces to be rased since a little money heer is difficult to be raised the theer is much to do with it.

The committee had, of course, to admit that the militia, their all-important supplement to the tiny regular army, could be unreliable in certain areas, as it had been in Campbell country during the rebellion, when most militia men turned out for Argyll. Their answer was explicitly to suggest the disbanding of the militia in disaffected areas.[27] Implicitly, they proposed to overwhelm trouble in such areas with militia units from 'sound' areas. That technique was well-established as the bottom line in internal security in Restoration Scotland.

During 1684, Argyllshire had been occupied by a force of Atholl militia with which the Marquis of Atholl had marched into the county to enforce his commission as its Lord Lieutenant. Though Atholl himself returned home after a couple of months, the bulk of his 1,000 men stayed on under his steward Patrick Stewart of Ballechin, the future Jacobite defender of Blair Castle in 1689. There was a central force at Inverary under Ballechin, with detachments at key points such as Argyll's house at Rosneth. Atholl led fresh levies, with a militia core, into the region in the spring of 1685, after being confirmed as its Lord Lieutenant,[28] to slight places likely to be seized in any hostile invasion, and it was he, with another big force of his own militia, who commanded the concentration of 3,000 or so men from reliable areas which met at Inverary in May 1688 to repel Argyll's incursion. Even after that weak rebellion had fizzled out and the loyal levies had been stood down in June 1685, Atholl was ordered to keep enough of his men embodied to crush the embers of revolt.

It was James VII who began the destruction of this useful militia-based security system. Disliking and distrusting the bulk of his subjects as Protestants and potential rebels, he wished to create a government not reliant on the will of subjects, so he logically looked to a professional army and grieved at the small number of Catholics he could find fit to insert in its officer corps. On 4 June 1685, he secured legislation from the Scots parliament abolishing the annual embodiment of the militia, ostensibly out of benign concern for the ease of his subjects, in reality in order to undermine the basic social compact of Restoration Scotland: the symbiotic relationship between Crown and nobility. James wanted no form of power-sharing.[29]

That fact proved his undoing. When, late in 1688, he faced the prospect of invasion by William III from the Netherlands, he tried to revive the force he had been so keen to see fall into desuetude. September saw orders issued to embody the militia, orders which, on the whole, the nobility and gentry seem to have tried to implement. Towards the end of that month, a royal letter countersigned by Lord Melfort, the unpopular favourite of King James and brother of Chancellor Perth, clearly anticipated moving the small Scots professional army into England. When, in the middle of October, the army did cross the Border to reinforce the English troops concentrated near London under Lord Favesham, the Scots executive simultaneously decided to cut the embodied militia to a quarter of its strength, ordering men like Atholl to dismiss with thanks the bulk of the gentry who had turned out.[30] Confused and ill-treated, Scottish militia forces started to disintegrate as an effective internal security facility. They neither prevented the *coup* by a Whig minority which seized control of the Scottish government in the aftermath of the successful Williamite seizure of power in England, nor did they prove available to the ardent Williamites who repeatedly tried to mobilise them, but in the end had to fight the 1689–92 civil war with professional and *ad hoc* volunteer units. Some of the latter may have included ex-militiamen; indeed, they virtually must have, but militia units these were not.[31]

Thereafter, the Scots militia slid into the same abyss of neglect which overcame the less important English militia forces after 1688. Williamite regimes trusted their subjects as little as had King James. Stuart of Goodtrees, who was reputed to have taken key military decisions under James, became Lord Advocate to William. The personnel of the executive in Scotland, in fact, changed amazingly little. Nor did the deplorable lack of any effective home-defence force, which had marked the final years of James, cease to be a problem after 1692. If anything, it became worse. William III created the British Army by embodying all Scots professional units in the same structure as managed his English professional forces, but his interests were purely Continental. What he wanted from Scotland was cannon-fodder for Flanders.

With a London-controlled executive which deeply distrusted, with some justice, the temper and loyalty of large parts of the nation, Scotland under William and Anne was unlikely to see a serious attempt by its monarchs to reactivate the old traditions of universal military obligation for all fencible men, traditions which had been the essential background for the militia of Charles II. Indeed, the last blast on that particular trumpet came logically enough from a Scots legislature locked in fierce conflict with the royal executive. The Act of Security passed in 1704 enacted

> . . . that the whole protestant heretors and all the burghs within the same [kingdom] shall furthwith provide themselves with fire arms for all the fencible men who are Protestants within their respective bounds . . . and the said heretors and burghs are hereby impowered and ordained to discipline and exercise their said fencible men once in the moneth at least . . .[32]

However, with the successful forcing through of an incorporating Act of Union in 1707, this attempt to create a mass militia to resist the twin threats of political and military aggression from Westminster and from the Popish Pretender faded into oblivion.

The last use of the royal veto on a piece of legislation (which was by no means the end of the right to veto as a serious political factor) was, in fact, on 11 March 1707/8, when Queen Anne indicated her rejection of 'An Act for settling the Militia of that Part of Great Britain called Scotland'.[33] This was hardly surprising, given that on the same occasion the Queen informed the Lords that

> I think it necessary to acquaint you, That I have received Advices this Morning from Ostend, that the French Fleet sailed from Dunkirk, Tuesday, at three in the Morning, Northward, with the Pretender on Board.[34]

This operation was the start of the abortive French descent on Scotland usually referred to as the '08. It failed because the naval commander, Admiral de Forbin, did not seem to have understood the role of the invasion in French grand strategy. He eventually preferred to save his ships by flight when the sacrifice of the ships would have allowed James Francis Edward Stuart to seize a virtually undefended Scotland, where the French knew full well the scale of dissatisfaction amongst the nobility because they had been in touch with them through their spy, Colonel Nathaniel Hooke. A Scottish attack on the Tyne-Tees coalfield, the source of London's fuel, might have forced England to the negotiating table at a peace conference.[35] Queen Anne preferred running high military risks to arming politically unreliable Scots.

In the event, Westminster was luckier than it deserved to be over the '08, and the same may be said of the '15 where, once again, a virtually undefended Scotland proved appallingly vulnerable to a Jacobite rising which was not even linked with a French invasion, but consisted of noblemen, lairds and their armed tenants. Admittedly, Highland clansmen were fierce fighters, but trained soldiers they were not. Only the Earl of Mar could have made so little of by far the greatest chance ever offered to the Jacobite cause.

After his discomfiture, steps were taken to create some sort of internal security system. That Jacobites were unenthusiastic about any such measures goes without saying. In 1714, the Scots Jacobite MP, Lockhart of Carnwath, had vocally opposed an attempt to create an English-type militia in Scotland, *i.e.* one controlled totally by Lords Lieutenants of the counties, all of whom would have been hand-picked Hanoverian trusties, assuming that sufficient noblemen of such conviction could have been found, which is by no means certain.[36] In practice, the Westminster legislature was pathologically suspicious of any proposals to arm and train Scotsmen, but, of course, there was always the option of using the power of the Crown to raise independent units under reliable leadership. In 1725, six independent companies were raised by royal warrant in the Highlands under Simon, Lord Lovat, Sir Duncan Campbell of Lochnell, Colonel William Grant of Ballindalloch, John Campbell of Carrick, Colin Campbell of Skipness, and George Munro of Culcairn. Augmented in 1727, these companies were an obvious target for an ambitious officer anxious to curry favour by inventing a new regiment. Major Scipio Duroure, Major of Brigade to the Forces in North Britain, made the suggestion that they be regimented as early as 1731 to General Wade, but only in October 1739 were they further augmented and incorporated into the 43rd (later 42nd) regiment of the line. The government violated the terms of enlistment and the regiment promptly and creditably mutinied. Wade had learned long before that men like Simon Fraser were neither financially honest nor politically reliable enough to be left in charge of an independent company.[37]

Since the regular troops which had crushed the '19 so smartly under General Wightman had, by 1744, almost all been withdrawn from Scotland to flight in Flanders, the country was yet again left virtually defenceless by Westminster and fell prey to a small minority of predominantly Highland Jacobites in the '45. Loyal Scots Whigs did not fail to point out that the Jacobite army was itself little more than a raw, but courageous, militia. A group of rising young Presbyterian clergy were left with the conviction that the refusal to arm a Scots militia was not only dangerous, but also degrading to their nation.[38]

One of the odd features of the eloquent and learned recent work by John Robertson on *The Scottish Enlightenment and the Militia Issue* is that, although it rightly sees the long-running dispute over the militia issue in eighteenth-century Scotland as being dominated by the arguments of Andrew Fletcher of Saltoun, as expressed in a series of publications starting with his *A Discourse concerning Militias and Standing Armies*, published in London in 1697, and reappearing in a slightly revised version as *A Discourse of Government with relation to Militias* in Edinburgh in 1698, it is silent about the practical role of the militia in the Restoration Scotland in which Fletcher had been politically active. This is all the odder since only the Restoration context makes sense of much of Fletcher's writing and, incidentally, shows how less remote from reality it is than is often assumed, despite the high-flying artificial mode of discourse adopted by Fletcher. It is simply not the case that nothing of any interest happened in Scotland before 1707. Nor is it true that the Scottish Enlightenment may be arbitrarily defined as two or three of its least typical figures such as the secular-minded David Hume and Adam Smith.[39]

A glance at the far more representative and clerical 'Moderate Literati' of Edinburgh as a whole shows how unusual was the stance of Hume and Smith on the militia issue. With their sustained intellectual dishonesty in the political field, neither of these men was prepared to admit that they were opposed to any meaningful participation by the subjects of Westminster in either their own government or their own defence. Hypocritically, Smith and Hume joined the Poker or Militia Club formed in 1762 to stir up support for a Scottish militia, and then tried to undercut the agitation from within by arguments such as the irrelevance of amateurs in an age when the principle of division of labour had made warfare a matter for trained professional specialists. What is wrong with this argument is that this is not what militia were primarily for. They were, first and foremost, an insurance against a *coup-d'état* in Scotland by a determined political minority, such as Covenanters in the late-seventeenth century, Jacobites after 1707. Secondly, of course, as the Restoration and its end showed, they were a marvellously sobering influence on a high-handed and irresponsible executive. Because the Hanoverian Whig ascendancy in Great Britain between 1714 and 1760 was for much of that time an unpopular minority regime, it had to use its regulars like militia, scattering them in penny packets round the country to hold down popular unrest. As a result, in the first couple of years of any Continental War, the British Army tended to perform very badly because it was not endowed with a grasp of precisely those large-scale military procedures so vaunted by Adam Smith. The only war in which British regulars made a good tactical start was the War of American Independence, but then they were fighting against men who were themselves often the products of provincial militias.[40]

The literati of Edinburgh, led by the Reverend Alexander Carlyle, Minister of Inveresk and author of *The Question Relating to a Scots Militia Considered*, which appeared early in 1760, were probably right to think that the militia issue was a key one and a test of how far an enlightened non-Jacobite Scotland was to be allowed to cultivate the self-respect and civic virtue which could only come from participation in defence and government. That is why, as well as literati like Carlyle, Adam Fergusson and Principal Robertson, the proposal was backed by rising Scots men of business at Westminster like Dempster of Dunnichen, Gilbert Elliot of Minto, Sir Adam Fergusson and even, in the mid-1770s, by John Viscount Mountstuart, eldest son of the Earl of Bute. By 1776, the issue was a particularly sore one because the Jacobite threat was as dead as a dodo and there was no question of the loyalty to Westminster in its misguided and catastrophic American war of virtually the entire Scottish ruling class. The agitation of the 1770s failed, and so did a further flurry of propaganda in the early 1780s. Of course, the Moderate Literati only approved of public virtue if displayed in defence of the *status quo*, but even that limited opportunity was not available to Scots. Logically enough, those members of this group who survived to see the establishment of a Scots militia in the French wars of the later 1790s did not much approve of it, on the grounds that it was more of an equivalent of the naval press gang than the sort of body they had themselves envisaged.[41] That the ordinary people shared this view was underlined by the widespread rioting in Scotland in August and September 1797 following the passage of the Scottish Militia Act which many Scots objected to both as an act of administrative tyranny and an attempt to stiffen a war effort, the success of which would primarily benefit the rich and the ultra-conservative.[42]

The whole concept of a national militia drawn from the fencible men of Scotland to serve both as a home security force and as a school of civic virtue, not to mention an implicit check on the activities of an irresponsible or tyrannical executive, failed to take into account the relentless determination of the Westminster-based elite to shake free from any form of implicit social contract which circumscribed their power and ability to rule. The Elder Pitt did contrive to rejuvenate the English militia system, up to a point, after 1759, but the salutary experience of having to back down before Irish and American gentlemen supported by their own militias did not endear the idea of a national Scottish militia to King George III or his fellow Westminster politicians. Ultra-conservative Scots like John Ramsay of Ochtertyre had opposed the original Poker Club agitation on the grounds that he did not trust the lower orders with arms. So far from being worried about the Jacobite problem, Ramsay thought regiments of monoglot Gaelic-speakers officered by 'sound' (*i.e.* ultra-reactionary) nobles might form a useful bulwark for property and privilege. Much later, during the Napoleonic Wars of the early nineteenth century, Ramsay retained the same cast of mind. He was paranoid and hysterical about Frenchmen coming to strip him of the privilege, wealth and social power which he regarded as his by Divine Right. He both feared and despised the country people around him as clodhopping Sancho Panzas, far too easily stirred up to mischief. He recognised their hatred of the new balloted militia, but he retained his own deep-seated dislike for any militia whatsoever, assuring his friends that it would prove a 'rope of sand' in any real crisis.[43]

When the word 'fencible' was used of military formations raised in late-eighteenth or early-nineteenth century Scotland, it had, in fact, lost all connotations which linked it with the idea of a universal obligation to defend the rights and liberties of a coherent national community. With the establishment of English county militia regiments after 1759, the year of the last French attempt to organise a Jacobite-led invasion of Britain, some sop to Scottish opinion was essential, so the Elder Pitt made proposals to the Earl of Sutherland that he raise a fencible regiment on his vast Highland estates. Sutherland needed only nine days after arriving on his estates with his letters of service to assemble at Dunrobin a regiment of 1,100 men, which he marched into Perth in May 1760. That other political trusty, the Duke of Argyll, raised a second fencible regiment in the same year. Twenty-two of its thirty-seven officers were called Campbell. Similar units were raised from the third year of the War of American Independence, and again on an even larger scale during the French Revolutionary War, the last Highland fencible unit being embodied in 1799. The fact that they were only obliged to serve in Britain, and that they by no means automatically agreed to the predictable pressure from Westminster to act as feeders to regular regiments, made them unpopular with government, but they were hardly a popular force either, for they were clearly designed to act as a conservative internal garrison, as much against the majority of their fellow-Scots as against the French.[44] From an era when they regarded their own control of a national militia as essential, propertied and privileged Scots had moved to reliance on a central monopoly of decision taking and organised violence, in London.

NOTES

1. The original form of the Roberts article was his inaugural lecture, published as *The Military Revolution, 1560–1660* (Belfast, 1956), later reprinted with some additions in M. Roberts, *Essays in Swedish History* (London, 1967), 195–225.
2. G. Parker, 'The "Military Revolution" 1560–1660: a myth?', *Journal of Modern History*, 48 (1976), 195–214.

3. G. N. Clark, *The Seventeenth Century* (2nd edn., Oxford, 1960), 104.

4. J. P. Kenyon, *The Stuart Constitution 1603–1688* (2nd edn., Cambridge, 1986), 2, where in a footnote the author says rightly that it is 'strange that this [*i.e.* the centrality of the militia] is still a matter for debate'.

5. John Childs, *The Army of Charles II* (London, 1976), 8–10.

6. Charles Dalton, *The Scots Army 1661–1688* (London and Edinburgh, 1909), 2–4.

7. Gordon Donaldson, *Scotland: James V to James VII* (Edinburgh, 1971), 358.

8. Walter Makey, *The Church of the Covenant 1637–1651* (Edinburgh, 1979).

9. Julia Buckroyd, *The Life of James Sharp, Archbishop of St Andrews 1618–1679* (Edinburgh, 1987).

10. Alexander Robertson, *The Life of Sir Robert Moray (1608–1673)* (London, 1922), 128–134.

11. *APS*, VII, 480–1.

12. J. R. Western, *The English Militia in the Eighteenth Century: the story of a political issue 1660–1802* (London, 1965), 162.

13. See the 'Prefatory Note' in J. R. Western, *Monarchy and Revolution: the English State in the 1680s* (London, 1972).

14. Robertson, *Life of Sir Robert Moray, loc. cit.*

15. *RPC*, 3rd series, II, xiii–xvi, 438–42, 533, 547–8. The shires originally listed were Roxburgh and Selkirk; Berwick; Edinburghshire; Haddington; Linlithgow and Peebles; Edinburgh, Leith and Canongate; Stirling and Clackmannan; Fife and Kinross; Perth; Forfar; Kincardine and Earl Marischall's part of Aberdeenshire; and Argyll.

16. *Ibid.*, 3rd series, III, 308–9, 241–9.

17. *Ibid.*, 3rd series, IV, 45–6.

18. *Ibid.*, 3rd series, IV, 245–6.

19. *Ibid.*, 3rd series, IV, 270–1, 287, 290, 311, 406, 651.

20. Dalton, *The Scots Army*, 40–3.

21. John R. Elder, *The Highland Host of 1678* (Aberdeen, 1914) is the basic work, though over-captivated by Wodrow.

22. John Childs, *The Army of Charles II*, esp. Chapter XI: 'Scotland and Ireland'.

23. Dalton, *The Scots Army*, 44–57.

24. Sir William Purves, *Revenue of the Scottish Crown, 1681*, ed. D. Murray Rose (Edinburgh, 1897), 82.

25. *RPC*, 3rd series, VI, xix–xxii.

26. *Ibid.*, 3rd series, XI, 44–5, 81.

27. HMC, XV, Appendix, Part VIII (Mss of Duke of Buccleuch and Queensberry), 131–5. This report is very partially cited in Audrey Cunningham, *The Loyal Clans* (Cambridge, 1932), 304, totally out of context and with no apparent grasp of the significance of the document for Scottish history in general. If the overall approach of this work has come under criticism recently for violent bias, it must be added that the technical scholarship on which it is based is not of the first order.

28. *RPC*, 3rd series, XI, 31–2.

29. Andrew Ross, 'The Perthshire Militia of the Seventeenth and Eighteenth Centuries' in *A Military History of Perthshire 1660-1902*, ed. the Marchioness of Tullibardine (Perth, 1908), 117–19.

30. A. and H. Tayler, *John Graham of Claverhouse* (London, 1939), 191–3 for an account of the Scots militia and army in late 1688. For an example of the conveying of the decision to stand down all but a fourth part of the embodied militia in October 1688 see *HMC*, XII, Appendix Part VIII (Mss of the Duke of Atholl and Earl of Home), 36 for letter from James, Earl of Perth, Lord Chancellor to Lord Murray, 16 October 1688.

31. Andrew Ross, 'Perthshire Militia', 121–2.

32. W. C. Dickinson and G. Donaldson, *A Source Book of Scottish History*, III (1567–1707) (2nd edn., Edinburgh, 1961), 476–7.

33. *Notes and Queries*, 12th series, V (1919), 155–6, establishes this fact.

34. Journal of the House of Lords, XVIII (1705–09), 506.

35. Extracts from the main contemporary sources for the '08 are printed conveniently in Charles S. Terry, ed., *The Chevalier de St George and the Jacobite Movements in the Favour 1701-1720* (London, 1901), Chapter III.

36. A. Ross, 'Perthshire Militia', 122.

37. H. D. MacWilliam, *A Black Watch Episode of the Year 1731* (Edinburgh, 1908); for Lord Lovat's comic-opera career as one of Wade's officers in command of independent companies, see Bruce P. Lenman, *The Jacobite Clans of the Great Glen 1650-1748* (London, 1984), 117–18.

38. Richard B. Sher, *Church and University in the Scottish Enlightenment* (Edinburgh, 1985), 37–44.

39. John Robertson, *The Scottish Enlightenment and the Militia Issue* (Edinburgh, 1985).

40. J. A. Houlding, *Fit for Service: the training of the British Army, 1715-1795* (Oxford, 1981).

41. Sher, *Church and University*, 232–40.

42. Kenneth J. Logue, *Popular Disturbances in Scotland 1780-1815* (Edinburgh, 1979), Chapter 3: 'The Militia Riots'.

43. For John Ramsay of Ochtertyre's early opposition to the Scottish militia agitation, see his remarks in *Scotland and Scotsmen in the Eighteenth Century from the MSS of John Ramsay Esq., of Ochtertyre*, ed. Alexander Allardyce (2 vols, Edinburgh, 1888), I, 332–5. For his sustained paranoia at a later period, see Barbara L. H. Horn, ed., *Letters of John Ramsay of Ochtertyre 1799-1812*, SHS, 4th series, vol. 3 (Edinburgh, 1966), esp. those to Elizabeth Graham on 18 July 1809 (which refers to the local militia as 'a rope of sand') and 12 July 1810, pp. 253 and 272 respectively.

44. Colonel David Stewart, *Sketches of the Character, Manners and Present State of the Highlanders of Scotland: with Details of the Military Service of the Highland Regiments* (2nd edn, Edinburgh, 1822), II, 299–396.

9

'WE ARE SAFE WHATEVER HAPPENS' — DOUGLAS HAIG, THE REVEREND GEORGE DUNCAN, AND THE CONDUCT OF WAR, 1916–1918

Gerard J. de Groot

On the eve of the Somme offensive in June 1916, General Sir Douglas Haig received a message from his deceased brother George which came to him via the hand of his sister Henrietta Jameson. (Mrs Jameson had, through a medium, maintained regular contact with George for a number of years.) The message read:

> I am so anxious to send a few lines to Douglas because I have been beside him and seen his earnest and good work for his army. Almighty God is his helper and guide and by the blessing of God a great soldier is allowed to be always near Douglas to advise him in his task. Napoleon is that soldier . . . And all the prayers of a great nation are united in asking God to guide His armies to victory . . . Our Douglas is the instrument he uses to crush the German invaders in France and Belgium. So tell Douglas with my love and blessing to go on as he is doing trusting to the mighty power above to shew him the way. And tell him he will not ask in vain.[1]

The historian should resist making too much of Haig's own involvement in spiritualism, which was nothing more than a harmless fascination. George's messages are nevertheless important, though their importance lies in their content rather than their source. Regardless of whether Haig believed in the possibility of communicating with the dead, he would have been receptive to the letters because they reinforced his preconceptions. He had no doubt that he would return from the war 'covered in glory'. More importantly, the belief that God was always by his side and that he was the instrument of Divine providence were matters of faith central to Haig's confidence in his ability to command.

Haig's belief in divine inspiration originated from his Scottish Presbyterian upbringing. As a small boy, his mother Rachel constantly reminded him of the 'All-seeing, loving eye ever upon you, my dear boy'.[2] When faced with an important decision, Douglas was exhorted to

'*seek to be directed* — and you may rest assured *God will shew you . . .*'
'Isn't it delightful', she wrote, 'to feel that you will be *wisely* directed
and that you may rest passive in the matter . . .'[3] But passivity in this
case did not imply complacency or idleness. Rather, in keeping with
Calvinist teachings, Haig grew up with a highly developed sense of the
spiritually purifying effects of hard work. When combined with his
natural ambition and self-assurance, this 'work ethic' made Haig into a
formidable soldier and servant of God.

Haig believed that his God-given abilities were essential to the
prosperity and survival of the British Empire. Since the Empire was by
definition God's Empire, serving it was the same as serving God. Haig's
conception of duty is evident in advice which he gave to a nephew who
was contemplating leaving the Army in order to take up a more
sedentary life as a farmer:

> It would be absurd for a lad of your years and without any real experience of
> the Empire and its inhabitants to settle down into a turnip grower in Fife.
> Leave these pursuits until you get into the doldering age! Meantime do your
> best to become a worthy citizen of the Empire. . . . It has been your *good
> fortune* not only to become a soldier, but to have served and risked your life
> for the Empire — you must continue to do so, and consider that it is a
> privilege . . . The gist of the whole thing is that I am anxious not only that you
> should realise your duty to your family, your Country and to Scotland, but
> also to the whole Empire — 'Aim High' as the Book says, 'perchance ye may
> attain'. Aim at being worthy of the British Empire and possibly in the
> evening of your life you may be able to own to yourself that you are fit to
> settle down in Fife. At present you are not, so be active and busy. . . . Don't
> let the lives of mediocrities about you deflect you from your determination to
> belong to the few who can command or guide or benefit our great Empire.
> Believe me, the reservoir of such men is not boundless. As our Empire grows,
> so is there a greater demand for them, and it behooves everyone to do his
> little and try and qualify for as high a position as possible. It is not ambition.
> This is *duty*.[4]

In other words, to fail to achieve one's full potential was a sin. Thus,
religion transformed what might ordinarily have been coarse or ruthless
ambition into a noble, Christian sense of duty. Otherwise devious deeds
were cleansed and purified if carried out in the service of God and
England.

There were many in the Army intellectually superior to Haig. But no
soldier could match him in energy or dedication. Since the Army valued
character at least as much as intellect, his rise was rapid.[5] This rise in
turn reinforced his belief that he was someone special, chosen by God.

Unlike Oliver Cromwell — who also saw himself as a divine instrument — he seems never to have questioned why he in particular had been singled out by God for a special purpose.[6] Religion made things simple for Haig; it provided life with order, meaning and justice, and left no room for self-doubt. Moral questions usually associated with war never surfaced; a Christian soldier was by definition morally pure. The colonial wars in which Haig fought were justified because they extended the righteous, benevolent, Christian influence of the British Empire. Likewise, when Britain went to war in 1914, Haig did not worry about questions of war guilt. Germany and her allies were clearly the aggressors, and therefore the transgressors of God's commandments. They were evil. This was in every sense a just and holy war.

Religion brought meaning and order to an otherwise incomprehensible war. Haig, a cavalryman, expected mobility — breached defences, turned flanks and glorious cavalry charges. He encountered instead stalemate, trenches and mud. An ordinary man would have been unnerved by this situation. But Haig remained calm. He drew constant solace from II Chronicles, Chapter 20, Verse 15: 'Be not afraid nor dismayed by reasons of this great multitude; for the battle is not yours but God's.' Referring to this passage in a letter to the Principal Chaplain, Reverend J. M. Simms, Haig wrote: 'This I have truly felt and so my courage and belief in Victory have never failed me.'[7] The unfathomable nature of the war was simply evidence of God's mystery and power.

Unfortunately, the first sixteen months of the war provided little evidence of God's blessing. But Haig's faith did not flag. His belief that the war was being directed from above did not prevent him from blaming British reverses on the Commander-in-Chief, Sir John French. In other words, the spiritual and the temporal sometimes came into conflict. Though Haig believed in a higher, perfect order, he had to live in an imperfect world and had to come to terms with its imperfections. Thus, while British successes were attributed to the hand of God, failures were often blamed on human error. When French's failures grew too numerous, Haig decided to act. Evidence of the Commander's incapacity was conveyed to politicians and royalty. Since Haig was French's logical successor, his actions might seem suspect. But undermining French would have been seen by him as a patriotic (not to mention Christian) duty. When Haig arrived at GHQ as the new Commander-in-Chief in December 1915, he wrote that he was 'astonished at the feeling of relief which is manifested at Sir J's departure . . . all seem to expect success as the result of my arrival, and somehow give me the idea that they think I am "meant to win" by some superior Power'.[8]

Prior to assuming command, Haig's religion provided a sense of order and meaning, but little in the way of comfort or inspiration. By the standards of the age, he was not overly religious. Spiritual matters did not, for instance, intrude into his letters or diary. Though he attended church regularly, he seldom commented upon the sermons or upon other religious issues. Suddenly all this changed. On 2 January 1916, Haig noted in his diary that he

attended the Scotch Church at 9:35 a.m. . . . . A most earnest young Scotch man, George Duncan, conducted the service. He told us that in our prayers we should be as natural as possible and tell the Almighty exactly what we feel we want. The nation is now learning to pray . . . nothing can withstand the prayers of a great united people. The congregation was greatly impressed, and one could have heard a pin drop during the service. So different to the coughing and restlessness which goes on in Church in peace time.[9]

Thereafter, Haig attended the Presbyterian service almost every Sunday. 'The half hour of worship', wrote Duncan, 'was not merely something he valued; it was apparently something which must not be missed.'[10] Thus, at the time when the strains of Haig's responsibilities became greatest, in stepped Duncan, who provided Haig with the spiritual comfort and moral reinforcement previously lacking in his religious worship.

Angular, clumsy, rather shy and soft-spoken, Duncan was thirty years old when he arrived at GHQ. Fresh from post-graduate work in Britain and Germany, he had no experience of preaching, and little of society. He admitted that 'I knew next to nothing about Army life when . . . I was selected for a commission as a temporary Chaplain to the Forces.'[11] He looked more like a young, suitably eccentric university don than a potential Messiah. (It was, in fact, to academia that he went after the war, earning some renown as a New Testament scholar and principal of St Mary's College, St Andrews.) His preaching was noted more for its soft-spoken, mellifluous expression and perspicacious rationality than for any fire or brimstone. Sermons inspired contemplation more than adoration; Duncan persuaded rather than exhorted. It was not a formula which inspired universal appeal, but it suited Haig perfectly. He admitted to Duncan that it had been 'a hard trial before I came across you'.[12] Thereafter, Haig refused to part with him. Orders from the Chaplain General for the young padre's transfer were rescinded by Haig. When Duncan requested a transfer to active service at the front he was persuaded to withdraw it by Simms, who referred to Duncan as 'a gift of God to our great Chief'. Simms wrote:

> No one in this great campaign has the same claim to our very best as our Chief — for he bears a well nigh crushing burden — and I bless God night and day that he has found a chaplain whom he is not afraid to say does help him to bear up under the load and how mortal man can desire a better, nobler, greater task for his war work I can't imagine.[13]

When GHQ was moved to Montreuil in March 1916, Duncan was moved with it.[14] When the Chief took leave, so did the chaplain. After the Sunday service, Duncan usually dined at Haig's table. The padre was in every sense Haig's personal preacher. Hardly a Sunday passed without Haig recording his reflections upon the sermon. The words of Duncan became the ways of Haig.

Duncan, who was orphaned at an early age, had a peculiar knack for attracting the patronage of eminent men, of whom Haig was only the most noteworthy. It is possible that he sought a father-figure or that he seemed in need of fatherly guidance. In return, Duncan gave his mentors unquestioning loyalty and respect bordering on adoration.[15] His diaries, for instance, overflow with praise for Haig, whom he likened to 'an old Homeric hero'.[16] Haig's tribulations became his own, as evidenced by the diary entry for 3 June 1916:

> One felt the Chief looked less alert in body and mind today than usual. Generally he looks as if he carried the responsibility lightly and he hasn't a care in the world, but the burden is never absent; and one knows how all sections of the staff here — and even the French — look to him and rely on him. Well may we pray for those to whom has been committed the leadership of our armies . . .[17]

Two weeks later, Duncan was pleased to record a different impression of Haig: 'As he shook hands before going out, his eyes looked deep into mine. One was glad to see how fresh he looked today.'[18] Haig's demeanour was a wind in which Duncan's moods would swing.

Duncan's mission, as he perceived it, was not just to serve God, but also to serve Haig. 'The preacher', he confessed to his diary, 'is not concerned with military details; but he ought to be able to read the signs of the times.'[19] Thus, like any good chaplain, he tailored his messages to suit the course which the war was taking. But he also carefully tailored

Figure 1. Haig's Messiah: the Reverend George Duncan in the Church Hut. Duncan's sermons helped to sustain Haig's belief that he was fighting a holy war on behalf of a chosen race.

them to suit Haig. On a Sunday in late February 1917, Duncan noticed that 'the Chief looked much older than I had ever seen him before'.[20] Consequently, a week later, the padre 'spoke on the Transfiguration — a great subject and (as I felt when I selected it) relevant to him in the present situation'. Afterwards, Haig 'looked his old self, fresh and alert'. Duncan was thrilled when 'I got a very cordial and approving smile from the Chief as he left'.[21] But the formula did not always work. Upon his return from the Calais Conference (at which Lloyd George had tried to transfer control of the British Army to the French commander Nivelle), Haig seemed almost overwhelmed by the weight of his responsibility. Duncan recorded that on the following Sunday 'I spoke on "If thy hand ensnare thee, hew it off", a Lenten sermon, but perhaps what the Chief needs rather is something that is aglow with confident hope.'[22]

It is worthwhile to examine in some detail the nature of Duncan's religious message, in order to understand how this harmonised with Haig's beliefs and his vision of the war. But in doing so, the historian encounters a problem relating to the reliability of the evidence. Copies of Duncan's sermons are not available. The padre's diaries only provide the briefest of sketches of each Sunday's message, usually in the form of a reference to the lesson for that day. The only detail available comes from Haig's diaries, but his accounts are by nature impressionistic. Haig, in common with any worshipper in any time, heard what he wanted to hear from the sermons and recorded what he wanted to record. As will be seen, it seems that on occasion the message Duncan wished to convey was significantly different from that which Haig absorbed. But the problem should not trouble the historian. In fact, as far as this study is concerned, discrepancies are as revealing as veracity. Haig's diaries might not be the best record of Duncan's sermons, but they are a very accurate and revealing account of the effect which those sermons had. The impressions, not the literal truth, is what is important here.

Haig's faith, according to Duncan, 'was not the product of some fanciful theory; it sprang from a calm recognition of the challenges and needs of everyday life'.[23] When those challenges were greatest, so too was his reliance upon God. After 1916, religion became 'a vital element in his life'; Duncan felt that he began 'to view in a more definitely religious light both the issues at stake in the war and the part which he himself was being called to play in it'.[24] When it was most necessary for Haig to make sense of the massive losses and the recurring setbacks, Duncan's 'fine manly sermon[s]' provided the necessary explanation.[25] Luminaries who visited GHQ were taken by Haig to see Duncan — the secret weapon, the chaplain who, according to the commander, 'could make anyone fight!'.[26]

In his diary, Haig recorded how Duncan emphasised 'the need from which all of us suffer of having nourishment for the spiritual side of life'.[27] This nourishment could be gained through a 'personal and practical religion. First pray to be told what is God's will. Secondly, believe that God is working in us for a particular purpose. Thirdly, that being so, have no fear lest any evil may befall you.'[28] On another Sunday,

Mr Duncan preached from St John. 'My peace I leave with you.' He spoke of life in general, how it is made up of anxieties and worries — and yet through it all, if we only have acquired certain qualities, we shall have that 'peace'. The war has educated many of us, so that we have found that peace of mind. Few indeed of us, before the dangers, the anxieties and the hardships of the war had been felt, had any idea of what that peace really means.[29]

This peace of mind has often been misunderstood by Haig's critics. Confronted with his apparent stoicism, they have concluded that he must have been impervious to failure and insensitive to suffering. He was neither. Failed offensives troubled him; massive casualties caused him considerable anguish. But no misfortune could overwhelm his absolute faith in God's grace.

Since, according to Haig, Britain was 'fighting for Christ and the freedom of mankind', it was obvious that 'a good Chaplain is as valuable as a good general'. The duty of the chaplain was to 'preach to the troops about the objects of Great Britain in carrying on this war. We have no selfish motive, but are fighting for the good of humanity.'[30] This meant that religion had to be taken into the trenches. Haig therefore rescinded, upon assuming command, restrictions upon padres entering the front lines. They subsequently began to share in the horrors of the war — began to die in greater numbers — and the soldiers' opinions of them consequently improved. Army commanders were instructed, in selecting clergymen, to look for 'large minded, sympathetic men . . . who realise *the great cause* for which we are fighting. Men who can imbue their hearers with enthusiasm. Any clergyman who is not fit for his work must be sent home.'[31] Though generally satisfied with the quality of religious provision, Haig thought the Church of England padres were too prone to 'squabbl[e] terribly amongst themselves over High Church and Low Church methods.'[32] The Archbishop of Canterbury was told that 'we cannot tolerate any narrow sectarian ideas. We must all be united whether we are clerics or ordinary troops.'[33]

One important lesson which Haig insisted chaplains should impart related to the price of victory — in other words the number of casualties which Britain would have to endure. Duncan referred to this subject on many occasions, most notably on 16 July 1916, during the heavy fighting on the Somme. Haig recorded his impressions of the sermon:

Anything worth having has always to be paid for fully. In this war, our object is something very great. The future of the world depends on our success. So we must fully spend all we have, energy, life, money, everything, in fact, without counting the cost. Our objects cannot be attained without the greatest sacrifice from each one of us.[34]

'We lament too much over death', Duncan supposedly stressed in another sermon. 'We should regard it as a welcome change to another room.'[35] This is probably an example of Haig hearing what he wanted to hear from Duncan's sermons, or, alternatively, recording a message out of context. There is no doubt that Duncan believed that the noble, Christian cause for which the British were fighting justified the losses. He naturally believed (and preached) that the fallen would receive God's grace in the afterlife. But it is difficult to believe that he ever meant to suggest that his congregation should not grieve over the losses. Haig's account makes him seem devoid of earthly sentiment — like an ayatollah — which he never was nor intended to be. He was, according to his son, 'an excessively emotional man who until the end of his life bitterly lamented the early death of his parents and elder brother, not to mention many of his friends in the war'.[36]

Haig always accepted that victory would entail great loss of life. Massive casualties did not, however, deter him. His occasional reflections upon this subject are revealing. In March 1916, he referred to a speech by the Emperor Baber to his troops on 16 March 1527 when fighting the Lord of Mewar, Rana Sanga: 'The most High God has been propitious to us in such a crisis that if we fall in the field, we die the death of martyrs; if we survive, we rise victorious the avengers of the cause of God.' This, Haig concluded, was 'the root matter of the present war'.[37] On the subject of granting rewards to his men, Haig once commented that their 'chief reward was their own feeling of satisfaction at having done their duty'.[38] In Haig's view, sacrifice provided its own reward and death, the ultimate sacrifice, the ultimate reward. In July 1917, Duncan likewise confided that he 'sometimes felt a process of selection was going on by which the best were being picked out for some special service beyond the grave'.[39] Haig recalled how the padre, preaching from The Acts, stressed that it was important to 'Remember [that] your lives are not your own, but purchased at a price . . . The Empire is living thanks to the gallant lives which have and are being expended in this war. After the war none of us can be the same as before it!'[40]

War, according to Duncan and Haig, was a process of purgation. The sacrifice would not only contribute to the defeat of the Germans, it would also, more importantly, cleanse and purify Britain. Haig's diary relates how Duncan referred to 'the change which must come over us all after the War, and . . . the new state which England must assume if she is to continue to progress in civilisation'.⁴¹ After 400,000 men had fallen on the Somme, the padre apparently promised that 'this Great War was accomplishing the preparation of the world for better living. It was ruthlessly sweeping away all shams, and in a larger sphere, was performing what was done by John the Baptist centuries ago for the Jews and the coming of the Lord'.⁴² Haig was particularly receptive to this idea of a glorious rebirth. He was 'greatly struck' by an American newspaper proprietor who predicted that after the war 'England would be the greatest gainer, the whole Empire would be wielded together into one great whole, and imbued with a higher spirit. On the other hand, the United States, though more money had been amassed, would decline because of the spirit of luxury and extravagance which was being developed.'⁴³

Haig's vision of a society purified and enriched by war naturally depended upon British victory. Of this he had no doubts. The British were a chosen race, therefore defeat was inconceivable. The only uncertainty related to the time required to achieve victory. Duncan, apparently respectful of German strength, repeatedly spoke of the need for patience. Four weeks before the launch of the Somme offensive, Haig's first major action, the padre took as his text a letter from St John to the Christians at Smyrna: 'Be ye faithful unto the end. To you shall be given a crown of everlasting life.' Afterwards, Haig summarised Duncan's message:

> The contents of the letter might have been addressed to the British Army in France today. We must look forward to still harder times, to the necessity for redoubled efforts, but in the end all will be well. How different are our feelings today to those with which the British people and the men in the Army began the War. Then, many people prophesied a race to Berlin, with the Russian steam roller etc. Now we were beginning to learn our lessons, and to be sobered by hard experience and to be patient.⁴⁴

Contrary to the above evidence, Haig did not at first accept the possibility of a long struggle. His self-assurance led him to believe that he could immediately succeed where Sir John French had dismally failed. The Germans, he insisted, could be defeated with one bold offensive. Forty thousand casualties on Day 1 of the Somme offensive did not convince him otherwise. After a week of horribly destructive and depressingly inconclusive fighting, a surprisingly sanguine Haig was still able to predict that 'In another fortnight, with divine help . . . some decisive results will be obtained'.[45] But God kept Haig waiting.

The Somme failure made Haig marginally more circumspect. He still spoke of dramatic breakthroughs, but at the same time stressed the need for patience. As the war progressed, victory became more elusive, endurance more important. It was a somewhat chastened Haig who told his wife, prior to the attack on Messines in June 1917, that 'We ought to take the ridge without much difficulty, but then as you already know, nothing is certain in war. Success lies in a Higher Power than me.'[46] A modest victory followed and God was duly thanked. When, subsequently, Haig's high hopes were smothered in the deep mud of Passchendaele, he took solace in Duncan's promise that '*At the right time* the Lord [will] bring about a great victory . . . we must be able to endure and not be impatient'.[47] In March 1918, the German Army (which Haig had assumed was a demoralised wreck) broke through the allied lines and advanced as far as forty miles, by far the deepest penetration of the war. Though Haig's optimism was unaffected by this startling defeat, it did lead to a realisation that God worked in mysterious ways. 'If one has full confidence that everything is being directed from above *on the best lines*, then there is no reason for fussing', he told his wife on 11 April 1918. 'Do the best we can, and I am confident that everything will come out right in time. But we must be patient, fully realising that *our* ways may not always be the ways chosen by the Divine Power for achieving the wished for end.'[48]

Because Haig was confident that the course of the war was being directed from above, he did not have to question his methods of command. Failures which under French had been blamed on human error were now the will of God. As he explained to his wife before the launch of an attack, 'I feel that everything possible for us to do to achieve success has been done. But whether or not we are successful lies in the Power above. But *I do feel* that in my plans I have been helped by a Power that is not my own. So I am easy in my mind and ready to do my best whatever happens.'[49] The belief in divine direction meant that Haig refused to take credit for the occasional successes which came his way. 'It isn't me', he would insist when Duncan tried to congratulate him on a victory.[50] When he won a particularly difficult argument with the troublesome French commander Joffre, he concluded that he 'had been given some power not always in me'.[51] Likewise, after the British victory at Arras in 1917, he wrote: 'I know quite well that I am being used as a tool in the hands of the Divine Power and that my strength is not my own, so I am not at all conceited, and you may rest assured that I am not likely to forget to whom belongs the honour and glory for *all* our good work and success.'[52]

Late in 1918, Haig's faith was rewarded. The German Army, worn out by its own offensive, could not withstand Haig's counter-punch. Surrender quickly followed. True to character, Haig related to his wife how

> the vast majority of our countrymen are fully alive to what has been done by the Army under my orders, and are grateful to me in a very surprising way. But I scarcely feel that I deserve this gratitude, for as the Old Testament says 'the battle is not yours but God's', and I feel that I have only been the instrument to carry out the almighty's intentions.[53]

When he learned that the Kaiser had fled to Holland and that German soldiers had fired on their officers, he reflected that 'If the war had gone against us, no doubt our King would have had to go, and probably our Army would have become insubordinate like the German Army. cf, John Bunyan's remark on seeing a man on his way to be hanged, "But for the Grace of God, John Bunyan would have been in that man's place."'[54] Victory confirmed what Haig had always accepted as a matter of faith: God was benevolently inclined toward the British Army.

What were the consequences to Britain's Army of having a Commander in Chief who believed himself an agent of God? Before examining this question it is important to stress that there is no evidence to suggest that at the time Duncan had any knowledge of this aspect of Haig's faith. As has been seen, Haig's feeling that he was 'meant to win' predated Duncan's arrival.[55] If the chaplain encouraged this belief he must have done so unconsciously. In fact, it seems that after the war Duncan became somewhat sensitive on this issue and felt the need to defend himself and Haig. In *Douglas Haig As I Knew Him*, he wrote:

> I have often been asked the question: 'How far is it true that Haig regarded himself as God's appointed agent for the winning of the war?' Never during the whole time I was with him did I hear language of that kind from his lips. I am also certain that, if he ever allowed himself to entertain such a thought, he did so in all humility, not out of egotism or wishful thinking, but with a sober grasp of the situation as he saw it.[56]

The above suggests that the current between Duncan and Haig travelled in only one direction. Haig absorbed the chaplain's sermons, but did not discuss his reaction to them. His faith remained private. This would be in keeping with the character of the man; Haig was basically a loner who did not reveal his innermost feelings to anyone. When Haig and Duncan dined together the two men discussed the course of the war, the role of the Church or other general topics, but not how these affected Haig. On 22 July 1917, Duncan observed how 'there was a steady straight look on [Haig] as on the man who had much to meditate on before the action began: but one *never* sees him oppressed by his meditation'.[57] When Duncan once suggested that Haig might like to 'stay behind some Sunday for Communion', he quickly realised that he had strayed into forbidden territory. 'I'm afraid I took him unawares: for his natural shyness overtook him and he could just mumble "No, no, I don't think so." . . . He seemed disinclined to continue the conversation, and simply shook hands again and said goodbye, and disappeared into his room'.[58]

Duncan's lack of awareness aside, there is no doubt that Haig believed himself divinely inspired and that this belief influenced his method of command. It would not be too reckless to suggest that a self-proclaimed agent of God might be inattentive to the ordinary events on the battlefield and might lose a sense of individual responsibility. Aware that Haig was open to such criticism, Duncan wrote that 'so far from relieving him for a moment of his responsibilities', Haig's faith 'rather impelled him to take them the more seriously'.[59] The assurances unfortunately fall wide of the mark. Haig's dedication to his command, and the energy he devoted to it, are beyond dispute. Anything other than a totally committed effort would not have been in keeping with his vision of himself as God's industrious servant, and his Protestant attitude toward work. But this does not mean that his religious beliefs were without adverse effects upon his command. As Basil Liddell Hart has argued, Haig's

> sense of a divine call . . . had inevitable ill-effects — it was difficult for a man so sure of his inspiration to question his own calculations, to give due weight to the ideas which differed from his own and to data which did not fit in with his conclusions.

Liddell Hart concluded that 'the sense of a divine call naturally grew [into a] sense of divine right'.[60] The judgement is unfortunately typical

CHURCH NOTICE.

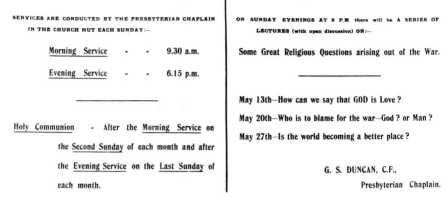

SERVICES ARE CONDUCTED BY THE PRESBYTERIAN CHAPLAIN
IN THE CHURCH HUT EACH SUNDAY:—

Morning Service   -   -   9.30 a.m.

Evening Service   -   -   6.15 p.m.

Holy Communion   -   After the Morning Service on
the Second Sunday of each month and after
the Evening Service on the Last Sunday of
each month.

ON SUNDAY EVENINGS AT 8 P.M. there will be A SERIES OF
LECTURES (with open discussion) ON:—

Some Great Religious Questions arising out of the War.

May 13th—How can we say that GOD is Love ?

May 20th—Who is to blame for the war—God ? or Man ?

May 27th—Is the world becoming a better place ?

G. S. DUNCAN, C.F.,
Presbyterian Chaplain.

Figure 2. One of Duncan's church notices, announcing services and lectures. (St Andrews University Photographic Collection).

of the author's tendency to debase perfectly valid points by venturing into unnecessary, misleading hyperbole. Divine right suggests an omnipotent, authoritarian commander — which Haig definitely was not. He has, in fact, been justifiably criticised for giving too much freedom to subordinates in the determination of tactics. In other words, chaos and contradiction resulted because Haig was insufficiently despotic.

Leaving aside the question of divine right, it is worthwhile to examine Liddell Hart's more valid criticisms relating to Haig's religious beliefs. The evidence does suggest that he was unreceptive to adverse intelligence and to advice which contradicted preconceptions. He was, to an extent, out of touch with reality (if 'reality' is taken to mean what was actually going on at the front). For instance, he never came to terms with the fact that mobility was virtually impossible and that there was no significant role for his beloved cavalry. On 17 November 1918 he concluded that he had won the war because 'I insisted always in keeping as much Cavalry as possible because I believed in Victory, and that arm alone can reap the fruits of Victory!'[61] This unrealistic vision of the war cannot be explained solely by Haig's belief that he was being directed by an all-powerful and infallible God. Sluggishness in coming to terms with the real war was not exclusive to Haig; less religious commanders were equally pig-headed. There are many explanations for

Haig's clouded vision. But as this paper is concerned with religion, it seems wise to explore the obfuscating effects of his beliefs, whilst bearing in mind that the emphasis upon this factor should not obscure the importance of others.

Haig has often been criticised for being overly optimistic. That he was so is beyond doubt; whether or not it was an impediment to effective command is a matter of judgement. But it is important to make a distinction between optimism and faith. Optimism is the tendency to assume a positive interpretation of received data. To use an example from Haig's papers, when he heard that the meat content in the ubiquitous German sausage was falling perilously low, he optimistically assumed that the German soldier must be on the verge of complete moral and physical collapse. Faith, on the other hand, is an act of trust, an assumption — made without material evidence — that all is well. Haig's papers also reveal examples of faith. For instance, on the eve of the Somme offensive, he told his wife that

> The men are in splendid spirits. Several have said that they have never before been so instructed and informed of the nature of the operation ahead of them. The wire has never been so well cut, nor the Artillery preparation so thorough.[62]

The true picture was drastically different. Haig could not have known his men's true feelings. The size of his Army and his inevitable separation from the front precluded any real intimacy. Faith in a benevolent God caused Haig to assume that his men felt as confident and secure as he did. This same faith inspired the belief that the front had been well-prepared for the attack. In fact it had not. Machine guns were not neutralised; wire remained uncut. Intelligence to this effect had been passed to GHQ but was either not imparted to Haig or not believed by him. The problem with Haig's faith was that it was often blind.

Thus, Haig's religion did occasionally obscure the real war. If intelligence gathered from the front conflicted with Haig's vision of the war, he often either ignored or subconsciously misinterpreted it. As if to preempt such criticism, Haig recorded some advice from Duncan which he found particularly cogent:

> the difficulties of any problem depends very much on the way the individual regards it. But we must not be optimistic . . . simply by shutting our eyes to the truth, but, through confidence in God's help, believe that we can and will overcome what opposes us.[63]

In other words, faith was at least as important as facts, a belief which
is perhaps basic to Christian thinking. Confident of God's blessing,
Haig never doubted that the British would eventually win. With the end
predetermined, events along the way diminished in importance. If
intelligence was occasionally ignored, it was because Haig believed that
the goodness of God was a more reliable indicator of the way the war
would be resolved.

In November 1916, Haig noted with profound interest Duncan's
warning that 'We have all had . . . enough of good advice. What we
wanted now was some help.' The padre told his congregation to 'Have
patience, do your best and look above for help.'[64] Whilst it would be
impossible to establish a causal link between Duncan's words and
Haig's receptivity to advice, it is clear that suggestions from outside
experts did not always find fertile ground at GHQ. When the War
Office produced a less optimistic report on the state of the German
Army than that of Haig's own intelligence unit, he commented that 'I
cannot think why the War Office Intelligence Department gives such a
wrong picture of the situation except that General McDonogh [sic]
(D.M.I.) is a Roman Catholic and is (perhaps unconsciously) influenced
by information which reaches him from tainted (i.e. Catholic) sources.'[65]
Adverse information, if it was to alter Haig's vision of the war, had first
to overcome his natural optimism, his stubbornness, his self-assurance,
the predilection of his subordinates to protect him, and of course his
faith in a benevolent, all-powerful God. These obstacles were virtually
impenetrable. Those who disagreed with Haig found it difficult to
maintain their opposition in the euphoria of headquarters. For instance,
in September 1917 the Chief of the Imperial General Staff, Sir William
Robertson, arrived at GHQ intent upon a change in strategy. The
morning after his arrival, Haig noted that 'A night's reflection and
Duncan's words of thanksgiving for our recent victory seemed to have
had a good effect' on Robertson, who appeared 'less pessimistic and
seemed to realise that the German Army was in reduced circumstances'.[66]

During a Sunday sermon in February 1917, Duncan, according to
Haig,

> laid stress on the need from which all of us suffer of having nourishment for
> the spiritual side of life . . . We must feel that this life leads naturally into the
> next — 'we must feel that if we go down into the Valley of Death, [Christ] is
> there'. We must really feel Christ in us, so that we are safe whatever
> happens.[67]

It would be relatively easy to argue that the spiritual nourishment which the Reverend George Duncan provided led to a dangerous detachment from the real war. The belief that 'we are safe whatever happens' suggests a frightening lack of respect for earthly hazards. In other words, Haig's certainty in life everlasting may have caused him to be reckless with lives temporal. But to concentrate on the ill-effects of Haig's deep religious conviction is to see but one side of the issue. The Great War was a ghastly, horrifying, utterly demoralising conflict. A commander of imagination and heightened sensitivity, a man who felt the utter tragedy of every death and who could sense the impairment to society which so much destruction would cause, might not have had the strength to lead the British Army to victory. It is a sad fact that in order to win, Britain needed Haig and Haig needed Duncan. Losses required justification; victory had to seem worthwhile. Haig may have been misguided, but in being so he was the type of commander which this terrible war demanded.

NOTES

1. George Haig (Henrietta Jameson) to Douglas Haig, 6 January 1916. Haig MSS, National Library of Scotland, Acc. 3155, No. 347(24). All quotations from the Haig Papers are from NLS Acc. 3155. To simplify further citations, therefore, only the volume number will be cited. I am grateful to the Earl Haig for permission to quote from his father's papers and for his helpful comments on this article.
2. Rachel Haig to Douglas Haig, 15 May 1874. Haig MSS, Vol. 3(a).
3. Rachel Haig to Douglas Haig, 25 February 1879.
4. Quoted in A. Duff Cooper, *Haig* (London 1935), pp. 90–92.
5. Technically speaking, his rise became rapid only after 1898, when, as a result of his service in the Sudan Campaign, his energy and dedication were noticed by his superiors.
6. I am grateful to my colleague Professor A. F. Upton for directing my attention to the very important differences between Haig's sense of predestination and that of Cromwell.
7. Haig to Reverend J. M. Simms, Duncan MSS, University of St Andrews, MS 37090/3/63.
8. Haig to Lady Haig, 27 December 1915. Haig MSS, No. 141.
9. Haig Diary, 2 January 1916. (Haig MSS).
10. G. Duncan, *Douglas Haig As I Knew Him* (London, 1966), p. 43.
11. *Ibid.*, p. 18.
12. *Ibid.*, p. 22.

13. J. M. Simms to Duncan, 4, 8 August 1917. Duncan MSS, 37090/3/77, 78.
14. One of the first priorities which Haig assigned to the GHQ camp commandant after the move to Montreuil was the location of premises in which Duncan could hold his services. A suitably unassuming hut was bought for 50 francs.
15. I am grateful to Professor Douglas Duncan for information on the life of his father, for donating his father's papers to the University of St Andrews and for permitting me to quote from those papers.
16. Duncan Diary, 24 July 1916. Duncan MSS, 37090/3/61, 62.
17. Duncan Diary, 3 June 1916.
18. Duncan Diary, 18 June 1916.
19. *Ibid.*
20. Duncan Diary, 4 March 1917. Duncan was referring to the way Haig had looked on the previous Sunday.
21. *Ibid.*
22. Duncan Diary, 25 February 1917.
23. Duncan, op. cit., p. 123.
24. *Ibid.*, pp. 21–22.
25. Haig Diary, 17 September 1916.
26. Duncan Diary, 29 April 1917.
27. Haig Diary, 11 February 1917.
28. Haig Diary, 29 April 1917.
29. Haig Diary, 15 October 1916.
30. Haig Diary, 29 May 1916.
31. Haig Diary, 15 January 1916.
32. Haig Diary, 30 March 1916.
33. Haig Diary, 29 May 1916.
34. Haig Diary, 16 July 1916.
35. Haig Diary, 23 April 1916.
36. Douglas Duncan to the author, 25 February 1989.
37. Haig Diary, 16 February 1916.
38. Haig Diary, 6 November 1915.
39. Duncan Diary, 22 July 1917.
40. Haig Diary, 19 March 1916.
41. Haig Diary, 28 January 1917.
42. Haig Diary, 24 September 1916.
43. Haig Diary, 5 October 1916.
44. Haig Diary, 4 June 1916.
45. Haig to Lady Haig, 8 July 1916.
46. Haig to Lady Haig, 5 June 1917.
47. Haig Diary, 30 September 1917.
48. Haig to Lady Haig, 11 April 1918.
49. Haig to Lady Haig, 30 June 1916.
50. Duncan Diary, 29 April 1917.
51. Haig Diary, 14 February 1916.
52. Haig to Lady Haig, 20 April 1917.

53. Haig to Lady Haig, 17 November 1918.
54. Haig Diary, 11 November 1918.
55. See Haig to Lady Haig, 27 December 1915, previously cited.
56. Duncan, op. cit., p. 125.
57. Duncan Diary, 22 July 1917.
58. *Ibid.*
59. Duncan, op. cit., p. 121.
60. Liddell Hart, *Through the Fog of War* (London, 1938), pp. 55–56.
61. Haig to Simms, 17 November 1918, previously cited.
62. Haig to Lady Haig, 30 June 1916.
63. Haig Diary, 9 July 1916.
64. Haig Diary, 5 November 1916.
65. Haig Diary, 15 October 1917.
66. Haig Diary, 10 September 1917.
67. Haig Diary, 11 February 1917.

INDEX

212